ArtScroll Mesorah Series®

Expositions on Jewish Liturgy and Thought

Rabbi Nosson Scherman / Rabbi Meir Zlotowitz
General Editors

hoshanos

THE HOSHANA PRAYERS / A NEW TRANSLATION WITH A COMMENTARY ANTHOLOGIZED FROM TALMUDIC, MIDRASHIC, AND RABBINICAL SOURCES.

Published by
Mesorah Publications, ltd

YESHIVA OF THE TELSHE ALUMNI

A Tale of Two Cities: Telshe and Riverdale

Telshe began in a Lithuanian hamlet called Telshe, in 1875. It was founded by Rabbi Eliezer Gordon, and in a time when the yeshiva movement was blossoming in Eastern Europe, the Telshe Yeshiva took its place at the forefront of the great yeshivos of the period. Its rigid standards of academic excellence and its illustrious roshei yeshiva were a magnet for many thousands of students from all over Europe, even for a number of students from faraway America. In 1941, Nazi troops entered the town of Telshe and killed most of the faculty and student body, but the great Telshe Yeshiva would not die.

Riverdale In 1980, the great and immortal tradition of Telshe came to the New York Metropolitan Area, as the Yeshiva of the Telshe Alumni was founded in suburban New Jersey. A few years later, it found its permanent home in Riverdale, where it was taken to heart by a warm and vibrant Jewish community.

Within a few short years, YTA emerged as a national Torah institution with a reputation for perfection, in the spirit of its Lithuanian forebear. Renewed was the intensity of Torah study. Renewed was the joy of accomplishment. Renewed was the emphasis on character development. Renewed was the concern for the entire Jewish community.

The yeshiva's intense program attracted boys from throughout the United States and Canada. Drawn by its analytical method of Torah study and emphasis on scholarship, they are trained to become future educators and leaders. Molded by a distinguished and charismatic faculty, Riverdale's students have established a new standard of excellence in the century-old tradition of Telshe.

The yeshiva and the Riverdale community are inseparable. More than 125 members of the community benefit from structured Torah sessions and lectures given by the yeshiva's faculty, or by participating in evening programs where they study with a partner or on their own.

Come visit YTA in Riverdale

You'll see faculty and students alive and aglow in the classic manner of Torah growth and greatness. You'll see physicians, professionals, and business people coming for their regular shiur in the Yeshiva. You'll see cleanliness and order. You'll feel the sense of mission that permeates the entire institution.

When the landmark Gibson House, overlooking the Hudson River, became available, the yeshiva seized the opportunity to acquire the building. It sits on four acres of land, directly across from the current facilities of the Yeshiva of the Telshe Alumni. The two buildings will adequately house the yeshiva's student body – now 150 students – and provide for the yeshiva's future needs.

Now this great and growing institution needs your help to grow and carry on its mission.

The Yeshiva of the Telshe Alumni has proven itself. It has earned your support.

Won't you become a generous partner in this magnificent institution?

Translated and compiled by
Rabbi Avie Gold

*An Overview /
 From Humble Willow to Highest Heaven*
by Rabbi Nosson Scherman

FIRST EDITION
First Impression . . . July 1980
Second Impression . . . August, 1981
SECOND EDITION
First Impression . . . July 1994

Published and Distributed by
MESORAH PUBLICATIONS, Ltd.
4401 Second Avenue
Brooklyn New York 11232

Distributed in Europe by
J. LEHMANN HEBREW BOOKSELLERS
20 Cambridge Terrace
Gateshead, Tyne and Wear
England NE8 1RP

Distributed in Israel by
SIFRIATI / A. GITLER — BOOKS
4 Bilu Street
P.O.B. 14075
Tel Aviv 61140

Distributed in Australia & New Zealand by
GOLD'S BOOK & GIFT CO.
36 William Street
Balaclava 3183, Vic., Australia

Distributed in South Africa by
KOLLEL BOOKSHOP
22 Muller Street
Yeoville 2198, Johannesburg, South Africa

ARTSCROLL MESORAH SERIES®
HOSHANOS

© Copyright 1980, 1994 by MESORAH PUBLICATIONS, Ltd.
4401 Second Avenue / Brooklyn, N.Y. 11232 / (718) 921-9000

ALL RIGHTS RESERVED.

This text, the new translation, Overviews, instructions, prefatory and associated textual contents and introductions — including the typographic layout, cover artwork, and ornamental graphics — have been designed, edited and revised as to content, form and style.

No part of this book may be reproduced
in any form — without **written** permission from the copyright holder,
except by a reviewer who wishes to quote brief passages in connection with a review written for inclusion in magazines or newspapers.

THE RIGHTS OF THE COPYRIGHT HOLDER WILL BE STRICTLY ENFORCED.

ISBN
0-89906-162-1 (hard cover)
0-89906-163-X (paperback)

Typography by Compuscribe at ArtScroll Studios, Ltd.
4401 Second Avenue / Brooklyn, N.Y. 11232 / (718) 921-9000

Printed in the United States of America by Noble Book Press
Bound by Sefercraft, Quality Bookbinders, Ltd. Brooklyn, N.Y.

Table of Contents

Author's Preface　vii

An Overview / From Humble Willow to Highest Heaven
  I. *Temple and Prophets*　xi
  II. *Symbols of Succos*　xviii
  III. *The Aravah*　xxiii
  IV. *Hoshana Rabbah*　xxviii

Hoshanos

	Ordering of the *Hoshana* Stanzas	34
Introductory stanza:	הוֹשַׁעְנָא לְמַעֲנָךְ / Please Save—For Your Sake	36
Hoshana 1*:	לְמַעַן אֲמִתָּךְ / For the Sake of Your Truth	38
	Hakafah-circuits and *Sefirah*-emanations	45
Hoshana 2:	אֶבֶן שְׁתִיָּה / Foundation Stone	46
Hoshana 3:	אוֹם אֲנִי חוֹמָה / Nation that Declares	50
Hoshana 4:	אֲדוֹן הַמּוֹשִׁיעַ / Lord Who Saves	56
Hoshana 5:	אָדָם וּבְהֵמָה / Man and Beast	60
Hoshana 6:	אֲדָמָה מֵאֶרֶר / Ground from Accursedness	62
Hoshana 7:	לְמַעַן אֵיתָן / In the Merit of the Courageous One	66
Hoshana 8:	אֶעֱרוֹךְ שׁוּעִי / I shall Arrange My Prayer	76
Hoshana 9:	אֵ-ל לְמוֹשָׁעוֹת / O God! Bring about Salvations	78
Hoshana 10:	כְּהוֹשַׁעְתָּ אֵלִים / As You Saved the Terebinths	84
	אֲנִי וָהוֹ הוֹשִׁיעָה נָּא / ANI VAHO, Bring Salvation Now	84
	הוֹשִׁיעָה אֶת־עַמֶּךָ / Save Your Nation	90
Hoshana 11 *(for the Sabbath):*	אוֹם נְצוּרָה / Nation Protected	92
Hoshana 12 *(for the Sabbath):*	כְּהוֹשַׁעְתָּ אָדָם / As You Saved Adam	96
Hoshana 13:	תִּתְנֵנוּ / Establish Us	106
Hoshana 14:	אָנָּא אֱזוֹן / Please Hearken	108
Hoshana 15:	תָּעִינוּ / We have Strayed	112
Hoshana 16:	לְמַעַן תָּמִים / In the Merit of Him Who Was Perfect	116
Hoshana 17:	תַּעֲנֶה אֱמוּנִים / Answer the Faithful	132
Hoshana 18:	אָז כְּעֵינֵי עֲבָדִים / Then, Like the Eyes of Slaves	138
	שַׁעֲרֵי שָׁמַיִם פְּתַח / Open the Gates of Heaven	140
Hoshana 19:	קוֹל מְבַשֵּׂר / The Voice of the Herald	142
	קַדִּישׁ / Kaddish	148
	יְהִי רָצוֹן / May It be Favorable	150

Appendix / The Custom of Hakafos on Succos and Hoshana Rabbah　155
Bibliography　158

---

* The numbers assigned to the *hoshanos* are merely for convenience in cross-referencing and have no other significance. For the particular *hoshana* of each day see pp. 34-35.

Preface

Bimah, *Torah and Jew merge in the center of the synagogue, the* מִקְדָּשׁ מְעַט, *miniature sanctuary, to form an altar — an altar representative of the one which stood in the courtyard of the Holy Temple in Jerusalem. The nation circles this altar praying for the rebuilding of its counterpart along with the entire Torah complex.*

How many of us circling the bimah *are aware of the cosmic implications of our circuits? How many of us chanting the Hoshana prayers are aware of the broad range of Talmudic and Midrashic interpretations contained in the stiches? Rashi, the "Father of Commentaries," saw fit to write a commentary on the* Hoshanos. *Obviously, Rashi considered such an undertaking at least on a par with his commentaries on Talmud and Scripture or he would not have expended time on it before completing the other two.*

In my limited way I have attempted to bring meaning to the cryptic phraseology of the paytan *by anthologizing from the vast array of commentaries to the* siddur *while adding a few notes of my own.*

I offer fervent prayers of thanksgiving to the מְלַמֵּד תּוֹרָה לְעַמּוֹ יִשְׂרָאֵל, *for allowing me to complete this work in His honor. At the same time I acknowledge the many gardeners who helped nurture the seed once it was planted:*

RABBI MEIR ZLOTOWITZ *suggested the undertaking and followed through with constant prodding and encouragement;* RABBI NOSSON SCHERMAN *personally edited the entire manuscript;* REB SHEAH BRANDER's *talents have created the beautiful frontipiece and the graphic arrangement of the book;* RABBI HERSH GOLDWURM *wrote the appendix and helped compile the bibliography;* RABBI MOSHE LIPSHITZ, *chief librarian of the Central Torah Library of Borough Park, helped select source materials.*

MRS. FAIGIE WEINBAUM *read the galleys and page proofs;* MISS PAULA KATZ *and* MRS. SURIE APPEL *typeset the book from manuscript through editorial changes until the final product.*

May all of them be granted their hearts' desires and be judged worthy of seeing the arrival of the Messiah, speedily in our days, Amen.

Both thanks and apologies are due my עֵזֶר כְּנֶגְדִּי, Nechie, who ably shouldered the double burden of being both mother and father to our children, נ״י, especially during the final weeks of preparing the book for print.

יהי רצון מלפניך שכשם שעזרתני לסיים ספר זו, כך תעזרני להתחיל ספרים אחרים ולסיימם. ללמוד וללמד מתוך הרחבה. לשמור ולעשות ולקיים את כל דברי תלמוד תורתך באהבה. וזכות כל החכמים הנזכרים בספר זו יעמד לי ולאשתי ולזרעי שלא תמוש התורה הקדושה מפינו מעתה ועד עולם אמן.

אברהם יצחק גאלד

ד׳ מנחם אב תש״מ
4 Av 5740

לזכר נשמת אבי מורי

ר׳ יעקב ב״ר אברהם יצחק ז״ל

יעקב איש תם ישב באהל של שם טוב

שהלך לעולמו י״ג מר-חשון תשל״ז

תנצב״ה

An Overview —
From Humble Willow to Highest Heaven

בְּכָל יוֹם הָיוּ מַקִּיפִין אֶת הַמִּזְבֵּחַ פַּעַם אַחַת...אֶת לוּלָבֵיהֶם...וְאֶתְרוֹגֵיהֶם בִּידֵיהֶם...וְאוֹתוֹ הַיּוֹם מַקִּיפִין שֶׁבַע פְּעָמִים.
אָמַר ר׳ חִיָּא, זֵכֶר לִירִיחוֹ.
הָא תִּינַח בִּזְמַן שֶׁבֵּית הַמִּקְדָּשׁ קַיָּם. בִּזְמַן הַזֶּה חַזַּן הַכְּנֶסֶת עוֹמֵד כְּמַלְאָךְ אֱלֹהִים וְסֵפֶר תּוֹרָה בִּזְרוֹעוֹ וְהָעָם מַקִּיפִין אוֹתוֹ דּוּגְמַת מִזְבֵּחַ.

Every day [of Succos] they would go around the altar...with their lulavim and esrogim in their hands...and on that day [Hoshana Rabbah] they would go around it seven times.

R' Chiya said, 'It was to commemorate the [miracle at Jericho].'

That was possible when the Temple stood. Nowadays, the representative of the congregation stands like an angel of God with a Torah Scroll in his arm, and the people go around him as if he were the altar (Yalkut, Tehillim 703).

I. Temple and Prophets

A Vestige When the Temple stood, its altar was the focus of a nation seeking God's help and His blessing of prosperity. The Temple is gone, but the focus remains. At the table where the Torah is read stands a man holding a Torah Scroll — and he represents the altar. Around him walk his fellow Jews, *lulav* and *esrog* in hand, saying הוֹשַׁעְנָא, *Please save!*, just as their ancestors did in the sacred precincts of old.

At the table where the Torah is read stands a man holding a Torah Scroll — and he represents the altar.

The Temple is gone. The altar is gone. The offerings are gone. The water libations of Succos are gone.

But the Torah remains — אֵין לָנוּ שִׁיּוּר רַק הַתּוֹרָה הַזֹּאת, *we have no remnant save for this Torah* (Yom

[xi]   Introduction

Kippur liturgy). In the person of a man holding the Torah, the existence of Israel is embodied. The *bimah*, the table from which the Torah is read, represents the altar's extension into every realm of life and every corner of the universe.

> *There is hardly a vestige of the Temple service left to us in our long exile, but the circuits around the altar remain.*

There is hardly a vestige of the Temple service left to us in our long exile, but the circuits around the altar remain — for the Torah remains, *lulav* and *esrog* remain, the *Hoshana* prayer remains. And so we remain linked to the Temple that once was and will be again *(Be'ur HaGra, Orach Chaim* 660:1).

What took place in the Temple during those sanctity-saturated days of Succos? How is it reminiscent of the conquest of Jericho? What is the basis of our observance today? Why does so much of the *Hoshana* service revolve around the humble *aravah*, the willow branch? What is the profound significance of Hoshana Rabbah?

In the Temple On Succos, in the days when the Temple stood, Jews would go down to Motza, a valley below Jerusalem, and pick huge *aravah* branches, each eleven cubits long (approximately 17-22 feet). The branches would be placed upright on the יְסוֹד, *base,* of the altar on all four sides. They would extend a cubit over the altar with their tips hanging over its top. To the joyous sound of trumpet blasts, Jews would enter the courtyard and encircle the altar once on each of the first six days of Succos. On the seventh day, Hoshana Rabbah, they would encircle the altar seven times. As they made their daily circuits they would pray אָנָּא ה' הוֹשִׁיעָה נָּא אָנָּא ה' הַצְלִיחָה נָּא, *Please HASHEM, bring salvation now! Please, HASHEM, bring success now! (Psalms* 118:25). According to R' Yehudah, they would say אֲנִי וָהוֹ הוֹשִׁיעָה נָּא, *ANI VAHO* [i.e., two mystical Names of God, see comm. to *hoshana* 10] *bring salvation now!*

> *According to most tannaim, this part of the Temple service was conveyed to Moses at Sinai.*

According to most tannaim, this part of the Temple service was conveyed to Moses at Sinai [וְהֲלָכָה לְמֹשֶׁה מִסִּינַי] and, though it is not specified in Scripture, it has the status of Torah law; according to Abba Shaul, it is ordained by Scripture *(Succah* 34a,

44a). But it was limited to the Temple Courtyard; in the rest of *Eretz Yisrael*, Jews could not take part in this observance.

The *exact* procedure of circuits in the Temple is not clear to us. Access to the area west of the altar (between it and the Temple building) is forbidden to all except *Kohanim*. Therefore, most commentators maintain that only the *Kohanim* marched around the altar, while the rest of the throng stood in the Courtyard and observed. *R' Sherira Gaon* writes that the Israelites and Levites stood in place on three sides of the altar. *Ohr Zarua* contends that the *mitzvah* was so great that even Israelites were admitted to the western area in order to take part in the circuits of the altar. (See Appendix to this volume.) Furthermore, the Sages *(Succah* 43b) disagree on whether the procession around the altar was done holding the Four Species or willow branches. *Rambam, Ritva,* and *Ran,* however, maintain that even if only the Four Species were held *during* the circuit, the willows were taken afterward. For a full exposition of these views, see ArtScroll Mishnah, *Succah* 4:5.

Ohr Zarua contends that the mitzvah was so great that even Israelites were admitted to the western area in order to take part in the circuits.

Israel Remembers

When the Second Temple was built, the *aravah* services were broadened. The prophets Chaggai, Zechariah, and Malachi, who were members of the Great Assembly, instituted the custom that on Hoshana Rabbah, Jews could take part in the *aravah* service wherever they were, even outside the Temple *(Succah* 44a-b, see *Rosh; Tosefos Yom Tov).*

After the Temple was destroyed, the entire practice of circuits and the *aravah* service came to an end — for a while.

But the people of Israel do not forget. Just as the spiritual genius of the people, thanks to its prophets, extended the *aravah* service throughout the land in happier times, so the collective soul of Israel would not remain stifled in the tragedy of exile. We do not know precisely when, but during the time of the *gaonim* who headed the great academies of Babylon after the end of the Talmudic era, a new spirit arose: 'Let us make a זֵכֶר לְמִקְדָּשׁ, *a reminder of the Temple.'*

But the people of Israel do not forget, so the collective soul of Israel would not remain stifled in the tragedy of exile.

> Has not Yechezkel taught us that our every synagogue and study hall is מִקְדָּשׁ מְעַט, a miniature Sanctuary?

The Sanctuary is gone, but its nation lives on. And wherever we have been exiled, God's Presence is exiled with us. Has not Yechezkel taught us that our every synagogue and study hall is מִקְדָּשׁ מְעַט, a miniature Sanctuary (Ezekiel 11:16)?

So Holy Arks were opened and Torah Scrolls were withdrawn and taken to the *bimah*. Around them, congregations with *lulav* and *esrog* in hand made their circuits and prayed for God's help. Surely they remembered R' Chiya's teaching *(Yalkut Tehillim 730)* that a representative of the congregation holding a Torah scroll is tantamount to the altar itself. Already in the times of R' Saadiah Gaon and R' Hai Gaon the custom was widespread, and *Rambam (Hilchos Lulav 7:23)* says that all Jewish communities march around the *bimah* on each day of Succos in commemoration of Temple days and on the seventh day of Succos, the *aravah*-bundle was taken separately and beaten on the ground, just as it had been in the Temple during the First Commonwealth and throughout the land during the time of the Second Commonwealth.

> The prayers we recite during our circuits are called Hoshanos because their constant refrain is הוֹשַׁעְנָא, [Hoshana], please save.

The prayers we recite during our circuits are called *Hoshanos* because their constant refrain — reminiscent of the one used in the Temple — is הוֹשַׁעְנָא, [*Hoshana*], *please save*. The medieval *paytanim*, primarily the great R' Elazar HaKalir, composed a host of beautiful acrostic prayers for each day of the *Hoshana* service, but the primary theme of them all is the constantly repeated plea, '*Hoshana!*'

Custom of Prophets

> There is a prophetic strain in Israel.

'A custom of the prophets.' This is how R' Yehoshua ben Levi describes the general adoption of the *aravah* custom.* The prophets did not institute it as a *mitzvah*; they formulated a *custom* which, apparently, they left for Israel to adopt or not to adopt. Perhaps there is something deeply significant in the Talmud's description of it as 'a custom of the prophets.'

There is a prophetic strain in Israel. When Hillel

---

* R' Yochanan's view that the prophets ordained it as a *mitzvah* is not adopted by the consensus of commentators; therefore no blessing is recited for its performance. See commentators to *Succah* 44a.

An Overview / From Humble Willow to Highest Heaven

the Elder was asked how knives should be brought to the Temple for the slaughter of the Pesach sacrifice when *erev* Pesach was on the Sabbath, he replied that he had forgotten, but

הַנַּח לָהֶם לְיִשְׂרָאֵל אִם אֵין נְבִיאִים הֵן בְּנֵי נְבִיאִים הֵן

> Let Israel be; if they are not prophets, they are children of prophets (Pesachim 66a).

Indeed, the next day, the law was decided; the Sages observed columns of people converging on the Temple following the halachic tradition maintained by ordinary Jewish families for who knows how many generations.

Hillel called his people 'children of prophets' though several centuries had elapsed since prophecy had departed from Israel. *Maharsha* explains that there were still old men and women who would recall what had been done years ago in similar circumstances, but, surely, Hillel must have meant more than that when he applied the concept of prophecy to the situation — a good memory is a far cry from prophecy.

The human being who merits God's direct communication through prophecy is not the same afterwards. Nor is the nation. *Ramban* and others frequently enunciate a major principle in comprehending the course of the Jewish nation: כָּל מַה שֶּׁאֵירַע לָאָבוֹת סִימָן לַבָּנִים, *everything that happened to the Patriarchs is a portent for the children* (see Overview, ArtScroll *Bereishis*   ). This is true not only with regard to the foreshadowed epochs, but also with regard to the indelible imprint left on the national character by the deeds of our forefathers. Israel's designation as God's Chosen People infused within it a spirit of prophecy, of majesty. There is a spark of Abraham, of Moses, of Samuel, of Elijah in every descendant of the nation they inspired. It is because of this instinct for holiness that Hillel described the nation of Israel as the offspring of prophets.

The law revealed to Moses called for circuits of the altar only in the Temple. Throughout the period of the First Commonwealth, neither judges nor prophets nor kings saw a need to extend the *aravah* ritual to the rest of *Eretz Yisrael*. Was it because *all* Jews made their pilgrimages to the Temple every Succos? Surely most of them did, but even in Solomon's golden era there must have been many who could not. The sheer size of *Eretz Yisrael* in those days was far greater than the area settled by those who returned from Babylon to build the Second Temple; what of those who could not make the trip every time? It would seem that the need for the *aravah* observance was more pronounced during the time of the Second Temple than it was during the First.

It would seem that the need for the aravah observance was more pronounced during the time of the Second Temple than it was during the First.

In earlier times, the holiness of the Temple was greater, prophecy was felt and heard throughout the land, the spiritual reverberations from the Temple had a tangible effect even on those who could not be present. When Chaggai, Zechariah, and Malachi returned and saw the reduced state of the people, they perceived that a circuit of the altar could work its effect only on those gathered in the Temple, but not in Lod, Modi'in, the Galil. They introduced a custom. Strange. They were members of the אַנְשֵׁי כְּנֶסֶת הַגְּדֹלָה, *Men of the Great Assembly*, which consisted of approximately one hundred-twenty sages. That Assembly instituted the daily prayers and a host of other regulations and ordinances. Why did not the entire body introduce the custom?

When Chaggai, Zechariah, and Malachi returned and saw the reduced state of the people, they introduced a custom.

The answer lies in the fact that the Talmud ascribes the broadened *aravah* custom only to 'prophets' and that, in the halachically adopted view of R' Yehoshua ben Levi, the custom was not required of the people.

Children of Prophets

In addition to the few living prophets who survived the end of the prophetic age, there was a prophetic strain in the *people* — 'let Israel be; if they are not prophets, they are children of prophets.' Should there be a nationwide *aravah* service? Chaggai, Zechariah, and Malachi took the lead, but the choice was left to the nation — the *prophetic* nation. Buried

> Buried in Israel's psyche is a prophetic legacy, a chord that is attuned to the spiritual needs of the people.

in Israel's psyche is a prophetic legacy, a chord that is attuned to the spiritual needs of the people. Israel chose to make circuits around its Torah Scrolls in acknowledgment that it needed the influence of Torah to complement the influence of the Temple.

When the Temple was gone, the circuits of the altar — and of the *bimah* — were no more. But Israel remained the descendants of prophets. In community after community, country after country, the custom was revived until no village or hamlet was without it. And so, today, wherever there are Jews, their synagogues feature an 'altar' at their center, an altar built of *bimah*, Torah, and Jew; and around the altar a nation walks with *lulav* and *esrog* in hand chanting its prayer for salvation.

The exiled nation's continuing need for this source of strength is reflected also in another aspect of the *Hoshana* liturgy. As noted above, the Mishnah (*Succah* 4:5) states that the circuits in the Temple included the refrain, אָנָּא ה' הוֹשִׁיעָה נָּא אָנָּא ה' הַצְלִיחָה נָּא, *Please HASHEM, bring salvation now! Please HASHEM, bring success now.* There is a minority opinion in the Mishnah, R' Yehudah's, according to which the refrain is אֲנִי וָהוֹ הוֹשִׁיעָה נָּא, *ANI VAHO, bring salvation now! Rashi (Succah 45a)* explains the meaning of the strange formula *ANI VAHO*. Its numerical value equals that of אָנָּא ה', *please HASHEM* — each totals seventy-eight — so R' Yehudah's formula is equivalent to that of the Rabbis. Moreover, *ANI* and *VAHO* are Names of God (see comm. to *hoshana* 10) — thus we invoke two sacred Names in this plea for help.

> ANI *and* VAHO *are Names of God — thus we invoke two sacred Names in this plea for help.*

It would seem that the Halachah should follow the majority view; indeed, *Rambam (Hilchos Lulav* 7:23) cites only the opinion of the Rabbis and does not mention R' Yehudah's. Nevertheless, the text of the liturgies adopted in our *Hoshana* service reads *ANI VAHO.* Why? We can find a clue to the answer in *Tosafos (Succah* 45a s.v. אני), who explains why R' Yehudah chose only these two from among God's many Names.

It is not merely a matter of Names, *Tosafos* ex-

God is not oblivious nor apathetic to Jewish suffering; He suffers with us, as it were.

plains, it is what they represent. God is not oblivious nor apathetic to Jewish suffering; He suffers with us, as it were. *Isaiah* (63:9) says: בְּכָל־צָרָתָם לוֹ צָר, *their every distress was His distress*, upon which the Midrash comments:

כְּבָר נִשְׁבַּעְתִּי לְבָנַי שֶׁאֱהֵא עִמָּהֶם בְּצָרָה
I have sworn to My children [Israel] that I will be with them in distress (Midrash Eichah 2).

God knows no rest when Israel's sins force Him to disperse them, to afflict them, to impoverish them. His Glory, too, is in exile. In two prophetic verses, He testifies to this condition of *Shechinah* in exile: וַאֲנִי בְּתוֹךְ־הַגּוֹלָה, *and I* [אֲנִי] *was among the exiles (Ezekiel 1:1)* — this refers to God Himself, as it were, Who joined the exiles being led from Jerusalem. The second verse is וְהוּא־אָסוּר בָּאזִקִּים בְּתוֹךְ כָּל־גָּלוּת יְרוּשָׁלַיִם וִיהוּדָה הַמֻּגְלִים בָּבֶלָה, *and He* [וְהוּא] *was bound in chains among all the exiles of Jerusalem and Judah who were exiled to Babylon (Jeremiah 40:1)* — this, too, refers to God Himself, Whose own majesty, as it were, is fettered in the chains of His people's exile *(Pesichta, Eichah Rabbasi 34).*

The two Names ANI *and* VAHO *are God's 'exile' Names. When we pray* ANI VAHO, *bring salvation now, we pray not for ourselves, but for God.*

Thus the two Names *ANI* [אֲנִי=*I*] and *VAHO* [from וְהוּא=*and He*] are God's 'exile' Names. When we pray *ANI VAHO, bring salvation now,* we pray not for ourselves, but for God. May *He* be helped by His Own exile being ended — if one may so express it. This prayer is in the tradition of Israel's most devout people who study, pray, and perform the *mitzvos* only because it is God's will that they do so, not because they will derive personal benefit from serving Him. We pray not for ourselves, but for Him.

II. Symbols of Succos

The Complete Man

Yesod V'Shoresh HaAvodah writes that the *hakafah*-circuits of the *Hoshana* service have a profound influence on the Heavenly spheres, an influence that cannot be grasped by ordinary human intelligence. But 'its periphery', as he puts it, can be perceived if we understand that the cosmic effects of this *mitzvah* emanate from the nature of its performance. It combines three factors: Man, Speech, and Deed. The fusion of the three alludes to the word אָדָם, literally *Adam-man*, but actually much more than that. For it is the responsibility of every individual man to raise himself back up to the august spiritual height of Adam before his sin (see *Overview* to ArtScroll *Bereishis* vol. I).

<small>Man, Speech, and Deed. These concepts are symbolized by the individual Jew as he makes his way around the bimah.</small>

Man, Speech, and Deed. These concepts are symbolized by the individual Jew as he makes his way around the *bimah*, intoning his *Hoshana* prayers, and holding the Four Species as he does so. This combination of Man, Speech, and Deed forms the word, and concept of, אָדָם, *man* at his greatest.

The א represents אָדָם, *the human being*; ד represents דִּיבּוּר, *the power of intelligent speech*, the power that *Targum* defines as man's quintessential characteristic as 'a living being' (see *Bereishis* 2:7); מ represents מַעֲשֶׂה, *deed*, the readiness to bring the abstract into the concrete by using man's physical powers to utilize earth, flesh, and blood in God's service. One who combines all three characteristics establishes himself as a total person, a Jew who dedicates himself, in mind and deed, to the goal represented by the *bimah*.

Organs Unite

The 'deed' aspect of this complete man is symbolized by the Four Species — and the implications of that *mitzvah* are profound, indeed. *Vayikra Rabbah* (ch. 30) lists a host of symbolisms contained in the Four Species. Many of them refer to the heavenly realms and are beyond human comprehension, but others are closer to our own perceptions. *R' Bachya* (*Leviticus* 23:40) cites a few of them and explains their implications. Among them are these:

<small>The species resemble major organs of the human body.</small>

— The species resemble major organs of the human body. The myrtle leaf is shaped like an eye and the *esrog* like a heart. As the Sages have taught, these two organs can unite in a perverted partnership of sin. The eye sees and the heart lusts with the result that the person's better instincts are inundated by the power of his temptations. The willow leaf is shaped like a mouth, the organ of speech, which is the tool of Torah, prayer, and encouragement, but which is so often corrupted into a weapon that tears away at man's spiritual fiber. The straight, tall *lulav* resembles man's spinal column, the organ through which all the brain's impulses are conveyed to the rest of the body. By combining these species in the performance of a *mitzvah*, we symbolize our repentance and desire for atonement. Every sin finds atonement when man takes a tool he once used for evil and converts it to good. One who had squandered funds on gluttony and debauchery must use his wealth to support worthy causes. One whose barbed mouth had inflicted pain on defenseless victims must learn to use the divine gift of speech for holy and helpful ends. The taking of the Four Species, which symbolize major organs, represents this resolve to utilize the body and its emotional and intellectual drive for the good — and, thereby, the *mitzvah* is an instrument of atonement.

— There is another organism in addition to the individual human body: the national organism of Israel with its many kinds of people. The Four Species symbolize them all. The *esrog* is a desirable food containing both טַעַם וְרֵיחַ, *taste and pleasant aroma*; it symbolizes righteous people who possess both Torah and good deeds. The *lulav*, the branch of a date palm, is odorless but it produces nourishing food; it symbolizes the scholar who possesses Torah knowledge but is deficient in good deeds. The fragrant, tasteless myrtle leaf represents common people who possess good deeds, but lack Torah scholarship. Finally, the odorless, tasteless willow leaf symbolizes someone who lacks both Torah and good deeds. The nation is often — too often — divided, but God wishes it to be a *community* of Israel. When all segments of Israel come together in the service of the common goal of national dedication to His will, then *everyone* belongs, from the august *esrog* to the lowly willow. And when every shade and manner of Jew joins with every other in pursuit

An Overview / From Humble Willow to Highest Heaven

of that goal, then God accepts their common repentance.

Time of Judgment Succos in general and Hoshana Rabbah in particular are periods of judgment in two ways: one specific and the other general.

Despite the awesome nature of the Ten Days of Repentance between Rosh Hashanah and Yom Kippur, not all is decided during this period of general judgment.

Despite the awesome nature of the Ten Days of Repentance between Rosh Hashanah and Yom Kippur, not all is decided during this period of general judgment. Once the overall decisions have been made for humanity as a whole and for each individual in particular, God determines what will be done with regard to *particular* needs. On Pesach He judges man with regard to the grain crops, on Shavuos with regard to fruit crops, and on Succos with regard to water supply *(Rosh Hashanah* 16a; see ArtScroll Mishnah, *Rosh Hashanah* 1:2).

The decision regarding water is not rendered until the end of Succos; for this reason, certain specific *mitzvos* of Succos revolve around water: in the Temple, water libations were offered at the altar; the *mitzvah* of the Four Species is performed with plants that depend on abundant water for their existence; and the willow, which assumes the spotlight on the climactic day of the water-judgment, Hoshana Rabbah, is identified by the Torah as a plant that grows alongside streams [*Leviticus* 23:40].

But Hoshana Rabbah has a significance broader than the universal need for water. The *Zohar* describes it as a judgment day akin to Yom Kippur itself, the day when the judgment of Yom Kippur is sealed finally, and the parchments containing the decrees are handed to angels who deliver them.

Hoshana Rabbah assumes special importance as a day of prayer and repentance. It is in this light that we must examine the aravah service.

Consequently, Hoshana Rabbah assumes special importance as a day of prayer and repentance. Because it is unique to Hoshana Rabbah, it is in this light that we must examine the *aravah* service.

Commentators (cited by *Sefer HaToda'ah*) explain this process of 'angels, parchments, and seals' that the *Zohar* associates with Hoshana Rabbah. God's kingdom can be better comprehended by us if we compare its procedure to that of a human government.

> When a merciful king passes judgment on his subjects, he seeks ways to avoid punishing them.

When a merciful king passes judgment on his subjects, he seeks ways to avoid punishing them. They may have erred, even rebelled, but perhaps there were extenuating circumstances. Even better, perhaps they feel a degree of remorse that guarantees a future better than the past, often for the very reason that the lessons of the flawed past will help mold a better future. Examining the case before him, if the king finds grounds for vindication or mercy, he dismisses the indictment and declares the defendant innocent. If not — there is still hope. The offender may have witnesses who will come forward in his behalf. There is always time to condemn and punish.

> There is always time to condemn and punish. Delay cannot hurt; a hasty decision may be irrevocable. So the king waits.

Delay cannot hurt; a hasty decision may be irrevocable. So the king waits. Time goes by, and if grounds for mercy are found indeed, the relieved king hands down his decision for acquittal. But even if the evidence mounts against the defendant and the verdict must be guilty, the king still has an option. The verdict does not take effect until it is inscribed, sealed and delivered — perhaps in the interval the defendant will repent or a defender will come forward. If not, the verdicts are handed to the officers of the court for delivery. If the verdict is favorable, it cannot be reversed, but if not — there is *still* hope. If the messenger comes to the convict's home and finds him joyously engaged in the service of the king and devotedly carrying out his laws, he returns to his monarch and says, 'Surely, he *was* guilty, but now he is a changed man.' The king agrees and tears up the verdict.

The Heavenly kingdom is similar. On Rosh Hashanah all people are judged. The righteous are given a favorable judgment, those found wanting — but not totally evil — are given until Yom Kippur to repent. If they fail to do so, the verdict against them is written and sealed, but not yet delivered. That is not done until Hoshana Rabbah, a day when Jews assemble in prayer, dedication and supplication. The joy of Succos reaches its climax not in dissolution but in devotion. God in His mercy finds ample reason to tear up the parchment bearing harsh sentences, as it were, and replace them with brighter tidings. This period of reprieve extends until the morning of Shemini Atzeres when Israel tarries for another period of rejoicing before God. The Four Species have been laid aside, the *aravah*-bundle has done its work, the succah is empty — but Israel remains with the intense joy it feels at having been privileged to serve God with love and awe. Then, even the guilty can mesh with the righteous and have their own spark of goodness break through the heavy overlays of sin that have obscured it for so long.

Even the guilty can mesh with the righteous and have their own spark of goodness break through the heavy overlays of sin.

III. The Aravah*

שִׁירוּ לֵאלֹהִים זַמְּרוּ שְׁמוֹ סֹלּוּ לָרֹכֵב בָּעֲרָבוֹת
בְּיָהּ שְׁמוֹ וְעִלְזוּ לְפָנָיו

Sing to God, make music for His Name, extol Him Who rides in Aravos, with YAH, His Name, and exult before Him (Psalms 68:5).

Master of Heaven

This verse calls upon Israel to express its grateful joy to God for the two events that singled us out as His nation — the Exodus and the Giving of the Torah.

This verse calls upon Israel to express its grateful joy to God for the two events that singled us out as His nation — the Exodus and the Giving of the Torah at Sinai. Events of such magnitude are associated only with His Ineffable Name — we thank Him for the Exodus by making music for His Name, the great Name which identifies Him in His infinity and unity. And for His gift of the Torah, we thank Him by acknowledging Him as the One Who dominates the *Aravos*. The Sages teach that there are seven heavens and the highest of them is *Aravos* (*Chagigah* 12b). By acknowledging Him as Master of *Aravos*, we declare Him to be above every manifestation of existence, even something as powerful and lofty as the highest sphere of heaven.

Vilna Gaon (see *Siddur HaGra* to *Ya'aleh V'Yavo*) explains the significance of the 'seven heavens'. Rather than tangible, measurable physical pheno-

---

* This section is based on *Kad HaKemach* of R' Bachya.

mena, they must be understood as seven spiritual levels which man must ascend by constantly refining his service of God. These layers separating man from God were created by human sin, and they can be removed only by repentance and raising the level of our performance. *Aravos* is the highest level; the Sages in *Chagigah* 12b describe it as אוֹצָר הַנְּשָׁמוֹת, *the treasury* [where God keeps pure] *souls*. *Aravos* represents the highest attainable degree of closeness to God; it is the level at which man's service is done with total sincerity, for God's sake alone [לִשְׁמָה]. Man's spiritual level is determined by his deeds on earth; *human* service alone can bring us to the point where our souls can testify that we have imbedded them in God's *Aravos*. Such is the magnitude of man's potential, and because God gave us the Torah through which we can realize this potential, we thank Him as the Master of *Aravos (Michtav MeEliyahu* III).

Aravos represents the highest attainable degree of closeness to God.

Moreover, by saying that He dominates even the *Aravos with YAH His Name*, we declare that God created everything יֵשׁ מֵאַיִן, *ex nihilo*, for the Sages teach *(Menachos* 29b) that God fashioned the universe with the letters of His Name יָה, *YAH* — with the *yud* He made the spiritual world, with the *he* he made the material world. This awesome power and majesty of God was revealed to Israel with unprecedented fullness at Sinai when God identified Himself, as it were, to Israel with the words אָנֹכִי ה' אֱלֹהֶיךָ, *I am HASHEM your God (Exodus* 20:2). Then we were 'shown' our Maker and given the source of all spiritual joy — of all truly *meaningful* joy — the Torah. Therefore, in thanking and praising Him for the Torah, we are urged וְעָלְזוּ לְפָנָיו, *and exult before Him*, for Torah study gladdens the heart of anyone who allows it to penetrate his heart and dispel the fog of delusion that blinds his eyes and deadens his mind.

Hoshana Rabbah's mitzvah of the aravah has the special purpose of alluding to the Creator of Aravos.

Hoshana Rabbah's *mitzvah* of the *aravah* has the special purpose of alluding to the Creator of *Aravos*. The day is called יוֹם הַחוֹתָם הַגָּדוֹל, *Day of the Great Seal*, because on it God completes the task of sealing

An Overview / From Humble Willow to Highest Heaven

the results of the Judgment Days. But the 'seal' characteristic of the day has further implications.

Confluence of Symbols

R' Bachya notes that Hoshana Rabbah is the twenty-first day from Rosh Hashanah, when Adam and Eve were created. It is also the twenty-sixth day from the beginning of Creation, for God created heaven and earth on the twenty-fifth of Elul.

Thus, Hoshana Rabbah is both day number twenty-one and day number twenty-six, two numbers with profound symbolism.

Thus, Hoshana Rabbah is both day number twenty-one and day number twenty-six, two numbers with profound symbolism. Twenty-one is the numerical value of the Name יהו with which, the Kabbalists teach, God fixed the three-dimensional nature of physical creation, stamping Himself as King of the universe in all its directions — east, west, north, south, up and down (see also comm. p. 152).

Twenty-six is the numerical value of the Four-letter Name that expresses His essence, the Name that is described as שְׁמוֹ הַגָּדוֹל, *His* **Great** *Name*. When a person or thing is described by the word גָּדוֹל, *great* — or its Aramaic translation, רַבָּה or רַבָּא — the implication is that its holiness extends to the very pinnacle of greatness, God's own Great Name. Such things as Moses, the Temple, the *Kohen Gadol* are described this way. And so is Hoshana Rabbah —

Let no one think that the title of the day refers to nothing more than the multitude of its Hoshana *prayers — though that, too, is implied.*

literally the *Great* Hoshana. Let no one think that the title of the day refers to nothing more than the multitude of its *Hoshana* prayers — though that, too, is implied in the name (*Chayei Adam* 153) — there is much more in this day of awesome holiness (see also R' Bachya to Deut. 33:21).

Yet another thing happens on Hoshana Rabbah. When the Temple stood, a unique order of sacrifices was offered on Succos (*Numbers* 29:12-34): a total of seventy bullocks as burnt offerings. Their purpose was to protect the seventy nations of the world from suffering, to seek atonement for them, and to seek peace for all peoples (*Bamidbar Rabbah* 21). R' Yehoshua ben Levi exclaims: If only the nations had known how beneficial to *them* the Temple was, they would have surrounded it with legions to protect it!

Though for their *benefit*, the offerings also called

upon God to *diminish* the power and stature of the nations that flouted His word. For although Adam and later Noah were intended to be the patriarchs of a human race that would serve God equally well and be of equal spiritual stature, humanity fell short and Abraham assumed the role that should have belonged to everyone (see Overviews to *Bereishis* and *Noah*). The hope for the future of mankind was then changed: its goal became that the power of rebellious nations would be broken, that Israel would fulfill its mission as the nation of God and His Torah, and that all humanity would allow itself to be led by Israel. Of these seventy burnt offerings of Succos, thirteen bullocks were sacrificed on the first day of the festival, twelve the second day, eleven the third, and so until, on Hoshana Rabbah, there were only seven. Thus, Hoshana Rabbah, the day of the smallest number of offerings, represents the final downfall of rebellious nations, just as the entire Succos festival represents their progressive slide from dominance.

Hoshana Rabbah, the day of the smallest number of offerings, represents the final downfall of rebellious nations.

Jericho There was another occasion when Israel's religious service was instrumental in bringing down the resistance of an enemy that refused to acknowledge God's mastery over creation. The first Canaanite city faced by Joshua and Israel was Jericho, a fortress protected by impregnable walls backed by a powerful army (see *Joshua* 6). God told Joshua to have the Jewish army, led by seven *Kohanim* and the Ark, circle the city once a day for six days. On the seventh day, they were to circle Jericho seven times, then the *Kohanim* were to blow their shofars, and the mighty wall would collapse.

The first Canaanite city faced by Joshua and Israel was Jericho.

In the Temple, too, a procession circled the altar once a day for the first six days of Succos, and seven times on Hoshana Rabbah. On that last day, Israel completed its decreasing order of seventy sacrifices that served to invoke God's protection on the nations, and also invoked the greatest benefit they could gain — that they be shorn of their illusory power and become subservient to the nation that

An Overview / From Humble Willow to Highest Heaven

represented God's will on earth. So the circuits of the altar and of the *bimah* are both evocative of Jericho, not merely in commemoration of an ancient event, but of the continuing goal of human history: that evil disappear and mankind recognize the purpose for which it was created.

First it was Jericho. Then it was all seventy nations. Now it is primarily Edom, the embodiment of evil, descendant of Esau and Amalek, initiator of the current, final exile that has plunged man into nearly twenty centuries of darkness.

Hoshana Rabbah brings with it the confluence of many factors of profound spiritual significance: the twenty-first day of Tishrei, symbolizing the Name that gave shape and dimension to the universe; the twenty-sixth day from the start of creation, symbolizing the Great Name; the day when God applies the final seal to the judgment of Yom Kippur; the day when seventy offerings are completed and when seven circuits are made around the altar/*bimah*; the day that recalls the miracle at Jericho and portends the glorious day when far greater forces of evil than Jericho will suffer their downfall, leading to a triumph that will dwarf Joshua's.

When that day comes, Isaiah's prophecy will be fulfilled יְשֻׂשׂוּם מִדְבָּר וְצִיָּה וְתָגֵל עֲרָבָה וְתִפְרַח כַּחֲבַצָּלֶת, *the arid desert will be joyous and* [עֲרָבָה] *the wilderness will exult and blossom like a rose* (Isaiah 35:1).

The word *aravah* means wilderness, it means willow, and it alludes to the *Aravos*, the spiritual realm that is closest to God. The prophets and sages and the collective genius of the people of Israel chose the *aravah* branch for the particular *mitzvah* of this portentous day. The *aravah* proclaims God as Master of the *Aravos*, and its message will one day — finally — be heard universally. Then, the final redemption will come, and Zion, whose spiritual magnificence had been reduced to a desert-like aridity, to an unproductive wilderness, will blossom with a new birth of spiritual splendor.

IV. Hoshana Rabbah

Prayer As we saw above, the *aravah* symbolizes an organ of the human body and an organ of the national body. It alludes to the mouth and to the simple folk who lack both learning and deeds. That the Sages chose Hoshana Rabbah as the day for these allusions, and the *aravah* as the symbol best suited to the day is clearly not coincidental.

Hoshana Rabbah is a day of many prayers, and the *aravah* — resembling the mouth and lips, the organs of prayer — is the aptest symbol of the day's theme. Different nations have different characteristics. No less a personage than Isaac defined the difference between his two sons, the two trends of humanity: הַקֹּל קוֹל יַעֲקֹב וְהַיָּדַיִם יְדֵי עֵשָׂו, *the voice is Jacob's voice, but the hands are Esau's hands* (Genesis 27:22). The Talmud observes that whenever a prayer is effective, a descendant of Jacob must be among those who uttered it; when a war is won, Esau's descendants must have had a hand in it *(Gittin 57b).* The secret of Israel's strength, the leitmotif of its identity, is the voice that utters words of prayer. For prayer is hardly a mouthing of liturgy, it is an expression of the inner Jew whose faith and reliance is in God.

> The secret of Israel's strength, the leitmotif of its identity, is the voice that utters words of prayer.

Ideally, the mouth should be the tool of the great Torah scholar, who uses it to expound, clarify, and teach the wisdom of God. But not every Jew reaches that pinnacle. Many can offer little Torah knowledge and few deeds. Often, even their faith seems doubtful. But in the severest tests and the worst times, their lips have given expression to the legacy of Jacob, even if they could say little more than הוֹשַׁעְנָא, *Please save!*

> In the severest tests and the worst times, their lips have given expression to the legacy of Jacob.

The masters of Kabbalah have taught that even the humblest *succah* is visited by seven אוּשְׁפִּיזִין, *guests,* during Succos, one each day. They are the spirits of the seven shepherds of Israel: Abraham, Isaac, Jacob, Moses, Aaron, Joseph, and David. The guest of the seventh day is David, composer of

An Overview / From Humble Willow to Highest Heaven [xxviii]

Despite his greatness and accomplishments, David is uniquely symbolic of prayer.

Psalms and sweet singer of Israel. Despite his greatness and accomplishments, David is uniquely symbolic of prayer, he said: וַאֲנִי תְפִלָּה, *I am [the embodiment] of prayer (Psalms* 109:4). At its highest level, prayer is not the printed page nor the uttered words; prayer is the *person* who pours out his heart to God. As the Sages taught, there is service done with the hands and service done with the heart; the service of the heart is prayer.

Power of Community

At bottom, no one can claim that his deeds are so worthy as to *compel* God to accede to his wishes. Even the greatest man is only a human with the limitations implied by the term. For him to expect his humble store of spiritual accomplishment to tip God's scale is like the village magnate comparing himself with Rothschild. Still we know that it is God's will that we serve Him and it is His desire to reward us for our humble attainments, because they represent a great effort on our part and because He has chosen to make our success or failure the principal consideration in how He will guide the functioning of the universe. Another consideration is in our favor: God has chosen the totality of Israel as His nation. No matter how substantial the accomplishment of an individual, it is far more significant if he serves God along with the community and regards himself as a cog in Israel's common destiny.

So even the Jew who is both a scholar and a *tzaddik* — symbolized by the *esrog* — recognizes that his accomplishments are magnified immeasurably when he joins himself to the nation. The Four Species of Succos are held together, for all kinds of people are part of a national unit, from the righteous *esrog* to the insignificant *aravah*, just as the mouth and heart are part of the same body. And more: the righteous person knows that he, too, must depend on prayer for his salvation.

The Four Species of Succos are held together, for all kinds of people are part of a national unit, from the righteous esrog to the insignificant aravah.

On Hoshana Rabbah, therefore, when the opportunities for achieving God's help are so auspicious, the prophets and sages laid aside the *esrog* with its perfection, the *lulav* with its Torah, the myrtle with its good deeds, and picked up a bundle of *aravos*. *Of course*, it represents the very highest of the heavens — but how does one scale the heavens? Hoshana Rabbah offers its own unique way: Through prayer. Through being part of Israel. Through recognizing that God longs for the repentance and prayer of *every* Jew, even the humblest *(Sfas Emes)*.

Patriarchs and Festivals

The Midrash teaches that the three pilgrimage festivals commemorate the three Patriarchs. *Tur Orach Chaim* (417) explains the source for this statement: Pesach reminds us of Abraham who told Sarah to bake matzos for the three visiting angels (*Genesis* 18:6); Shavuos is for Isaac because the shofar blast at Sinai was in the merit of the horn of the ram which replaced Isaac on the altar of the *Akeidah*, and Succos recalls Jacob who made סֻכּוֹת, *succah*-tents for his flocks (*Genesis* 33:17, Overview to ArtScroll *Vayeitzei*).

Just as each of the Patriarchs contributed his own particular blessing to the nation, so each festival has its own contribution to make to the well-being of the people. We express this idea in the festival *Shemoneh Esrei* when we say וְהַשִּׂיאֵנוּ ה' אֱלֹהֵינוּ אֶת־בִּרְכַּת מוֹעֲדֶיךָ, *Bestow upon us, HASHEM, our God, the blessing of Your festivals;* each festival has its own blessing, and we pray that we may deserve it.

As we find in the Mishnah (*Rosh Hashanah* 1:2), Pesach is the judgment time for crops, Shavuos for fruit, and Succos for rain. Although these are material blessings, it is a basic principle of our belief that every tangible benefit is not an end to itself, but a physical manifestation of a higher, spiritual reality.

Sh'lah HaKadosh gives us an insight into this principle. The human eye is a distillation in physical form of the ability to perceive and understand, and ultimately of God's knowledge of all that occurs. Thus, when someone listens to an explanation of a complicated idea and exclaims 'I see', it is not a figure of speech; he *does* see in a higher sense. Similarly we can legitimately say that we 'see' something which is

An Overview / From Humble Willow to Highest Heaven   [xxx]

being done in seclusion thousands of miles away. And one with well-developed powers of analysis can 'see' far better than an uncomprehending eyewitness.

<small>The true definition of rain is God's power to stimulate the growth of vegetation.</small>

When we say 'rain', we think of saturated clouds releasing drops of water. But the true definition of rain is God's power to stimulate the growth of vegetation. In a similar vein, the Sages speak of טַל שֶׁל תְּחִיָּה, *life-giving dew*, with which God resuscitates the dead. 'Dew' is not a wonder drug and the 'life-giving dew' is not the morning moisture that blankets the earth, but both are essentially the same: God has the power to confer life on man, animal, and vegetable. This Divine power is distilled into rain and dew in ordinary, human terms. So, too, the blessings of Abraham, Isaac, and Jacob, as explained in the festivals, speak of grain, fruit, and water, but in their true sense they are kindness, service, truth, Torah, holiness, and all the other noble virtues that are part of our Patriarchal legacy.

In *Genesis* the Torah relates the blessings of the Patriarchs and it concludes *Deuteronomy* with the blessings of Moses. *Sfas Emes* comments that just as each festival manifests, in the realm of time, the spiritual content and legacy of one Patriarch, so the legacy of Moses is reflected in a festival. Shemini Atzeres is the festival of Moses, the transmitter of Torah to Israel. Moses absorbed the teachings of the Patriarchs; to them he added his own, and bequeathed the whole to Israel.

<small>The essence of Moses is related to the essence of Jacob. This is symbolized by the unique nature of Shemini Atzeres.</small>

The *Zohar* teaches that the essence of Moses is related to the essence of Jacob. This is symbolized by the unique nature of Shemini Atzeres, which is simultaneously both a separate festival and related to Succos; Jacob's blessing of truth flowed into Moses' blessing of Torah *(R' Gedaliah Schorr* in *Ohr Gedalyahu).*

The Aravah and the People

It is noteworthy that the festival of Jacob includes the very *mitzvos* which stress the unity of the Jewish people. Of the three Patriarchs, Jacob was the only one whose family was perfect in its entirety.

Abraham gave birth to an Ishmael and the children of Keturah, Isaac had an Esau; but Jacob's children were righteous without exception and became the pillars of the nation. Jacob's blessings to his children reveal how diverse they were, nevertheless each was essential to the integrity of the nation. The Four Species of Succos point up how every facet of Israel thrives best when it is united with all the others. And Hoshana Rabbah with its emphasis on the lowly *aravah* shows best of all how Israel can no more dispense with its common folk than it can be without its finest.

The Four Species of Succos point up how every facet of Israel thrives best when it is united with all the others.

The *aravah* people are an extension of Jacob whose identity lay in his 'voice'. When Israel is united in this manner, when it shows its appreciation of every offspring of Jacob, when it proves its understanding that its ultimate salvation is in the hands of God, when it stands at the climax of its judgment season with *aravah* in hand — then it is worthy of the gift of Moses, and to ascend to the realm of *Aravos*.

Then it is worthy of the gift of Moses, and to ascend to the realm of Aravos.

סדר הושענות

✥ Ordering of the Hoshana Stanzas

An introductory stanza of four verses opens the *Hoshana* service whenever it is recited. On each of the first six days of the festival, one of ten stanzas (called *hoshanos*) is said, followed by a standard concluding stanza. On the seventh day, Hoshana Rabbah, seven *hoshanos* are recited.

The following chart records the generally accepted order of *hoshanos* for the first six days. Some rites, however (among them *Tehillas Hashem*[1] and *Avodas Yisrael*[2]), follow a different order.]

The varying order of *hoshanos* for each of the days up to Hoshana Rabbah is based on five principles (listed by *Levushei Srad* 663):

(A) According to our calendar [formulated in 4118 (358 C.E.) by R' Hillel HaSheini, son of R' Yehuda Nesia *(Seder HaDoros)*], the first day of the Succos festival can fall only on Monday, Tuesday, Thursday, or the Sabbath. Thus only four charts are needed.

(B) The *hoshana* לְמַעַן אֲמִתָּךְ, *For the Sake of Your Truth*, lists attributes of the Shechinah, [Divine Presence], and therefore takes preference over all others; while אֶבֶן שְׁתִיָּה, *Foundation Stone*, describes the *Beis HaMikdash* [Holy Temple] and is recited on the second day of the festival. (This order applies except when the first day of Succos falls on the Sabbath [see (C) and (D) below].)

(C) A special *hoshana* referring to the various commandments and laws of the Sabbath is always said on that day: אוֹם נְצוּרָה, *Nation Protected*.

(D) The *hoshana* אֶעֱרוֹךְ שׁוּעִי, *I Shall Arrange My Prayer*, contains the stich גִּלִּיתִי בְּצוֹם פִּשְׁעִי, *I have bared, on the fast day, my transgression*, which alludes to the וִדּוּי, *confession*, of Yom Kippur and should consequently be said as close to that day as possible. However, because it contains repeated supplications for forgiveness, this *hoshana* cannot be said on *Yom Tov* or the Sabbath. Hence it is said on the first Intermediate Day, unless it is the Sabbath, in which case the *hoshana* is postponed to Sunday. [Because the first Intermediate Day is always the same day of the week as Yom Kippur it is an appropriate time for the *hoshana* of confession *(R' Yisachar Dov of Belz)*; e.g., see page 35, fig. 4.]

(E) אָדוֹן הַמּוֹשִׁיעַ, *Lord Who Saves*, is in large part a prayer for rain. But rain is considered a symptom of curse during the *Succos* festival because rain makes it impossible to live in a *succah* [*Taanis* 1:1]; therefore this *hoshana* is delayed until the festival has almost ended.

---

1. *Chabad* (Lubavitch) Chassidim follow the order of Hoshana Rabbah on each of the first six days of Succos, regardless of the day of the week. Thus, for example *hoshana* 5, אָדָם וּבְהֵמָה, *Man and Beast*, is always read on the fifth day of Succos. On Shabbos the *Chabad* liturgy omits the *hoshana* service entirely, but the omitted *hoshana* is recited on Sunday, when two *hoshanos* are said *(Tehillas Hashem)*.

2. The order of *Avodas Yisrael* (used by many German communities) follows the days of the festival rather than the days of the week (except the Sabbath when אוֹם נְצוּרָה, *Nation Protected*, is said). For the five non-Sabbath days it is as follows:

First day: *hoshana* 8 — אֶעֱרוֹךְ שׁוּעִי, *I Shall Arrange My Prayer*.
Second day: *hoshana* 9 — אֵל לְמוֹשָׁעוֹת, *O God! Bring About Salvations*.
Third day: *hoshana* 3 — אוֹם אֲנִי חוֹמָה, *Nation that Declares, 'I Am a Wall!'*
Fourth day: *hoshana* 2 — אֶבֶן שְׁתִיָּה, *Foundation Stone*.
Fifth day: *hoshana* 6 — אֲדָמָה מֵאֶרֶר, *Ground From Accursedness*.

Figure 1: First Day Succos on Monday

S	M	T	W	T	F	S
14	15 למען אמתך FOR THE SAKE OF YOUR TRUTH	16 אבן שתיה FOUNDATION STONE	17 אערוך שועי I SHALL ARRANGE MY PRAYER	18 אום אני חומה NATION THAT DECLARES, 'I AM A WALL!'	19 אל למושעות O GOD! BRING ABOUT SALVATIONS	20 אום נצורה NATION PROTECTED
21 הושענא רבה HOSHANA RABBAH	22	23	24	25	26	27

Figure 2: First Day Succos on Tuesday

S	M	T	W	T	F	S
13	14	15 למען אמתך FOR THE SAKE OF YOUR TRUTH	16 אבן שתיה FOUNDATION STONE	17 אערוך שועי I SHALL ARRANGE MY PRAYER	18 * אל למושעות O GOD! BRING ABOUT SALVATIONS	19 אום נצורה NATION PROTECTED
20 אדון המושיע LORD WHO SAVES	21 הושענא רבה HOSHANA RABBAH	22	23	24	25	26

* Some liturgies substitute אוֹם אֲנִי חוֹמָה, *Nation That Declares*.

Figure 3: First Day Succos on Thursday

S	M	T	W	T	F	S
11	12	13	14	15 למען אמתך FOR THE SAKE OF YOUR TRUTH	16 אבן שתיה FOUNDATION STONE	17 אום נצורה NATION PROTECTED
18 אערוך שועי I SHALL ARRANGE MY PRAYER	19 אל למושעות O GOD! BRING ABOUT SALVATIONS	20 אדון המושיע LORD WHO SAVES	21 הושענא רבה HOSHANA RABBAH	22	23	24

Figure 4: First Day Succos on the Sabbath

S	M	T	W	T	F	S
9	10 יום הכפורים YOM KIPPUR	11	12	13	14	15 אום נצורה NATION PROTECTED
16 למען אמתך FOR THE SAKE OF YOUR TRUTH	17 אערוך שועי I SHALL ARRANGE MY PRAYER	18 אבן שתיה FOUNDATION STONE	19 אל למושעות O GOD! BRING ABOUT SALVATIONS	20 אדון המושיע LORD WHO SAVES	21 הושענא רבה HOSHANA RABBAH	22

❊ ❊ ❊

Immediately after either *Hallel* (*Nusach Sefard*) or *Musaf* (*Nusach Ashkenaz*) the Ark is opened. A Torah scroll is taken to the *bimah*, the Ark remaining open, until the conclusion of the *Hoshana* service. The four introductory stiches are read responsively, the congregation repeating each stich after the *chazzan*. Upon completing the introductory *hoshana*, the *chazzan*, followed by all males present who are carrying *lulav* and *esrog*, circles the *bimah* as he reads the day's *hoshana* responsively with the congregation. He should time his steps to complete one circuit as he recites the last stich of the *hoshana*.

הושענא למענך

Each day's Hoshana service begins with this introductory stanza chanted responsively. For the particular hoshana of each day see pp. 34-35.

הוֹשַׁעְנָא לְמַעַנְךָ אֱלֹהֵינוּ	הוֹשַׁעְנָא:
הוֹשַׁעְנָא לְמַעַנְךָ בּוֹרְאֵנוּ	הוֹשַׁעְנָא:
הוֹשַׁעְנָא לְמַעַנְךָ גּוֹאֲלֵנוּ	הוֹשַׁעְנָא:
הוֹשַׁעְנָא לְמַעַנְךָ דּוֹרְשֵׁנוּ	הוֹשַׁעְנָא:

הושענא למענך — Please Save — For Your Sake

Israel cries: *Not for our sake, HASHEM, not for our sake* — not because our deeds make us deserving — *but for Your Name's sake give honor, for the sake of Your loving-kindness and Your truth* (Psalms 115:1; Targum Yonasan).

God responds: לְמַעֲנִי לְמַעֲנִי אֶעֱשֶׂה, *For My sake, for My sake, shall I act ...* (Isaiah 48:11).

As long as Israel is in exile, the שְׁכִינָה [*Shechinah*] *manifestation of the Divine Presence*, is in exile with them — as the prophet declares: *In all their troubles, He is troubled* (Isaiah 63:9), and as God says: *I am with you in trouble* (Psalms 91:15). The Talmud discusses this at length:

Come and observe how beloved Israel is to the Holy One Blessed be He, for wherever they [Israel] are exiled, the *Shechinah* is with them ... and when they will be redeemed, the *Shechinah* will be [redeemed] with them ... This teaches that the Holy One Blessed be He returns with them from their exiles (*Taanis* 16a; *Megillah* 29a).

[The concept of *Shechinah* in exile is the theme of chs. 9-11 of *Ezekiel*. There, in response to the idol-worship of Israel, the *Shechinah* withdraws, first from the Temple and then from Jerusalem, presaging the destruction of the Temple and the expulsion of Israel from Jerusalem. Where sanctity is profaned, where purity is defiled, where wood, stone, and heavenly bodies replace their Creator as objects of worship, there the Divine Presence is not — indeed cannot be — manifest. Gradually, step by step, the *Shechinah* withdraws from Its residence. For God's dwelling is not within buildings, but within hearts and minds. When they have no room for Him, He departs (see ArtScroll ed. *Yechezkel*; see also comm. beginning of *hoshana* 10).

Yet, after the Divine Presence has completed Its departure from Jerusalem and the entire land, another facet of *Shechinah* in exile comes to light:

Thus says my Lord HASHEM/ELOHIM: *Though I have removed them far off among the nations, and though I have scattered them among the countries, yet I have been for them a small sanctuary* (מִקְדָּשׁ מְעַט) *in the countries where they came.* (Ezekiel 11:16).

Despite everything, God's Presence remains מִקְדָּשׁ מְעַט, a term which *Targum* renders *synagogue*. The synagogue is today's sanctuary of Divine worship, but it is מְעַט, *smaller, lesser,* than was Jerusalem's מִקְדָּשׁ, *Holy Temple*.]

But, 'says God,' anyone who joins in communal [i.e., synagogue] prayer is considered as having redeemed Me and My children from among the nations [of their exile] (*Berachos* 8a).

As we gather in the synagogue to join in prayer, we ask for redemption of the *Shechinah* and the nation — for the sake of God, Himself — that we may once again worship not merely in the present small sanctuary, but in the בַּיִת הַגָּדוֹל,

◄§ Please Save—For Your Sake

Each day's *Hoshana* service begins with this introductory stanza chanted responsively. For the particular *hoshana* of each day see pp. 34-35.

Please save—for Your sake, our God!   *Please save!*
Please save—for Your sake, our Creator!   *Please save!*
Please save—for Your sake, our Redeemer!   *Please save!*
Please save—for Your sake, our Attender!   *Please save!*

Great House (see II Chronicles 3:5), may it be rebuilt speedily in our days, Amen.

הוֹשַׁעְנָא — *Please save.*
[This word is compounded of the words הוֹשַׁע, *save,* and נָא, *please.* Indeed, many *siddurim* give it as two words.]

The translation of הוֹשַׁע as *save* is based on the verse: הוֹשַׁע עַבְדְּךָ אַתָּה אֱלֹהַי, *save Your servant, You, my God* (Psalms 86:2).

Alternatively, the word may be translated *turn toward* [i.e., show favor; accept] as in: וַיִּשַׁע ה׳, *HASHEM turned to Abel ... but to Cain ...* לֹא שָׁעָה, *He did not turn* (Genesis 4:4-5; Shaar HaShamayim).

The translation of נָא as *please* follows *Rashi,* who states often in his commentary to Torah [e.g., Genesis 22:2] that נָא is an expression of request.

Onkelos, however, almost invariably renders נָא as בְּעַן, *now;* thus, הוֹשַׁעְנָא would mean *save now.*

לְמַעַנְךָ — *For Your sake.*
This expression is an abridged version of the fuller phrase לְמַעַנְךָ אִם לֹא לְמַעֲנֵנוּ, *for Your sake, if not for ours,* which appears in the אָבִינוּ מַלְכֵּנוּ, *Our Father, our King,* prayer. It is an appeal to help us for His Own sake even if we are unworthy of such help on our own merits *(Beis Yaakov).*

אֱלֹהֵינוּ — *Our God.*
[This introductory *hoshana,* which pleads for redemption of the *Shechinah* from its exile, uses a different appellation for God in each of its four verses. These four Names begin with the first four letters of the *aleph-beis* respectively. Although the designation of אֱלֹהֵינוּ, *our God,* is obviously used here to fit the alphabetical ordering of this prayer, the question remains as to why this particular name is used, as opposed to, perhaps, אֲדֹנֵנוּ, *our Lord,* or אָבִינוּ, *our Father,* both of which begin with an א, *aleph,* and are commonly used as prayer openings. The reason is as follows:]

The verse שְׁמַע יִשְׂרָאֵל, *Hear* (or *listen*) *Israel,* speaks of God as אֱלֹהֵינוּ ה׳, *HASHEM is our God* — He is currently recognized by Israel as *our God,* but the idolatrous nations do not acknowledge His sovereignty. In the future, however, He will be recognized by everyone as ה׳ אֶחָד, *HASHEM is One* — the One God (*Rashi; Deuteronomy* 6:4).

Thus we pray, 'For Your sake, because only we recognize You as אֱלֹהֵינוּ, *our God* — save us, and bring closer the day when all the world will proclaim, "HASHEM is One"' (Shaar Yisas'char).

בּוֹרְאֵנוּ — *Our Creator.*
[Is God only *our* Creator, to the exclusion of all others? Did He not create the entire world and all its inhabitants?

Rashi (Genesis 1:1) teaches that the world was created for the sake of Torah and for the sake of Israel. Everything in the universe was created with a purpose — but the purpose of all purposes is that knowledge of God's Unity be disseminated to the inhabitants of the world. This goal can be achieved only by Israel — through its study and teaching of the Torah. Thus, although He did not create Israel exclusively, He created *for* Israel exclusively. Indeed, the same prophet, Isaiah, who alludes to God as בּוֹרֵא קְצוֹת הָאָרֶץ ה׳, *HASHEM, Creator of the ends of the earth* (40:28), and בּוֹרֵא הַשָּׁמַיִם וְנוֹטֵיהֶם ה׳, *HASHEM,*

לְמַעַן אֲמִתָּךְ

א לְמַעַן אֲמִתָּךְ. לְמַעַן בְּרִיתָךְ. לְמַעַן גָּדְלָךְ וְתִפְאַרְתָּךְ.
א-ג

Creator of the heavens and all that is suspended in them (42:5), also quotes God's reference to Himself as ... 'ה בּוֹרֵא יִשְׂרָאֵל, HASHEM ... Creator of Israel (43:15).

Relative to the Divine plan for creation, Israel is *all* of creation, because all of creation is for Israel. Thus we pray to *our* Creator that He redeem us for His sake, i.e., to enable us to fulfill the purpose of our creation — studying, teaching, and spreading the words of His Torah and knowledge of His Unity.]

גֹּאֲלֵנוּ — *Our Redeemer.*

[This word appears twice in Scripture, both times as an appellation for God: גֹּאֲלֵנוּ ה' צְבָאוֹת שְׁמוֹ קְדוֹשׁ יִשְׂרָאֵל, *Our Redeemer, His Name is HASHEM of hosts, the Holy One of Israel* (Isaiah 47:14); and אַתָּה ה' אָבִינוּ גֹּאֲלֵנוּ מֵעוֹלָם שְׁמֶךָ, *You HASHEM, our Father "our Redeemer" has eternally been Your Name* (Isaiah 63:16).

The use of the two appellations בּוֹרְאֵנוּ גֹּאֲלֵנוּ, *our Creator, our Redeemer,* in tandem is neither unique to the Hoshana service (the same usage appears in the fourth blessing of בִּרְכַּת הַמָּזוֹן, *Grace after Meals*) nor strictly an alphabetical convenience. The two titles represent two aspects of our recognition of God, two aspects that are expressed in the Sabbath liturgy. In the Friday evening Kiddush blessing, the Sabbath is alluded to as both זִכָּרוֹן לְמַעֲשֵׂה בְרֵאשִׁית, *a memorial to the act of Genesis,* and זֵכֶר לִיצִיאַת מִצְרַיִם, *a memorial to the Exodus from Egypt.* This dual symbolism of the Sabbath is based upon the different reasons for the rest day listed in the two versions of the Ten Commandments. Initially (*Exodus* 20:8-11) the Sabbath rest is explained by the Torah as a reminder that *He rested on the seventh day;* while in *Deuteronomy* (5:12-15) the Sabbath is explained as a device to make us remember that *you were a slave in the land of Egypt and HASHEM brought you forth.*

Ramban explains that the narration in Genesis demonstrates that God is the Creator, and that of the Exodus showed that He *retains* mastery over the world [contrary to those who acknowledge that there *was* an act of creation but that ח"ו since then the universe functions only under natural law.] He is the Redeemer and as such He manipulates nature to serve His Divine will, as at the Exodus. Thus is His mastery proven.

Israel's unique role does not stop at its declaration of God as the Creator. It must teach the world that He remains the Sovereign Ruler — He is not only our Creator, but also our Redeemer.]

דּוֹרְשֵׁנוּ — *Our Attender.*

This epithet for God is derived from the verse: אֶרֶץ אֲשֶׁר ה' אֱלֹהֶיךָ דֹּרֵשׁ אֹתָהּ, [*Eretz Yisrael is*] *a land which HASHEM, your God, tends* ... (*Deuteronomy* 11:12; *Shaar Yisas'char*).

King David also used this title for God when He told his son: *You, Solomon my son, know your father's God, and serve Him with a perfect heart ... for HASHEM tends* (דּוֹרֵשׁ) *all hearts* (*I Chronicles* 28:9). The sense of the expression is that He takes an interest in His people and His land, never totally abandoning them to the vagaries of blind fate.

Although our custom is to recite only four introductory stiches, there are liturgies in which this *hoshana* comprises twenty-two stiches, completing the entire twenty-two letter Hebrew alphabet (*Shaar HaShamayim*).

[Most liturgies add the word הוֹשַׁעְנָא, *please save,* to each stich — either before it (הוֹשַׁעְנָא לְמַעַן אֲמִתָּךְ), after it (לְמַעַן אֲמִתָּךְ הוֹשַׁעְנָא), or both (הוֹשַׁעְנָא לְמַעַן אֲמִתָּךְ הוֹשַׁעְנָא).]

◆§ For the Sake of Your Truth

1 ¹**F**or the sake of Your Truth, ² for the sake of Your
1-3 Covenant, ³ for the sake of Your Greatness and Your

◆§ לְמַעַן אֲמִתָּךְ — For the Sake of Your Truth

Most of the *hoshanas* are composed around general motifs.

This *hoshana* records various attributes of God; accordingly, it may be considered an extension of the introductory stanza which directly precedes it *(Rashi)*.

This prayer is recited on the first day of the festival (unless that day is a Sabbath). It is recited again during the first *hakafah*-circuit of *Hoshana Rabbah*, when the final verdict which was written on *Rosh HaShanah* and sealed on *Yom Kippur* is given its final seal — thus the verdict is validated by "a seal within a seal." Since the seal of God is אֱמֶת, Truth *(Shabbos 55a)*, it is fitting that the *hakafah*-circuits on the day of the final seal begin by calling upon the attribute of אֱמֶת, Truth *(Bnei Yisas'char)*.

1. אֲמִתָּךְ — *Your Truth.*

Pleading for God's salvation, King David cries *(Psalms 115:1): Not for our sake, HASHEM, not for our sake, but for Your Name's sake give honor — for the sake of Your Loving-kindness and Your Truth* [עַל חַסְדְּךָ וְעַל אֲמִתֶּךָ]. The Psalmist does not pray for himself; he asks that God's truth and glory be vindicated on earth. Like David, we pray for a salvation which will substantiate for all that He is the true God *(Tefillah Yesharah)*.

Another rendering is based on the alternative translation of נָא as *now* (see above p. 37). *Now*, during the long and difficult period of exile, we have seen the fulfillment of the prophecy: וְתַשְׁלֵךְ אֱמֶת אַרְצָה, *it will throw truth to the earth (Daniel 8:12)*. Truth has become ridiculed and despised — therefore we pray: *Save us now, for the sake of Your Truth (Beis Avraham)*.

2. בְּרִיתָךְ — *Your Covenant.*

Shmuel taught that תָּמָה זְכוּת אָבוֹת, *the merits of the Patriarchs have expired* [i.e., the merits accumulated through the righteousness of Abraham, Isaac, and Jacob have all been expended to achieve the salvation of Israel at times when it did not deserve God's intervention] *(Shabbos 55a)*. *Rabbeinu Tam (Tos., s.v.,* ושמואל*)*, however, deduces that although their merits have expired, בְּרִית אָבוֹת לֹא תָּמָה, **God's covenant** *with the Patriarchs has not expired*; meaning that His promise to them remains irrevocable because a promise made cannot be unilaterally rescinded. This may be seen in Scripture. After threatening to punish the wayward nation of Israel by *'bringing you to the land of your enemies,'* God assures them, *'I shall remember My covenant* [וְזָכַרְתִּי אֶת בְּרִיתִי] *with Jacob ... Isaac ... Abraham; I shall remember — and the land shall I remember (Leviticus 26:41-42)*. In this stich, we pray that God remember us and redeem us for the sake of this covenant *(Iyun Tefillah)*.

Indeed, we find an instance of the actual fulfillment of this covenant in the prophet's word *[II Kings 13:23]: HASHEM was compassionate with them, and He was merciful to them, and He attended to them for the sake of His covenant* [לְמַעַן בְּרִיתוֹ] *with Abraham, Isaac, and Jacob (Tefillah Yesharah)*.

3. גָּדְלָךְ וְתִפְאַרְתָּךְ — *Your Greatness and Your Splendor.*

In his last public declaration of God's praise, King David said: *To you HASHEM is the Greatness* [גְּדֻלָּה] *and the Power* [גְּבוּרָה] *and the Splendor* [תִּפְאֶרֶת] *and the Eternality* [נֵצַח] *and the Glory* [הוֹד] *... the Kingdom* [מַמְלָכָה] *and the Sovereignty over every ruler (I Chronicles 29:11)*. [For *Eternality*,

א לְמַעַן דָּתָךְ. לְמַעַן הוֹדָךְ. לְמַעַן וְעוּדָךְ. לְמַעַן זִכְרָךְ.
ד״א לְמַעַן חַסְדָּךְ. לְמַעַן טוּבָךְ. לְמַעַן יִחוּדָךְ. לְמַעַן כְּבוֹדָךְ.

Glory and *Kingdom*, see commentary to sts. 14, 5, 13 respectively.]

The present stich deviates from the rest of this stanza by combining two attributes, instead of listing only one. This anomaly is compounded by the exclusion of גְבוּרָה, *Power*, which (a) fits the alphabetical scheme whereas תִּפְאֶרֶת, *Splendor*, does not; and (b) follows immediately after *Greatness* in King David's formula.

Bnei Yisas'char explains as follows: Kabbalistically, the attributes of גְדוּלָה גְבוּרָה תִפְאֶרֶת, *Greatness, Power,* and *Splendor*, are equivalent to חֶסֶד דִּין אֱמֶת, *Loving-kindness, Justice,* and *Mercy*, respectively. The latter three are symbolic of the judges on the Heavenly Tribunal through which God passes judgment on His world; each one representing a different response to man's deeds. While Justice tends to strictness, Loving-kindness and Mercy lean toward leniency. Hence, we beseech God, *'Please save us because of Your Greatness/Loving-kindness and Your Glory/Mercy'* — the attributes of compassion which outweigh the severity of Power/Justice.

4. דָּתָךְ — *Your Mandate.*

God is described by the Torah as coming from Sinai toward Israel with אֵשׁ דָּת לָמוֹ, *a fiery mandate for them* (Deuteronomy 33:2). The Talmud and all major commentators understand the *fiery mandate* of this passage as alluding to the Torah. *Rashi* explains that the Torah is described as 'fiery' because it was (a) originally written with [letters of] black fire upon [a background of] white fire [see *Yerushalmi Shekalim* 6:1], and (b) given at Mount Sinai through smoke and fire [see *Exodus* 19:18].

5. הוֹדָךְ — *Your Glory.*

[This is one of the attributes mentioned in *I Chronicles* 29:11. See comm., st. 3.]

Praise the Name of HASHEM ... His Glory (הוֹדוֹ) *is upon earth and heaven. He elevates the power of His people ...* (Psalms 148:13-14). God's Glory is manifested upon heaven and earth — for all creatures, whether celestial or terrestrial, exist only through His supervision. His Glory will be best displayed to the entire universe when He raises up Israel from its downtrodden exile and gives His devout ones cause for joyous praise (*Radak*).

Shaar Yisas'char comments that the term *Glory* in our stich alludes to the Temple, for the *Zohar* relates the destruction of the Holy Temple to the defilement of God's הוֹד, *Glory*. Both blows, the destruction and the defilement, can be remedied through the same medium. Only through study of Torah can God's Glory be restored; and only through study of Torah can the Holy Temple be rebuilt.[1]

6. וְעוּדָךְ — *Your Meeting House.*

This is an allusion to the Meeting House par excellence — the Holy Temple where the *Shechinah* and Israel came together — and in particular the דְּבִיר, *hidden rendezvous* (see comm., *hoshana* 2 st. 4). This interpretation is based on the verse: *I shall designate a time* (וְנוֹעַדְתִּי) *for assembly there* (Exodus 25:22).

Agra d'Kallah understands the Scriptural verse in a completely different fashion. The root of וְנוֹעַדְתִּי, וְעַד, may

---

1. This also explains the juxtaposition of דָּתָךְ, *Your Mandate*, i.e., the Torah, with הוֹדָךְ, *Your Glory*, i.e., a rebuilt Jerusalem and Temple. Only through Your Mandate can Your Glory be restored.

This we learn from the prophet Jeremiah who mourned the destruction of the Holy Temple, lamenting: *Over this [tragedy] our hearts were sick* (דָּוֶה) (*Lamentations* 5:18). It is no accident that the word דָּוֶה, *sick*, comprises the same letters as הוֹד, *glory*, but in reverse order. When the Glory is overturned, sickness and destruction result. Return, repent, restore the overturned Glory — salvation and rebuilding follow.

1   *Splendor,* [4] *for the sake of Your Mandate,* [5] *for the sake of*
4-10   *Your Glory,* [6] *for the sake of Your Meeting House,* [7] *for the sake of Your Mention,* [8] *for the sake of Your Lovingkindness,* [9] *for the sake of Your Goodness,* [10] *for the sake of*

also be vocalized וָעֵד, *and more.* Kabbalah teaches that the goal of creation in general and every human action in particular is the unification of God's Name (see *Rashi, Exodus* 17:16). This goal may be achieved in one of two ways: the Superior Unification [יִחוּדָא עִילָּאָה] or the Inferior Unification [יִחוּדָא תַּתָּאָה]. The superior form is symbolized by the word אֶחָד, *Oneness,* representing an indivisible unity, as distinct from a sum of many characteristics. The inferior form is formulated in the word וָעֵד, *and more,* implying a sum of many parts, an accumulation of attributes resulting in a totality. The Inferior Unification is imperfect because God and His attributes cannot truly be taken as separate entities any more than a human being can be described as a collection of separate and unrelated characteristics; He and His attributes are one indivisible, perfect unity; it is only the limited nature of the human mind that prevents it from fully comprehending the Superior Unification. However, there will be a time when this Superior Unification will be fully realized; that time is described by the prophet as *that day on which HASHEM will be* [recognized by all the world as] אֶחָד, *One, and His Name will be* אֶחָד, *One* (*Zechariah* 14:9). The place of this realization will be the Holy Temple. Homiletically, this concept is found in the verse וְנוֹעַדְתִּי לְךָ שָׁם, *I will be manifest in My Totality* — in the Inferior Unification — *there,* eventually to develop into the Superior Unification.

[In this interpretation, we pray for salvation and the rebuilt Temple — so that our awareness of God's unity may grow there until the arrival of *that day, when HASHEM will be One and His Name will be One.*]

7. זִכְרְךָ — *Your Mention* [lit. memorial, remembrance].

Moses asked of God: *When I come to the children of Israel and say to them, 'The God of your ancestors has sent me to you,' and they will respond, 'What is His Name?' What shall I say to them?*

God replied: HASHEM, *God of Your ancestors ...* זֶה שְׁמִי, *This is My Name eternally,* וְזֶה זִכְרִי, *and this is My Mention in every generation* (*Exodus* 3:13,15).

[The Talmud finds this last passage difficult, for although the verse records only one name — the ineffable Four Letter Name — it repeats the demonstrative pronoun זֶה, *this,* indicating that two names are being alluded to.]

R' Avina explains the passage: The Holy One Blessed be He meant, 'Not as My Name is written, is it pronounced [or mentioned]. *This is My Name* alludes to the way we spell God's Name, י-ה-ו-ה; *this is My Mention* refers to the way we pronounce that Name, as if it were spelled אֲדֹנָי, *Adonai.*

Another verse states: *HASHEM will be the King over all the land; on that day HASHEM will be One and His Name will be One* (*Zechariah* 14:9). But does He not have One Name today? R' Nachman bar Yitzchak taught: The world of the future will be unlike the world of today. In the world of today God's Name is spelled one way and pronounced differently, whereas in the world of the future all will be one — the spelling and pronunciation will both be י-ה-ו-ה (*Pesachim* 50a).

[This means that we fail to perceive God's nature as it is expressed in the true pronunciation of His Name; therefore we may not utter it. But in time to come, there will be no contradiction between perception and reality.]

8-9. חַסְדְּךָ ... טוּבְךָ — *Your Lovingkindness ... Your Goodness.*

Lead me in Your Truth and teach me, for You are the God of my salvation [יִשְׁעִי] ... *recall not the sins of my youth*

א לְמַעַן לְמוּדָךְ. לְמַעַן מַלְכוּתָךְ. לְמַעַן נִצְחָךְ. לְמַעַן סוֹדָךְ.
יב-יט לְמַעַן עֻזָּךְ. לְמַעַן פְּאֵרָךְ. לְמַעַן צִדְקָתָךְ. לְמַעַן קְדֻשָּׁתָךְ.

and my iniquities; according to Your Loving-kindness [כְּחַסְדְּךָ] *may You remember me for the sake of Your Goodness* [לְמַעַן טוּבְךָ]*, HASHEM (Psalms 25:5,7).*

10. יִחוּדָךְ — *Your Oneness.*

[See *comm.* to sts. 6 and 7. See also *comm.* to אֱלֹהֵינוּ, *Our God*, p. 37.]

11. כְּבוֹדָךְ — *Your Honor.*

[Once again we follow the Psalmist's lead in praying: עָזְרֵנוּ אֱלֹהֵי יִשְׁעֵנוּ, *Assist us, O God of our salvation,* עַל־דְּבַר כְּבוֹד־שְׁמֶךָ, *for the sake of Your Name's Honor (Psalms 79:9).*]

12. לְמוּדָךְ — *Your Teaching.*

When the Jews at Mount Sinai heard the Divine Voice proclaim: *'I am HASHEM, your God, Who has brought you forth from the Land of Egypt ...'* they shuddered and stood at a distance. They said to Moses, *'You speak to us, that we may be able to accept your words; but let not God speak with us, lest we die!' (Exodus 20:2,15-16).*

The Holy One Blessed be He says: In This World the Jews were taught Torah by flesh and blood — that is by Moses — therefore, they forget what they have learned. For just as flesh and blood passes from the World, so his teachings pass ... But in the World to Come, Israel shall be taught Torah directly by the Holy One Blessed be He, as the prophets declare: *all your children shall be* לִמּוּדֵי ה׳, *taught by HASHEM (Isaiah 54:13)*; and *man shall no longer teach his fellow (Jeremiah 31:33).* Just as God is eternal so is His [direct] Teaching eternal. Torah taught in this way can never be forgotten *(Yalkut Shimoni II 479).*

13. מַלְכוּתָךְ — *Your Kingdom.*

[This is one of the attributes mentioned in *I Chronicles* 29:11. See *comm.* st. 3.]

On *Rosh HaShanah*, just before reciting the *Kaddish* before the *Musaf*, R' Levi Yitzchak of Berditchev would cry out: The czar of Russia claims that the world is his; the emperor of France claims that the world is his; so it is that every monarch claims possession of the world. But we, Your Jewish nation, say, ... יִתְגַּדַּל וְיִתְקַדַּשׁ, *May His great Name be exalted and sanctified in the world ...* וְיַמְלִיךְ מַלְכוּתֵהּ, *and may He establish His Kingship, and cause His Salvation to sprout ...*

Likewise, we pray for salvation which will lead to the day when *HASHEM shall be King over the entire earth (Zechariah 14:9;* see *comm.* st. 6; *Shaar Yisas'char*).

14. נִצְחָךְ — *Your Eternality.*

[This is one of the attributes mentioned in *I Chronicles* 29:11. See *comm.* st. 3.]

The word נֶצַח has many meanings, several of which are possible in the sense of our verse. Our translation is based upon the definition of נֶצַח as *forever*, as in *Isaiah* (25:8): בִּלַּע הַמָּוֶת לָנֶצַח, *He will swallow up death forever.* Alternative translations are *strength* (see *Isaiah* 63:6); *supervision* (see *Ezra* 3:9); and *victory* (see *I Samuel* 15:29).]

15. סוֹדָךְ — *Your Counsel.*

[The Psalmist proclaimed: אֲשֶׁר יַחְדָּו נַמְתִּיק סוֹד בְּבֵית אֱלֹהִים נְהַלֵּךְ בְּרָגֶשׁ, *Together we would share sweet counsel, in the House of God we would walk with multitudes (Psalms 55:15).* Rashi explains that "sweet counsel" refers to the intricacies of the Torah. Sweet counsel is attained in the Holy Temple in Jerusalem.

We pray for salvation from this oppressive exile, so that we can return to our land and rebuild the Holy Temple, there to share the sweetness of Your Counsel.]

An alternative rendering of סוֹדָךְ is *Your Secret*, i.e., the secrets revealed by prophecy *(Beis Yaakov)* [as in *Amos* 3:7, *God will do nothing until He has revealed* סוֹדוֹ, *His secret, to His servants the prophets (Amos 3:7)*. But, the Rab-

1 *Your Oneness,* **11** *for the sake of Your Honor,* **12** *for the sake*
11-19 *of Your Teaching,* **13** *for the sake of Your Kingdom,* **14** *for the sake of Your Eternality,* **15** *for the sake of Your Counsel,* **16** *for the sake of Your Strength,* **17** *for the sake of Your Beauty,* **18** *for the sake of Your Righteousness,* **19** *for the sake of Your*

bis teach, prophecy is confined to *Eretz Yisrael (Mechilta, Bo* 12:1). Thus, we beseech God to save us from exile and return us to our land with renewed spiritual greatness so that we may once again become privy to the secrets revealed only through His prophets.]

16. עֻזְּךָ — *Your Strength.*
[After the Exodus from Egypt and the miraculous deliverance of the fledgling nation through the Sea of Reeds, Moses and the Israelites sang: *Strength* (עָזִּי), *and praise of God has been my salvation (Exodus* 15:2).

Concerning the advent of Messiah, Micah prophesied: *He will arise and sustain his flock* בְּעֹז ה׳, *through HASHEM's Strength (Micah* 5:3).

The first redemption of the Jews — from Egypt — and their final redemption — in Messianic times — both depend on the attribute of Divine Strength. Thus, we pray along with the founder of the Davidic dynasty, which will reach its fulfillment in the person of King Messiah: *Turn to me, be gracious to me, give of Your Strength* (תְּנָה עֻזְּךָ) *give of Your Strength to Your servant and save Your maidservant's son (Psalms* 86:16).]

17. פְּאֵרְךָ — *Your Beauty.*
Our salvation is God's beauty *(Beis Yaakov),* as the prophet says in God's Name [*Isaiah* 46:13]: *I shall place salvation in Zion, to Israel* [I shall give] *My beauty (Tefillah Yesharah).*

פְּאֵר alludes to tefillin, as in *Ezekiel* 24:17, פְּאֵרְךָ חֲבוֹשׁ עָלֶיךָ, *bind your beauty* [i.e., your tefillin] *onto yourself*

(Berachos 11a).[1] But our stich speaks of *God's tefillin,* not Israel's; as if God wears tefillin, as it were. How is Israel's salvation connected to God's tefillin?

The Talmud teaches that just as Israel's tefillin contain verses which sing God's praises, so God's tefillin contain verses which sing Israel's praises. Thus said the Holy One Blessed be He to Israel: [in your tefillin] you declare My uniqueness to the world with the verse ... שְׁמַע יִשְׂרָאֵל, *Hear Israel, HASHEM is our God, HASHEM is One (Deuteronomy* 6:4) — likewise, in My tefillin, shall I declare your uniqueness to the world: *Who is like Your people Israel, a unique nation in the land (I Chronicles* 17:21). Another verse contained in God's tefillin is: *You are praiseworthy, Israel, a people saved by HASHEM (Deuteronomy* 33:29; *Berachos* 6a).

But as long as Israel is in exile, its condition seems to contradict this stich, and, so to speak, to render God's tefillin invalid. Our prayer, therefore, is that His tefillin — the praises of Israel — become valid again *(Beis Avraham).*

18. צִדְקָתָךְ — *Your Righteousness.*
The revelation of God's righteousness will be a by-product of Israel's redemption. As the prophets teach, כִּי קְרוֹבָה יְשׁוּעָתִי לָבוֹא וְצִדְקָתִי לְהִגָּלוֹת, *For My Salvation is soon to come, and My Righteousness to be revealed (Isaiah* 56:1). הוֹדִיעַ ה׳ יְשׁוּעָתוֹ לְעֵינֵי הַגּוֹיִם גִּלָּה צִדְקָתוֹ, *HASHEM has made His Salvation known, to the eyes of the nations He has revealed His Righteousness (Psalms* 98:2).

---

1. The juxtaposition of עֻזְּךָ, *Your Strength,* and פְּאֵרְךָ, *Your Beauty,* is noteworthy. As mentioned in the *commentary,* פְּאֵרְךָ חֲבוֹשׁ means *bind your tefillin;* but since the word פְּאֵר may also be translated *turban* (see *Ezekiel* 34:18) it must refer to the *tefillin* worn on the head. The word עֹז, *strength,* is also used to refer to tefillin. The prophet says: *HASHEM has sworn by His right hand and by the arm of* עֻזּוֹ, *His Strength (Isaiah* 62:8). The Sages interpret this passage: *His right hand* refers to the Torah (see *comm., v.* 4); *the arm of His Strength* is His tefillin [worn on the left arm] *(Berachos* 6a).

א לְמַעַן רַחֲמֶיךָ הָרַבִּים. לְמַעַן שְׁכִינָתָךְ. לְמַעַן תְּהִלָּתָךְ:
כ־כב

During the first six days of Succos turn to page 84. On Hoshana Rabbah continue:

כִּי־אָמַרְתִּי עוֹלָם חֶסֶד יִבָּנֶה:

(עֲנֵנָא בִּזְכוּתָא דְּאַבְרָהָם רַחִימָא עֲנֵנָא:)

19. קְדֻשָּׁתָךְ — *Your Sanctity.*

After describing the final salvation, the victory over Israel's last enemy, Gog, God declares [Ezekiel 38:23]: *And I shall be exalted and sanctified* [וְהִתְגַּדִּלְתִּי וְהִתְקַדִּשְׁתִּי] *in the eyes of many nations* (Tefillah Yesharah).

20. רַחֲמֶיךָ הָרַבִּים — *Your numerous Mercies.*

[Scripture spells out clearly that salvation is dependent upon God's numerous Mercies: וּבְרַחֲמֶיךָ הָרַבִּים, *and according to Your numerous Mercies You gave them saviors who saved them from their oppressors* (Nehemiah 9:27).

This stich deviates from the rest of this *hoshana* in that only here is an adjective used in conjunction with the attribute. No explanation is offered to explain this anomaly. Indeed, Rashi cites *Machzor Roma* which omits the word הָרַבִּים, *numerous.*]

21. שְׁכִינָתָךְ — *Your Shechinah.*

The word שְׁכִינָה [*Shechinah*], from שכן, *to dwell*, refers to the manifestation of the Divine Presence on earth.

The Talmud teaches: Come and observe how beloved Israel is to the Holy One Blessed be He. For wherever they are exiled the *Shechinah* is with them...and when they will eventually be redeemed, the *Shechinah* will be among them...for the Holy One Blessed be He returns with them from their exiles (Taanis 16a; Megillah 29a).

Save us for the sake of Your *Shechinah* — which is in exile with us (Beis Avraham).

[Alternatively, salvation is a prerequisite for *Shechinah* manifestation. וְשָׁכַנְתִּי, *and I shall dwell* (i.e., My Presence will be perceived) *among the children of Israel ... Then they will know that I am HASHEM, their God, Who has brought them forth from the land of Egypt* לְשָׁכְנִי, *to dwell, among them* (Exodus 29:45-46). Just as the redemption from Egypt was followed by manifestation of His Presence, so may we merit redemption followed by restoration of the *Shechinah* to our midst.]

22. תְּהִלָּתָךְ — *Your Praise.*

Our salvation is His Praise, as it is written: *to recount the Name of HASHEM in Zion,* וּתְהִלָּתוֹ, *and His Praise in Jerusalem* (Psalms 102:22; Ibn Ezra).

Ibn Yachya explains a different verse in similar fashion. *Who can tell of the mighty feats of HASHEM, make understood all of* תְּהִלָּתוֹ, *His Praise?* (Psalms 106:2). The *mighty feats* alludes to the creation of the world; *His Praise*, to the redemption from Egypt.

A different insight into תְּהִלַּת ה׳, *HASHEM's Praise*, can be gleaned from the Yom Kippur liturgy. One of the Thirteen Attributes of Mercy listed in Exodus (34:6-7) is אֶרֶךְ אַפַּיִם, *forbearance* [lit. *long of countenance*]. אַף, the singular form of אַפַּיִם, means *countenance, face* (see I Kings 1:23) or, more specifically, *nose* (see Genesis 2:7). Since a common sympton of anger is heavy breathing through the nose, an alternate meaning of אַף is *anger* (see Rashi, Exodus 15:8). Most translations of אֶרֶךְ אַפַּיִם understand the phrase in this latter manner and render *slow to anger* or *long suffering*.

If this opinion is correct, why does Scripture use the plural form אַפַּיִם, rather than the singular אַף? The Talmud explains that forbearance takes two forms: One is reserved for the righteous; the other, for the wicked (Eruvin 22a).

Tosafos elaborates. The beneficent face which shines upon the righteous is slow to appear, for the rewards of the righteous are not temporal, but eternal;

1
20-22

Sanctity, [20] for the sake of Your numerous Mercies, [21] for the sake of Your Shechinah, [22] for the sake of Your Praise.

During the first six days of Succos turn to page 84. On Hoshana Rabbah continue:

For I have said: The world shall be built with loving-kindness.
(Answer us, in the merit of beloved Abraham, answer us.)

and they are withheld until the World to Come. The wicked, too, are treated with forbearance, but of a different sort. The angry face of retribution is deferred to the World to Come, where the wicked suffer the fate which their evil deeds have earned them. This delay is also a display of Divine Mercy, for it allows time for repentance.

This dual nature of forbearance represented by the plural form of אֶרֶךְ אַפַּיִם is given as a praiseworthy attribute of God: It is Your manner, our God, to be forbearing to the wicked and to the righteous, and this is תְּהִלָּתֶךָ, Your Praise (Yom Kippur liturgy).

◆§ Hakafah-circuits and Sefirah-emanations

Man can have no conception of God Himself, for His true Being is beyond human intelligence. All we can know are His manifestations such as mercy, power, and judgment, and even these can come to us only through intermediaries. These intermediaries are called Sefiros, generally translated emanations (ArtScroll Zemiroth, p. 226).

Each of the seven hakafah-circuits of Hoshana Rabbah is related to one of the seven Sefirah-emanations which are represented respectively by the seven Patriarchs. These relationships are delineated in the chart below.

A Scriptural passage which mentions the applicable Sefirah is recited after each hakafah. Beis Yaakov then adds the phrase, Answer us in the merit of Abraham, [or Isaac, or Jacob and so on], answer us.

כִּי־אָמַרְתִּי... — For I have said...
This passage is recorded here as it appears in most liturgies. It is a fragment of a verse in Psalms (89:3) which reads in full: כִּי־אָמַרְתִּי עוֹלָם חֶסֶד יִבָּנֶה שָׁמַיִם תָּכִן אֱמוּנָתְךָ בָהֶם, For I have said: The world shall be built with loving-kindness — You shall prepare your faithfulness in the very heavens. Some siddurim (e.g., Beis Yaakov) cite the entire verse. Others (e.g., Avodas Yisrael) omit the first stich and say only: עוֹלָם חֶסֶד יִבָּנֶה, The world shall be built with loving-kindness.

עוֹלָם חֶסֶד יִבָּנֶה — The world shall be built with loving-kindness.
Rabban Yochanan ben Zakkai was once walking in Jerusalem followed by his disciple R' Yehoshua. When the latter spied the ruins of the Holy Temple he sighed, 'Woe unto us, for the Beis HaMikdash — the place where our sacrifices atoned for our sins — has been destroyed!'

Rabban Yochanan responded, 'My son, be not discouraged, for there is an

Hakafah-circuit	Sefirah-emanation	Patriarch
first	חֶסֶד, Loving-kindness	אַבְרָהָם, Abraham
second	גְבוּרָה, Power	יִצְחָק, Isaac
third	תִּפְאֶרֶת, Splendor	יַעֲקֹב, Jacob
fourth	נֶצַח, Eternality	מֹשֶׁה, Moses
fifth	הוֹד, Glory	אַהֲרֹן, Aaron
sixth	יְסוֹד, Foundation	יוֹסֵף, Joseph
seventh	מַלְכוּת, Kingship	דָּוִד, David

Hoshanos / **For the Sake of Your Truth**

אבן שתיה

ב א־ט אֶבֶן שְׁתִיָּה. בֵּית הַבְּחִירָה. גֹּרֶן אָרְנָן. דְּבִיר הַמֻּצְנָע. הַר הַמּוֹרִיָּה. וְהַר יֵרָאֶה. זְבוּל תִּפְאַרְתֶּךָ. חָנָה דָוִד. טוֹב

alternative means of attaining forgiveness, one that is just as effective as sacrifice — charitable acts of loving-kindness. For thus says God, *'I prefer loving-kindness and not sacrifices'* (Hosea 6:6); and, *'I have said: The world shall be built with loving-kindness'* (Yalkut II 522).

In one of the Heavenly palaces there are angels who are appointed to gather the acts of loving-kindness which Israel does in This World. When the Attribute of Divine Justice makes accusations against the nation, these angels immediately bring forth the kindnesses which they have amassed and display them before the Holy One Blessed be He — who desires loving-kindness. Then, despite their guilt, as long as they treat each other kindly, He is merciful with them *(Tomer Devorah)*.

[Thus, *the world* which was created for Israel (see *comm.* to בּוֹרְאֵנוּ, *Our Creator*, page 37) *shall be built*, i.e., maintained, *with loving-kindness* performed by the people of Israel.]

עוֹלָם — *The world.*

Our translation follows *Targum* (to *Psalms* 89:3). Most of the commentators, however, (notably *Rashi, Ibn Ezra, Radak*) render עוֹלָם as *eternity*. Thus the verse reads: *Loving-kindness be built* (i.e., established) *eternally*.

אֶבֶן שְׁתִיָּה — Foundation Stone

[All twenty-two stiches of this prayer are allusions to either the *Beis HaMikdash* or the city of Jerusalem in which it was located. Most of the descriptive expressions are of Scriptural derivation; the remainder are of Talmudic origin.]

The *kavanah*, purposeful concentration, of all these stiches is the same, namely: Please save (i.e., redeem) the *Beis HaMikdash* from its present desolation and desecration; from the wild foxes that prowl over it [see *Lamentations* 5:18] *(Beis Avraham)*; that it may be rebuilt, speedily in our days *(Shaar HaShamayim)*. [The commentary will be limited to expositions on the origins and implications of each allusion.]

1. אֶבֶן שְׁתִיָּה — *Foundation stone.*

There was a stone in the center of the Holy of Holies (upon which stood the Ark of the Covenant) ... It was known from the days of the early prophets [Samuel and David *(Rashi)*] and was called Foundation Stone, ... for from this spot the world sprang forth [meaning that the stone was the first part of earth to be created by God. It grew into the planet as we know it] *(Yoma 53b, 54b)*.

The Midrash traces this stone to a much earlier date. While Jacob was traveling to Charan from Beer Sheba, the sun set when he was at the very spot where Abraham had been willing to offer Isaac as a sacrifice. Jacob took twelve stones from the altar upon which his father had been bound and placed them around his head. These stones symbolized the twelve tribes which would eventually issue from him. But as he slept the stones fused into one huge stone, indicating that the twelve tribes would become one unified nation. When he awoke and discovered the miracle, he consecrated the unified stone by pouring oil over it. The Holy One Blessed be He then placed His right foot, so to speak, upon the stone, causing it to sink to the nethermost depth. There it became a foundation supporting the earth, and was called Foun-

✥ Foundation Stone

**2
1-8**

Foundation stone, ² chosen Temple, ³ Arnan's granary, ⁴ hidden rendezvous, ⁵ Mount Moriah, ⁶ Mount He-is-seen, ⁷ residence of Your Splendor, ⁸ where David resided,

dation Stone. Upon it was built the *Beis HaMikdash*, as Jacob pledged: *Then this stone which I have set up as a pillar shall become a house of God* (Genesis 28:22; *Pirkei d'R' Eliezer* ch. 35).

2. בֵּית הַבְּחִירָה — *[The] Chosen Temple.*
This frequently used Talmudic expression for the Temple (e.g., *Maaser Sheini* 5:12) is derived from the verse: *And HASHEM appeared to Solomon at night and said to him ... 'Now ...* בָּחַרְתִּי, אֶת הַבַּיִת הַזֶּה, *I have chosen this House [the Temple] that My Name shall be there eternally'* (II Chronicles 7:16).

3. גֹּרֶן אָרְנָן — *Arnan's granary.*
Upon the instruction of the prophet Gad, King David purchased Arnan's granary as the site for the erection of a מִזְבֵּחַ, *altar* (see II Samuel 24:18-25). Subsequently, *Solomon commenced building the Temple of HASHEM in Jerusalem, on Mount Moriah ... at the granary of Arnan the Jebusite* (II Chronicles 3:1).

4. דְּבִיר הַמְצֻנָּע — *Hidden rendezvous.*
This term refers to the Holy of Holies, in which stood the Ark, upon which the two *cheruvim* were placed. From between them the voice of God issued when He summoned Moses (*Rashi* to *Leviticus* 1:1). The chamber was called דְּבִיר [from דבר, *to speak*], alluding to the דְּבַר ה׳, *word of HASHEM*, which issued from within (*Beis Yaakov*).
Pesikta d'R' Kahana explains with a parable why the word of God issues from a secluded place:
A king would often stroll through the public gardens with his young daughter. Once she came of age, however, he regarded it undignified to converse with the princess in full view of his subjects. [*The complete glory of a princess is within* (Psalms 45:14).] He therefore had a private pavilion built where he would meet and converse with her.
Similarly, when Israel was a young, emerging nation, God wrought great overt miracles for all the world to see — the splitting of the sea, the receiving of the Torah — but once they matured as a nation, it became undignified to deal with them publicly, so He set aside the דְּבִיר הַמְצֻנָּע, *hidden rendezvous* (*Rashi*).

5-6. הַר הַמּוֹרִיָּה ... וְהַר יֵרָאֶה — *Mount Moriah ... (And) Mount He-is-seen.*
The mountain upon which the *Beis HaMikdash* was built is the very same mountain upon which the עֲקֵידַת יִצְחָק, *Binding of Isaac*, took place. God called to Abraham and said, '*Take your son ... Isaac, and get yourself to the land of Moriah; bring him up there as an offering upon one of the mountains ... And Abraham named that site HASHEM-will-appear, as it is said this day: on the Mount HASHEM-is-seen* (Genesis 22:2, 14). This site later became Arnan's granary (see stich 3 above), and was purchased by King David. Eventually, *Solomon commenced building the House of HASHEM in Jerusalem, on Mount Moriah ...* (II Chronicles 3:1).
Why was the mountain called מוֹרִיָּה, *Moriah* [lit., *teaching of God*]? ... For from there went forth teaching to Israel. As the prophet declared: *From out of Zion shall issue Torah* (lit., *teaching*) *and the word of HASHEM from Jerusalem* (Isaiah 2:3; *Taanis* 16a; *Rashi*). Indeed, the chamber of the Sanhedrin was situated in the Temple courtyard (*Rashi* to *Exodus* 21:1).

7. זְבֻל תִּפְאַרְתֶּךָ — *Residence of Your Splendor.*
After building the Temple, King Solomon said: *I have erected* בֵּית זְבֻל, *a*

[47] *Hoshanos*/**Foundation Stone**

ב הַלְּבָנוֹן. יְפֵה נוֹף מְשׂוֹשׂ כָּל־הָאָרֶץ. כְּלִילַת יֹפִי. לִינַת
יד-טז הַצֶּדֶק. מָכוֹן לְשִׁבְתֶּךָ. נָוֵה שַׁאֲנָן. סֻכַּת שָׁלֵם. עֲלִיַּת

house of residence, for You (I Kings 8:13; Rashi). Isaiah (63:15) expanded the description: וְבֵל קָדְשְׁךָ וְתִפְאַרְתֶּךָ, the residence of Your Holiness and Your Splendor (Tefillah Yesharah).

8. חָנָה דָוִד — *Where David resided.*
Standing *in the city where David resided*, Isaiah (29:1) prophesied about the impending destruction of the Temple.

9. טוּב הַלְּבָנוֹן — *Goodness of Lebanon.*
Moses beseeched God to permit him, entry into the Holy Land, that he might see הָהָר הַטּוֹב הַזֶּה וְהַלְּבָנֹן, *this good mountain and the Lebanon* (Deuteronomy 3:25).
Although the name Lebanon refers to a forest in which grew towering cedars, the Sages understand Moses' request as more than just the desire to visit a place. Lebanon alludes to the *Beis HaMikdash* ... And why is it called לְבָנוֹן, *Lebanon*, a word related to לָבָן, *white?* Because it cleanses the sins of Israel; as it is stated: *If your sins are as scarlet, as snow He will whiten them* (Isaiah 1:18; *Sifri* 3:25).
[Another reason why the Temple is called *Goodness of Lebanon* is that timber for the Temple was brought from the forest of Lebanon (see *I Kings* 5:20-28; *Song of Songs* 3:9). Since we may assume that only the best trees were felled for this purpose, *Goodness of Lebanon* is an apt appellation for the *Beis HaMikdash*.]

10. יְפֵה נוֹף מְשׂוֹשׂ כָּל־הָאָרֶץ — *Fairest of brides, joy of all the earth.*
This description of Mount Zion, upon which the Temple stood, appears verbatim in *Psalms* 48:3. *Rashi* who translates the obscure word נוֹף as *bride* bases his opinion upon a statement of R' Shimon ben Lakish (*Rosh HaShanah* 26a): In the precinct of Ken Nesheraya a bride is called *nynphe* [=*nymph*, Greek for bride].
Alternative interpretations of יְפֵה נוֹף are: *Fair as the spreading branches* (נוֹף) *of a tree* (Rashi citing Dunash); *fairest of sites* (see *Joshua* 17:11; Rashi citing Menachem); *fairest of climates* (Radak citing his father).

11. כְּלִילַת יֹפִי — *Perfectly beautiful.*
The juxtaposition of כְּלִילַת יֹפִי, *perfectly beautiful*, and מְשׂוֹשׂ כָּל הָאָרֶץ, *joy of all the earth*, is based on *Lamentations* 2:15. Jeremiah bewailed the destruction of Zion: *Could this be the city of which they said*, כְּלִילַת יֹפִי מָשׂוֹשׂ לְכָל־הָאָרֶץ, *perfectly beautiful, a joy to all the earth.*
The word כַּלָּה, *bride*, is related to כָּלִיל, *perfect.* A bride is called כַּלָּה because she is the epitome of beauty; on her wedding day, every bride is regarded as perfectly beautiful (*Metzudos* to *Jeremiah* 2:2). According to this interpretation we may extend our translation to *perfectly beautiful bride*, making this stich synonymous with the previous one, *fairest of brides.*
Strangely, the appellation כְּלִילַת יֹפִי, *perfectly beautiful*, is also used to describe the city of Tyre: *Tyre, you have said, 'I am perfectly beautiful!'* (*Ezekiel* 27:3). But there is a difference. Tyre spoke these words in self-praise — *I am* — others did not praise her in this manner. But with Zion such is not the case. It was, *The city of which they said, 'Perfectly beautiful!'* This is the meaning of the folk saying: [Believe] not what her mother says of her, but what her neighbors say of her (*Midrash Tehillim* 48:3).[1]

12. לִינַת הַצֶּדֶק — *Lodge of righteousness.*

1. A further difference between Jerusalem and Tyre may be discerned in the respective verses despite the identical expression being used about both cities. Realization of one's own beauty may lead to pride — a pride often manifested in jealousy. 'I am beautiful, you are ugly; therefore, I am worthy, you are worthless.' Such a pernicious pride and the beauty that engenders it are valueless to the world. Such beauty was Tyre's — *I am perfectly beautiful* —

2
9-18

⁹ *goodness of Lebanon,* ¹⁰ *fairest of brides, joy of all the earth,* ¹¹ *perfectly beautiful,* ¹² *lodge of righteousness,* ¹³ *prepared for Your dwelling,* ¹⁴ *tranquil abode,* ¹⁵ *tabernacle of Salem,* ¹⁶ *pilgrimage of the tribes,* ¹⁷ *valuable cornerstone,* ¹⁸ *the dis-*

[*Isaiah* (1:21) bemoans the spiritual and moral defilement of Jerusalem: *How has she become as a harlot, the loyal city which was once filled with justice,* צֶדֶק יָלִין בָּהּ, *righteousness once lodged in her, but now — murderers.*]

R' Yehuda ben R' Simon said: No man ever lodged overnight in Jerusalem while sin still stained his hands. How so? The *Tamid* [Daily Sacrifice] of the morning atoned for the sins of the night; and the *Tamid* of the afternoon atoned for the sins of the day *(Rashi citing Bamidbar Rabbah).*

Rashi's alternative interpretation of this expression is based upon *Sanhedrin* 32a and 35a: In cases calling for capital punishment, the court in Jerusalem would not issue a guilty verdict unless the matter was deliberated overnight; this to give ample opportunity to reflect on the possible righteousness of the defendant. Hence, the city is called, *lodge of righteousness.*

13. מָכוֹן לְשִׁבְתֶּךָ — *Prepared for Your dwelling.*

[Both Moses, in the Song at the Sea *(Exodus* 15:17), and Solomon, in his invocation at the Dedication of the Holy Temple *(I Kings* 8:13; *II Chronicles* 6:2), use this phrase to describe the Temple.]

The word מָכוֹן, may also be vocalized מְכֻוָּן, *corresponding,* thus offering an alternative interpretation. The Holy Temple on earth *corresponds* to the Throne of Glory in heaven *(Rashi to Exodus* 15:17).

14. נְוֵה שַׁאֲנָן — *Tranquil abode.*

The prophet proclaimed: *Your eyes will see Jerusalem* נְוֵה שַׁאֲנָן, *tranquil abode, unbreachable shelter … (Isaiah* 33:20).

15. סֻכַּת שָׁלֵם — *Tabernacle of Salem.*

Salem was an ancient name of Jerusalem. Abraham called the city יִרְאֶה, *Yireh* [=Jeru], as is stated *(Genesis* 22:14): *Abraham named that site HASHEM Yireh.*

Shem [son of Noah, also known as Malchi-zedek] called the place שָׁלֵם, *Shalem* [=Salem], as it is written (ibid. 14:18): *Malchi-zedek, king of Salem.*

Said the Holy One Blessed be He, 'If I call it *Yireh* [=Jeru] as Abraham did, then the righteous Shem will be distraught; but if I call it *Shalem* [=Salem], then the righteous Abraham will be distraught. Instead I will satisfy both of these righteous men by calling it *Yireh-Shalem* [=Jeru-Salem=Jerusalem] *(Midrash Rabbah to Genesis* 14:18).

As the Psalmist says: *Well-known in Judea is God, in Israel His name is great.* וַיְהִי בְשָׁלֵם סֻכּוֹ, *When in Salem was His Tabernacle, and His residence in Zion (Psalms* 76:2-3).

16. עֲלִיַּת שְׁבָטִים — *Pilgrimage of (the) tribes.*

[Literally, the word עֲלִיָּה means *elevation* or *ascending.* The specialized meaning of *pilgrimage* is based on the fact that Jerusalem is situated on hills; hence one ascends as he makes his pilgrimage to the Holy City. The Psalmist sings, *'I was joyful when they said to me, "To the House of HASHEM shall we go …" for there* עָלוּ שְׁבָטִים, *the tribes ascended … (Psalms* 122:1,4).]

Alternatively, עֲלִיָּה may mean *assessment,* for when David bought Arnan's granary he assessed each tribe fifty

no more, no less. The rest of the world is totally ignored. Only Tyre matters.

On the other hand, the pride evoked by one's beauty may be expressed in benevolent fashion. 'I am proud of the beauty with which the Creator endowed me. It makes me happy, and I shall share that happiness with others!' Such beauty was Jerusalem's — not merely did others call her *perfectly beautiful,* but she was also *a joy to all the world.*

ב שְׁבָטִים. פִּנַּת יְקָרַת. צִיּוֹן הַמְצֻיֶּנֶת. קֹדֶשׁ הַקֳּדָשִׁים.
יז-כב רְצוּף אַהֲבָה. שְׁכִינַת כְּבוֹדֶךְ. תֵּל תַּלְפִּיּוֹת:

During the first six days of Succos turn to page 84. On Hoshana Rabbah continue:

לְךָ זְרוֹעַ עִם־גְּבוּרָה, תָּעֹז יָדְךָ תָּרוּם יְמִינֶךָ:
(עֲנָנָא בִּזְכוּתָא דְיִצְחָק עֲקִידְתָּא עֲנָנָא:)

◈§ אום אני חומה

ג אוֹם אֲנִי חוֹמָה. בָּרָה כַּחַמָּה. גָּלָה וְסוּרָה. דָּמְתָה
א-ד

17. פִּנַּת יְקָרַת — *Valuable cornerstone.*

Therefore, thus says my Lord, HASHEM/ELOHIM, 'I have established in Zion a stone — a fortified stone — פִּנַּת יְקָרַת, *a valuable cornerstone ...* (Isaiah 28:16). The structure for which the 'cornerstone' would be used was the building where the Sanhedrin sat. Its role was to engage in Torah study, which is more valuable than pearls (Rashi). [This is a play on the similarity of sound between פִּנָּה, cornerstone, and פְּנִינָה, *pearl*.]

Alternatively, פִּנָּה may be derived from פָּנִים, *face*, and לִפְנוֹת, *to turn to*, or, *to face*. Accordingly, the Temple is described as precious place [יְקָרַת from יָקָר, *precious*], toward which all faces turn — all Jews face towards Jerusalem when they bow during *Shemoneh Esrei* (*Rashi; see Berachos* 31a).[1]

18. צִיּוֹן הַמְצֻיֶּנֶת — *The distinguished Zion.*

As it is written (Psalms 87:2): *HASHEM loves the gates of Zion* [or: *the distinguished gates*] (שַׁעֲרֵי צִיּוֹן). Rav Chisdah explained this as the gates distinguished by [the study of] halachah [שְׁעָרִים הַמְצֻיָּנִים בַּהֲלָכָה]. Thus, God loves the gates of [the academies where] halachah [is taught] more than the synagogues and study halls [where homiletical discourse and flowery orations may hamper the study of practical halachah (Maharsha)] (Berachos 8a).

Alternatively, the distinguishing marks of Zion may refer to the roadside markers placed by the exiles as they were being driven from Jerusalem, as a sign that even as they were leaving, the hope of eventual return remained in their breasts. The prophet cried to the exiles (Jeremiah 31:20): *Erect for yourselves markers* [צִיֻּנִים], *... take to your heart the road on which you travel* [into exile]; *you will return, Maiden of Israel, you will return to these your cities.*

19. קֹדֶשׁ הַקֳּדָשִׁים — *Holy of Holies.*

[This descriptive title for the inner sanctum of both the Tabernacle, which accompanied the Israelites on their journeys through the desert, and the Temple in Jerusalem is found numerous times in Scripture. (See, for example, Exodus 26:33 and I Kings 6:16). In either case, this chamber occupied the rear third of the edifice. The front area of the Temple was called הַקֹּדֶשׁ, *the Holy* (Exodus 26:33), while the screened-off section was the *Holy of Holies* and is identical to the דְּבִיר הַמֻּצְנָע, *hidden rendezvous*, mentioned in stich 4.]

20. רְצוּף אַהֲבָה — *Decked with love.*

An Aperion (meeting hall) *did King Solomon make for himself, of the timbers of Lebanon ... its insides* רְצוּף אַהֲבָה, *decked with love, for the daughters of Zion* (Song of Songs 3:9-10).

---

1. [The juxtaposition of this phrase with the preceding one is based on Scripture. When Nehemiah relates how the wall surrounding Jerusalem was rebuilt, the last section mentioned is called עֲלִיַּת הַפִּנָּה, *elevation of the cornerstone.* (See Nehemiah 3:31-32.)]

2 tinguished Zion, **19** Holy of Holies, **20** decked with love,
19-22 **21** resting place of Your Honor, **22** Hill of Talpios.

<small>During the first six days of Succos turn to page 84. On Hoshana Rabbah continue:</small>

Yours is the arm with Power, show the strength of Your hand, raise high Your right hand. (Answer us in the merit of Isaac who was bound on the altar, answer us.)

◆§ Nation that Declares

3   **1** **N**ation that declares, 'I am a wall!'
1-3   **2** Brilliant as the sun — **3** yet exiled and displaced.

Rashi explains that by condensing his *Shechinah*, as it were, between the two *cheruvim* [see comm. st. 4] God showed His love for Israel and the Temple they built in His honor.

22. תַּל תַּלְפִּיוֹת — *Hill of Talpios.*
As the Tower of David ... built לְתַלְפִּיוֹת, as Talpios (Song of Songs 4:4). The Temple is known as David's tower because he dedicated himself to making the preparations for its construction so that Solomon could build it without delay. The Temple was called *Talpios*, an adornment, because all gazed upon it to learn its forms and the beautiful masterwork of its design (*Rashi*).

Other interpretations offered for this rare word תַּלְפִּיוֹת, *Talpios,* include:
— landmark *(Ibn Yanach);*
— a place to hang swords (לִתְלוֹת פִּיוֹת) [i.e., a fortress] *(Ibn Ezra);*
— teaching, training ... to guide the traveler, for its height made it visible from afar *(Metzudos);*
— a hill (תֵל) to which all mouths (פִּיוֹת) turn in prayer [as King Solomon declared when He dedicated the *Beis HaMikdash* (I Kings 8:35-36); 'When they will pray towards this place and will praise Your Name ... then may You hearken from the heavens ...] *(Berachos* 30a).

... לְךָ זְרוֹעַ — *Yours is the arm ...* Psalms 89:14.

תָּעֹז יָדְךָ תָּרוּם יְמִינֶךָ — *Show the strength of Your hand, raise high Your right hand.*
Targum's interpolations make this verse eminently suitable as an epilogue to the *hoshana* which speaks of the Holy Temple: *Show the strength of Your hand* by redeeming Your nation; *raise high Your hand* and complete *Your Beis HaMikdash.*

◆§ אוֹם אֲנִי חוֹמָה — Nation that declares 'I am a wall!'

Many metaphors are used in Scripture and Rabbinic writing to describe the nation of Israel. During the third *hakafah*-circuit, which corresponds to the Patriarch Jacob (Israel), from whom the nation derived its name, an alphabetical catalogue of such metaphors is chanted in prayer for the nation's redemption and salvation *(Bnei Yisas'char).*

[Most of the epithets in this *Hoshana* are particularly applicable to Israel during its decline and exile. Material poverty is juxtaposed with spiritual wealth as the *paytan* paints a word-picture depicting the firm faith of God's chosen people.]

1. אוֹם אֲנִי חוֹמָה — *Nation* [that declares], *'I am a wall!'*
What shall we do for our sister on the day she is spoken of? If she be a wall, then we shall build a turret of silver upon her. But if she be a door,

ג לְתָמָר. הַהֲרוּגָה עָלֶיךָ. וְנֶחְשֶׁבֶת כְּצֹאן טִבְחָה. זְרוּיָה בֵּין
ה-יג מַכְעִיסֶיהָ. חֲבוּקָה וּדְבוּקָה בָּךְ. טוֹעֶנֶת עֻלָּךְ. יְחִידָה
לְיַחֲדָךְ. כְּבוּשָׁה בַּגּוֹלָה. לוֹמֶדֶת יִרְאָתָךְ. מְרוּטַת לֶחִי.

then we shall enclose her with panels of cedar.
'I am a wall!' (Shir HaShirim 8:8-10).

Rashi interprets: *'What shall we do,'* reflected the Heavenly Tribunal, *'for our sister,* Israel, *on the day she is spoken of* by the enemy nations who plot evil against her?

'If she be steadfast in her faith as *a wall* of the strongest metal, *then we shall build a turret of silver upon her* — i.e., we shall fortify her by rebuilding Jerusalem with its Holy Temple. *But if she be* influenced by every alien culture like *a door* swinging on its hinges this way and that, *then we shall enclose her* not with long lasting metal walls, but *with panels of cedar* — wooden boards which eventually rot from too much interaction with their surroundings — allowing the enemy to enter at will.'

At this point Israel responds, אֲנִי חוֹמָה, *I am a wall,* strong and stalwart in my love for God!'

2. בָּרָה כַּחַמָּה — *Brilliant as the sun.*

Israel is compared to the heavenly bodies — יָפָה כַלְּבָנָה, *beautiful as the moon,* בָּרָה כַּחַמָּה, *brilliant as the sun* (Shir HaShirim 6:10).

The dawn is preceded by darkness. Whatever light there is comes from the moon, itself but a small reflection of the sun's brilliance. Gradually, as the sun rises, darkness gives way to light; the moon's reflected splendor fades as the sun dazzles the earth in its full majesty. So it was during the era of the Second Temple. When the rebuilt *Beis HaMikdash* first gazed down upon the world from its lofty mountain, Israel was ruled by Zerubavel, an appointed governor — a mere reflection of majesty — serving at the pleasure of King Cyrus. Nevertheless, Israel was *beautiful as the moon.* But in later years, when the Hasmoneans rid the land of the alien Hellenist culture and established their own Jewish dynasty, the nation became בָּרָה כַּחַמָּה, *brilliant as the sun* (Rashi).

O return us to those days, not when we were merely a moonlike reflection of beauty, but when our brilliance rivaled even that of the sun.

3. גָּלָה וְסוּרָה — [Yet] *exiled and displaced.*

Both Diaspora Jews and those in *Eretz Yisrael* are alluded to in this stich (which is based on *Isaiah 49:21*). The former are גָּלָה, *exiled,* the latter סוּרָה, *displaced.* For even in *Eretz Yisrael* they cannot worship in the Temple (*Shaar HaShamayim*).

4. דָּמְתָה לְתָמָר — *(She is) likened to a palm tree.*

While every other nation prostrated itself before Nebuchadnezzar's statue, only Israel refused to pay tribute to an idol (see *Daniel* ch. 3; see also *hoshana* 7, st. 19). Her posture remained upright like a stately palm tree (*Rashi* to *Shir HaShirim 7:8*).

Alternatively תָּמָר is a proper noun, *Tamar,* and refers to Judah's daughter-in-law. When his two eldest sons, Er and Onan, died childless after being married to Tamar, Judah would not allow his third son, Shelah, to marry her [See ArtScroll *Bereishis* and *Overview* to *Ruth*]. Tamar, however, burned with the desire to bear children of Judah's lineage. Recognizing her sincerity, God brought about a chain of events which resulted in Tamar's bearing twins to Judah. From one of them, Peretz, descended David, the ancestor of Messiah. (See *Genesis* ch. 38 and *Rashi*; *Ruth* 4:18-22.)

Although we are *exiled and displaced,* we desire only to cleave to God. Our longing to serve Him is *likened unto Tamar's* desire to bear the seeds of monarchy. In the merit of following her example, may we be worthy of the advent of her scion, the Messiah from the house of David (*Bnei Yisas'char*).

3
4-14

⁴ *Likened to a palm tree —* ⁵ *yet murdered for Your sake*
⁶ *and regarded like sheep for slaughter.*
⁷ *Although scattered among her provocateurs,*
⁸ *she hugs and cleaves to You* ⁹ *and bears Your yoke—*
¹⁰ *unique in declaring Your Oneness.*
¹¹ *While vanquished in exile*
¹² *she learns Your awesomeness.*
¹³ *Plucked of cheek,* ¹⁴ *given over to the whippers,*

5־6. הַהֲרוּגָה עָלֶיךָ וְנֶחְשֶׁבֶת כְּצֹאן טִבְחָה — [*Yet*] *murdered for Your sake and regarded like sheep for slaughter.*

Even when You crushed us in the place of Tanim and shrouded us in the shadow of death — have we forgotten the Name of our God? Or extended our hands to a strange god? ...כִּי־עָלֶיךָ הֹרַגְנוּ כָל־הַיּוֹם, *Because for Your sake we are killed all day long,* נֶחְשַׁבְנוּ כְּצֹאן טִבְחָה, *we are regarded like sheep for slaughter. Awaken! Why do You seem to sleep, O my Lord? Arouse Yourself, forsake not forever! Arise — assist us! And redeem us by virtue of Your loving-kindness (Psalms 44:20-21, 23-24, 27).*

7. ...זְרוּיָה — [*Although*] *scattered...*

Like stiches 5-6, this one is based on Psalm 44, specifically v. 12: *You delivered us like sheep for devouring, and among the nations scattered us (Tefillah Yesharah).*

10. יְחִידָה לְיַחֲדָךְ — *Unique in* [*declaring*] *Your Oneness.*

[See comm., hoshana 1, sts. 6,7,17.]

11־12. כְּבוּשָׁה בַּגּוֹלָה לוֹמֶדֶת יִרְאָתָךְ — [*While*] *vanquished in exile she learns Your awesomeness.*

Whatever befalls a person should be viewed as a lesson in serving his Creator. If one's love is aroused when he views a desirable, beloved object, he should consider it nothing more than a means to attain a higher form of love — אַהֲבַת ה׳, *love for God.*

Similarly, if in the presence of royalty one is enveloped with a feeling of awe, he should learn proper יִרְאַת ה׳, *fear of the Lord,* from his experience *(Bnei Yisas'char* citing unnamed disciples of the *Baal Shem Tov).*[1]

13. מְרוּטַת לֶחִי — *Plucked of cheek.*

Beards are torn from cheeks. This is done not to inflict pain, but to insult and embarrass the victim *(Tosefta Bava Kama 9:11).* [It is noteworthy that one of the favorite tactics of Jew-baiters through the centuries, and especially the Nazis, שר״י, was to make sport of defenseless Jews by plucking their beards.]

The juxtaposition of stiches 11-15 is perhaps based on the Midrash: The prophets suffered personally from Israel's rebellious spirit. At times they were even beaten in response to their admonition, as *Isaiah 50:6* states: *My body have I given to the whippers* [נָתַתִּי לְמַכִּים] *and my cheeks to the pluckers* [וּלְחָיַי לְמֹרְטִים], *my face have I not turned aside (Tanchuma, Tazria 9).* In the spirit of מִדָּה כְּנֶגֶד מִדָּה, punishment suited *measure for measure* to fit the sin, Israel must bear the burden of physical pain and psychological insult which it had itself inflicted upon the

---

1. The story is told of a righteous man who would wear a lightweight garment while praying, even in the dead of winter. When asked how he was able to bear the cold, the *tzaddik* replied, 'My position often brings me into contact with the king. In his majesty's presence I have learned to suppress all extraneous feelings and emotions, except for the deep-seated awe which his august personage evokes. This awe I bring to my prayers. The fear of My Creator before whom I stand makes me oblivious to my surroundings and I feel not the slightest discomfort from the weather.'

Similarly, the very oppressiveness of our exile teaches us His awesomeness *(Beis Avraham).*

ג נְתוּנָה לְמַכִּים. סוֹבֶלֶת סִבְלָךְ. עֲנִיָּה סֹעֲרָה. פְּדוּיַת
יד-כב טוֹבִיָּה. צֹאן קָדָשִׁים. קְהִלּוֹת יַעֲקֹב. רְשׁוּמִים בְּשִׁמְךָ.
שׁוֹאֲגִים הוֹשַׁעְנָא. תְּמוּכִים עָלֶיךָ:

During the first six days of Succos turn to page 84. On Hoshana Rabbah continue:

תִּתֵּן אֱמֶת לְיַעֲקֹב, חֶסֶד לְאַבְרָהָם:
(עֲנָנָא בִּזְכוּתָא דְיַעֲקֹב שְׁלֵימָתָא עֲנָנָא:)

prophets. But, we pray, now that exiled, oppressed Israel has learned to recognize Your awesomeness — please save this nation.

16. עֲנִיָּה סֹעֲרָה — *A storm-tossed pauper.*

Her heart is stormy because of her troubles (Rashi to Isaiah 54:11).

17. טוֹבִיָּה — *Moses.*

Yocheved's first vision of her newborn baby Moses is described in Scripture: *And she saw that he was* טוֹב, *good* (Exodus 2:2). This teaches that she named him טוֹבִיָּה, Toviah [lit., God is good] (Sotah 12a).

18. צֹאן קָדָשִׁים — *Sacred sheep.*

The prophet compares Israel to sheep: *I shall increase them — the people — like sheep, like sacred sheep, like the sheep of Jerusalem* (Ezekiel 36:38). Not just ordinary sheep, but sheep that are: a) as numerous as the sheep which are brought to Jerusalem during the festival season (Metzudos); and b) sanctified in their entirety, like the sheep brought as עוֹלוֹת, *burnt offerings*, upon the altar in Jerusalem (Malbim).

19. קְהִלּוֹת יַעֲקֹב — *Congregations of Jacob.*

The Torah which Moses taught us, is a heritage to קְהִלַּת יַעֲקֹב, *the congregation of Jacob* (Deuteronomy 33:4). Although Scripture uses the singular קְהִלַּת, *congregation of,* the paytan uses the plural form קְהִלּוֹת, *congregations,* alluding to the tripartite make-up of the nation: Kohanim, Levites and Israelites (Iyun Tefillah).

The verse does not mention the Torah as the heritage of בֵּית יַעֲקֹב, *the Family of Jacob,* or זֶרַע יַעֲקֹב, *the offspring of Jacob.* The term קְהִלַּת יַעֲקֹב, *congregation of Jacob,* includes not only those who can trace their ancestry back to Jacob, but all who congregate in Torah academies, seeking to cleave to God. Even גֵרִים, *proselytes* are included (Ramban).

20. רְשׁוּמִים בְּשִׁמְךָ — *Inscribed with Your Name.*

The gentile nations mocked Israel's national census when each adult male Jew would be counted among the members of his tribe. 'These people think they are pure-blooded Jews, yet they are actually of Egyptian stock. The Jews delude themselves that Egyptian men did not prevail over their mothers. But if Egyptian taskmasters prevailed over the Israelites' bodies, surely they prevailed over their wives!'

In response to these gibes the Holy One Blessed be He surrounded the Israelite family names with His own. He divided one of His Holy Names, יָה, YAH, placing the letter ה before each family name, and the letter י after each name. Thus the family of Chanoch was called מִשְׁפַּחַת הַחֲנֹכִי, *family of HaChanochi.* With this in mind, the Psalmist described Israel as שִׁבְטֵי־יָהּ, *the tribes of YAH* (Psalms 122:4), i.e., the tribes whose legitimacy was attested by God by means of His Name יָה (Rashi to Numbers 26:5).

Alternatively, *inscribed with Your Name* alludes to the covenant of circumcision which is inscribed — i.e., carved — from their very flesh. The next stich — שׁוֹאֲגִים הוֹשַׁעְנָא, *they cry, 'Please save us!'* — recalls the custom [not found in the Ashkenazic rite, but retained in some (e.g., Aleppian) Sephardic rites] that those gathered at a circumcision call out in unison:

3
15-22

¹⁵ *she shoulders Your burden.*
¹⁶ *A storm-tossed pauper*
¹⁷ *is she who was redeemed by Moses.*
¹⁸ *Sacred sheep,* ¹⁹ *congregations of Jacob,*
²⁰ *Inscribed with Your Name,*
²¹ *they cry, 'Please save us!'* — ²² *they rely upon You!*

During the first six days of Succos turn to page 84. On Hoshana Rabbah continue:

Grant truth to Jacob, loving-kindness to Abraham.
(Answer us in the merit of the wholesome Jacob, answer us.)

אָנָּא ה' הוֹשִׁיעָה נָא, *We beseech You, HASHEM, save us now! (Psalms 118:25; Beis Avraham).*

21-22. שׁוֹאֲגִים הוֹשַׁעְנָא תְּמוּכִים עָלֶיךָ — *They cry, 'Please save us!' — they rely upon You!*

Service of the Creator may be directed inward or outward. One *tzaddik* may spend his days introspectively scrutinizing his every action and thought while seeking to perfect himself to his fullest potential. About the broader problems faced by the nation as a whole — poverty, drought, epidemic, pogrom — he merely shrugs, 'Whatever God decrees shall be! Who are we to attempt to change God's will?' Regarding such a person the story is told:

During an extremely oppressive period in which many vicious edicts were promulgated against European Jewry, the Baal Shem Tov stormed heaven and earth, leaving no stone unturned, in his search for any and every way to have these decrees annulled. A God-fearing man approached him, 'But this is the will of the Creator! Shouldn't we lovingly accept His will?'

'It is well that you were not living at the time of the Purim story,' replied the Baal Shem Tov. 'Had you been there, you would have told Mordechai, "But this is the will of the Creator! Shouldn't we lovingly accept His will?"'

Despite his narrow view of communal needs, this *tzaddik* cannot be faulted in his personal service of God. For that he is not only himself worthy of merit, but indeed the entire community benefits from his merits. [It was perhaps just such righteous people who Abraham thought could save Sodom with their personal merits (see *Genesis* 18:20-23).]

On the other hand, there is the *tzaddik* who ignores his own needs. For himself, he has complete faith that whatever God decrees shall be! But for the public welfare he will not rest until he has neutralized whatever ominous cloud hangs over his people. He will scour every corner of heaven or earth in his search for that meritorious deed which will tip the scales of Divine justice in his community's favor. שׁוֹאֲגִים הוֹשַׁעְנָא, *They cry, 'Please help us!'* describes the *tzaddikim* of the latter mold. They cry, they pray, they search for salvation. Of those who belong to the former type it may be said, תְּמוּכִים עָלֶיךָ, *they rely upon You!* In the merit of both of these groups, 'Please, save us now!' *(Shaar Yisas'char).*

תִּתֵּן אֱמֶת לְיַעֲקֹב חֶסֶד לְאַבְרָהָם — *Grant truth to Jacob, loving-kindness to Abraham.*

This passage is recorded here as it appears in most liturgies. It is a fragment of a verse in *Micah* (7:20) which continues: אֲשֶׁר־נִשְׁבַּעְתָּ לַאֲבֹתֵינוּ מִימֵי קֶדֶם, *as You swore to our fathers from ancient times.* Some *siddurim* (e.g., *Beis Yaakov*) cite the entire verse.

Although this third *hakafah*-circuit is personified by the Patriarch Jacob, it is the combination of חֶסֶד, *loving-kindness,* and אֱמֶת, *truth,* which elicits favorable judgment from the Heavenly Tribunal (see comm. *hoshana* 1, st. 3).

אֲדוֹן הַמּוֹשִׁיעַ

ד אָדוֹן הַמּוֹשִׁיעַ. בִּלְתְּךָ אֵין לְהוֹשִׁיעַ. גִּבּוֹר וְרַב
א-ט לְהוֹשִׁיעַ. דַּלּוֹתִי וְלִי יְהוֹשִׁיעַ. הָאֵל הַמּוֹשִׁיעַ. וּמַצִּיל
וּמוֹשִׁיעַ. זוֹעֲקֶיךָ תּוֹשִׁיעַ. חוֹכֶיךָ הוֹשִׁיעַ. טְלָאֶיךָ תַּשְׂבִּיעַ.

אֲדוֹן הַמּוֹשִׁיעַ — Lord Who Saves

Every part of Creation may be assigned to one of four kingdoms or categories of existence. In ascending spiritual order they are: דּוֹמֵם, mineral [lit. silent]; צוֹמֵחַ, vegetable [lit. sprouting]; חַי, animal [lit. living]; and מְדַבֵּר, human [lit. speaking].

In the Divine plan for the world, each member of one realm is capable of becoming elevated to a higher one. Indeed, this is the purpose of its existence. The soil, water, and air of the Mineral Kingdom are the nutrients which are absorbed by, and become one with, the plant life of the Vegetable Kingdom. Plants, in turn, serve as food and building blocks for the creatures of the Animal Kingdom. Finally, these become the fare of Man, subject of the Human Kingdom. Scripture alludes to this system of elevation: וְנָתַתִּי עֵשֶׂב בְּשָׂדְךָ לִבְהֶמְתֶּךָ וְאָכַלְתָּ וְשָׂבָעְתָּ, And I shall give grass [vegetable] in your field [mineral] for your cattle [animal] and you [Man] shall eat and be sated (Deut. 11:15).

But does this process of uplift end with man? Is man the perfect being? Certainly not — since the imagery of man's heart is evil from his youth (Genesis 8:21), man must raise himself from the evil which fills his heart — and the last words of the above verse (Deuteronomy 11:15) allude to the proper method to accomplish this end. The same phrase וְאָכַלְתָּ וְשָׂבָעְתָּ, and you shall eat and be sated, also appears as the opening of another verse in Deuteronomy (8:10). That verse continues וּבֵרַכְתָּ אֶת ה' אֱלֹהֶיךָ, and you shall bless HASHEM, your God ... Recitation of a blessing is the fulfillment of a Divine command [mitzvah]; and he who performs a mitzvah creates a friendly angel for himself (Avos 4:11). Kabbalah teaches that study of Torah provides the soul's sustenance, while the performance of mitzvos supplies its raiment. Man must use the baser elements of creation in the fulfillment of the Divine commandments, but he needs guidance to use them wisely. In the next three hoshanos we invoke Divine protection for the animal, vegetable and mineral realms, and we pray for our own welfare — Lord Who saves ... save now man and beast ... (and) the ground from accursedness.

2. בִּלְתְּךָ אֵין לְהוֹשִׁיעַ — Other than You there is no savior [lit., none who can save].

This stich is a paraphrase of God's own words: I am HASHEM, your God, [who has delivered you (Targum)] from the land of Egypt ... וּמוֹשִׁיעַ אַיִן בִּלְתִּי, there is no Savior other than Me (Hosea 13:4).

3. גִּבּוֹר וְרַב לְהוֹשִׁיעַ — [You are] powerful and abundantly able to save.

God's גְּבוּרָה, power, differs from that of flesh and blood. The powerful human is able to kill the living — but God's power resurrects the dead (Ikkarim 4:35). Thus, although You are powerful, Your power is not destructive but productive (Iyun Tefillah).

[The second benediction of Shemoneh Esrei may be understood in this manner: You are גִּבּוֹר, powerful eternally, My Lord, You revive the dead, and thereby You are רַב לְהוֹשִׁיעַ abundantly able to save.]

The expression רַב לְהוֹשִׁיעַ, abundantly able to save, is taken from Isaiah (63:1). The people will ask, 'Who is this

◆§ Lord Who Saves

4
1-10

¹ **L**ord Who saves, ² other than You there is no savior.
³ You are powerful and abundantly able to save.
⁴ I am impoverished, yet You shall save me.
⁵ God is the Savior, ⁶ He delivers and saves.
⁷ Those who cry to You — save;
⁸ those who yearn for You — save.
⁹ Satiate Your lambs; ¹⁰ cause an abundance of crops,

... Who subdues [the nations (Mahari Kara)] with His great strength?' To which God will respond, 'It is I, Who speaks in righteousness, abundantly able to save!' The people will inquire about the punishment dealt out by His great strength, and He will respond with salvations which stem from His mercy.

The *Zohar* (*Bo* 36b) teaches that God displays strict power and lenient lovingkindness at the same time, but not to the same people. *HASHEM will plague Egypt — He will afflict and He will heal* (*Isaiah* 19:22). Although most commentators understand both the plague and the cure to refer to Egypt, *Zohar* interprets that the very plague of Egypt will be a healing balm to Israel.

In similar fashion the Psalmist declares: *And all the pride of the wicked I shall cut down; exalted shall be the pride of the righteous* (*Psalms* 75:11). It is the very downfall of evil, brought about by the Divine Attribute of גְּבוּרָה, power, which exalts the righteous and brings about their salvation (*R' Yisachar Dov of Belz*).

Two alternative readings of this stich are: גִּבּוֹר וּמוֹשִׁיעַ, *You are powerful and You save* (*Avodas Yisroel; Tehillas HASHEM*); and גּוֹאֵל וּמוֹשִׁיעַ, *You redeem and You save* (*Machzor Roma*).

4. דַּלּוֹתִי וְלִי יְהוֹשִׁיעַ — *I am impoverished, yet You shall save me.*

Israel said to the Holy One Blessed be He: Although דַּלּוֹתִי, I am [spiritually] *impoverished*, and lacking in the performance of *mitzvos*, nevertheless, I am Yours. Therefore it is proper and fitting that לִי יְהוֹשִׁיעַ, *You shall save me* (*Psalms* 116:6; *Pesachim* 118b).

An alternative interpretation is based on the *Midrash*:

On five occasions King David cried, קוּמָה ה׳, *arise, HASHEM, and save me* (*Psalms* 3:8; 7:7; 9:20; 10:12; 17:13).

God answered him, 'David, My son, no matter how often you call upon me to rise up, I shall not do so except when I see the poor being robbed and hear the crying of the needy' (*Bereishis Rabbah* 75:1). Thus, because we are impoverished, You shall rise up to save us (*Divrei Yechezkel* cited in *Beis HaOtzar*).

7. זוֹעֲקֶיךָ תּוֹשִׁיעַ — *Those who cry to You — save.*

They cried [וַיִּזְעָקוּ] *to HASHEM when adversity overtook them, from their oppression He saved them* [יוֹשִׁיעֵם] (*Psalms* 107:13,19).

8. חוֹכֶיךָ הוֹשִׁיעַ — *Those who yearn for You — save.*[1]

As the prophet declares: *Praiseworthy are all who yearn* (חוֹכֵי) *for Him* (*Isaiah* 30:18).

9. טְלָאֶיךָ — *Your lambs.*

Thus my Lord HASHEM/ELOHIM will come in strength ... as a shepherd He will graze His flock, with His arm He will gather the lambs ... (*Isaiah*

---

1. *Shem Shlomo* uses a parable to explain the first eight stiches of this *hoshana*:
   A poor farmer owned only one small field from which he barely eked out a living. To make matters worse, his wicked neighbors allowed their flocks to graze on his field. Whatever would escape the animals, the farmers themselves would steal. As often as he mended fences,

ד יְבוּל לְהַשְׁפִּיעַ. כָּל־שִׂיחַ תַּדְשֵׁא וְתוֹשִׁיעַ. לְגֵיא בַּל
יד-כב תַּרְשִׁיעַ. מְגָדִים תַּמְתִּיק וְתוֹשִׁיעַ. נְשִׂיאִים לְהַסִּיעַ.
שְׂעִירִים לְהָנִיעַ. עֲנָנִים מִלְהַמְנִיעַ. פּוֹתֵחַ יָד וּמַשְׂבִּיעַ.
צְמֵאֶיךָ תַּשְׂבִּיעַ. קוֹרְאֶיךָ תּוֹשִׁיעַ. רְחוּמֶיךָ תּוֹשִׁיעַ.
שׁוֹחֲרֶיךָ הוֹשִׁיעַ. תְּמִימֶיךָ תּוֹשִׁיעַ:

During the first six days of Succos turn to page 84. On Hoshana Rabbah continue:

נְעָמוֹת בִּימִינְךָ נֶצַח:

(עִנְיָנָא בִּזְכוּתָא דְמֹשֶׁה רַעְיָא מְהֵימְנָא עֲנַנָּא:)

40:11). [See also comm. to *hoshana* 3, st. 18.]

10. יְבוּל — *Crops.*
Although the primary meaning of יְבוּל is *crops* (Leviticus 26:4), *Iyun Tefillah* notes that the term also alludes to many other necessities of communal life: freedom (Leviticus 25:10); water (Isaiah 44:4); and law and order (Isaiah 55:12).

11. כָּל־שִׂיחַ תַּדְשֵׁא — [*Of*] (*all*) *trees, of vegetation* [lit. *vegetation sprout forth*].
The *paytan* combines two verses (Genesis 2:5 and 1:11) describing the creation of trees and vegetation. The second verse uses the imperative תַּדְשֵׁא, *let vegetation sprout forth.* The *paytan* retains that form instead of using the noun דֶּשֶׁא, *vegetation* (*Iyun Tefillah*).

12. גֵיא — *The ground.*
גֵיא means *valley.* By extension it refers to the entire earth which is like a low valley lying between the high heavens (*Kol Bo*).

בַּל תַּרְשִׁיעַ — *Do not condemn.*

Fulfill that which You said to Noah (Genesis 8:21): *I will not continue to curse again the ground because of man* (*Iyun Tefillah*). For even if man sinned, why is the earth to be blamed? (*Kol Bo*)

14. נְשִׂיאִים — *Soaring clouds.*
Clouds are called נְשִׂיאִים literally, *elevated ones,* for they rise high above the earth (*Radak* to *Psalms* 135:7).
The Sages have another interpretation. The word נְשִׂיאִים may also mean *princes.* Moisture laden clouds bring about abundant crops which make farmers wealthy as princes (*Yerushalmi Taanis* 3:3).
R' Hirsch comments that clouds are likened to princes because rulers have the responsibility to use their power and wealth to serve the people from whom they derive their position. Clouds, too, have the function of returning to earth the moisture from which the clouds were formed.
נשא also means to *lift* or *carry.* The clouds lift the moisture from the ocean and carry it on high (*Shaar HaShamayim*).

so often did they breach them. Finally, in desperation, the poor victim sought help from some of the townsfolk.
'It is not my wont,' replied the first, 'to offer help to others. I worry about myself, you worry about yourself.'
The second responded more favorably, but also refused to assist him. 'Why do you ask me? I always get stuck with other people's troubles. Many others can help you; let them do it.'
'They are stronger than I am,' answered the third. 'I fear their reprisals.'
'You are a lazy, worthless person who deserves whatever they do,' rejoined the fourth.
The fifth also offered no aid. 'If I were to force your wicked neighbors to return all that they have stolen from you, it will be of no avail. Tomorrow they will be back and treat you even worse than before.'
The last potential redeemer said, 'You sound insincere to me. I do not believe that you are telling the truth. Your words lack feeling.'

4

11-22

¹¹ *of trees, of vegetation — save.*
¹² *Do not condemn the ground,*
¹³ *but sweeten the luscious fruits — save.*
¹⁴ *Let the wind bring the soaring clouds,*
¹⁵ *let the stormy rains be emplaced,*
¹⁶ *let the clouds not be withheld.*
¹⁷ *He Who opens a hand and satisfies*
¹⁸ *Your thirsty ones — satisfy;* ¹⁹ *Your callers — save;*
²⁰ *Your beloved — save;* ²¹ *Your seekers — save;*
²² *Your wholesome ones — save.*

During the first six days of Succos turn to page 84. On Hoshana Rabbah continue:

There is delight at Your right hand for eternity. (Answer us in the merit of Moses, the faithful shepherd, answer us.)

15. שְׂעִירִים — *Stormy rains.*

Rashi (Deuteronomy 32:2) relates this word to רוּחַ סְעָרָה, *storm wind*, but also cites *Onkelos* who renders *winds of rain*.

17. פּוֹתֵחַ יָד וּמַשְׂבִּיעַ — *He Who opens a hand and satisfies.*

This stich is an abridgment of Psalms 145:16 which reads: פּוֹתֵחַ אֶת־יָדֶךָ, *You open Your hand,* וּמַשְׂבִּיעַ לְכָל־חַי רָצוֹן, *and satisfy the desire of every living being (Kol Bo).*

Alternatively, this is a plea for salvation in the merit of those charitable people who open their hands to support and sustain the poor and the helpless *(Beis Avraham).*

18. צְמֵאֶיךָ — *Your thirsty ones.*

This refers to those who seek God and thirst for His presence. *You are my God, I seek You* (אֲשַׁחֲרֶךָּ). *My soul thirsts* (צָמְאָה) *for You (Psalms 63:2).*

20. רְחוּמֶיךָ — *Your beloved.*

God told the prophet Hosea to name his daughter לֹא רֻחָמָה, *Lo Ruchamah [Unbeloved]*, symbolizing Israel's estrangement from God. Once the nation returned to His worship, He changed her name to רֻחָמָה, *Ruchamah, [Beloved] (Hosea 1:6; 2:2).* Thus, רְחוּמֶיךָ means *Your. Ruchamah —* i.e., *Your beloved nation (Beis Yaakov).*

Avodas Yisrael has a variant reading: רַב לְהוֹשִׁיעַ, *Abundantly able to save.*

21. שׁוֹחֲרֶיךָ — *Your seekers.*

[See comm. to st. 18.]

Alternatively, this refers to those who awake in the middle of the night to pray for salvation (תִּקּוּן חֲצוֹת). Such righteous people may be described as those who awaken the שַׁחַר, *dawn (Beis Avraham).* [Such was the custom of King David. *Awake, O my soul, awake ...* אָעִירָה שָּׁחַר, *I shall awaken the dawn (Psalms 57:9).*]

Israel is surrounded by enemies, each availing himself of every opportunity to steal whatever it produces — indeed, even the land itself. But, when Israel turns to You for help, O God, You make no excuses.

You are wont to help the oppressed — אֲדוֹן הַמּוֹשִׁיעַ, *Lord Who saves.*

You do not send us elsewhere, for בִּלְתְּךָ אֵין לְהוֹשִׁיעַ, *other than You there is no savior.*

You do not fear reprisals — גִּבּוֹר וְרַב לְהוֹשִׁיעַ, *You are powerful and abundantly able to help.*

You do not call us worthless and undeserving for although דַּלּוֹתִי, *we are [I am] impoverished*, וְלִי יְהוֹשִׁיעַ, *yet You shall save us [me].*

You do not fear that Your efforts at salvation will be wasted when the evil oppressors renew their attacks, for You are הָאֵל הַמּוֹשִׁיעַ, *God, the Savior,* וּמַצִּיל וּמוֹשִׁיעַ, *Who delivers and saves —* with a salvation which cannot be overturned by mortals.

Finally, You hear our cries and probe our hearts, You know that we are זוֹעֲקֶיךָ, *those who cry to You,* and חוֹכֶיךָ, *those who yearn for You (quoted by Shaar Yisas'char).*

אדם ובהמה

ה א-יב אָדָם וּבְהֵמָה. בָּשָׂר וְרוּחַ וּנְשָׁמָה. גִּיד וְעֶצֶם וְקַרְמָה. דְּמוּת וְצֶלֶם וְרִקְמָה. הוֹד לַהֶבֶל דָּמָה. וְנִמְשַׁל כַּבְּהֵמוֹת נִדְמָה. זִיו וְתֹאַר וְקוֹמָה. חִדּוּשׁ פְּנֵי אֲדָמָה. טִיעַת עֲצֵי נְשָׁמָה. יְקָבִים וְקָמָה. כְּרָמִים וְשִׁקְמָה. לְתֵבֵל הַמְסִימָה.

נְעִמוֹת — There is delight ...

This passage is recorded here as it appears in most liturgies. It is a fragment of *Psalms* 16:11 which reads in full: תּוֹדִיעֵנִי אֹרַח חַיִּים, *You will reveal to me the path of life*, שֹׂבַע שְׂמָחוֹת אֶת־פָּנֶיךָ, *the fullness of joys in Your Presence; there is delight at Your right hand for eternity*. Some *siddurim* (e.g., *Beis Yaakov*) cite the entire verse. [See commentary to *hoshana* 1, st. 14.]

אָדָם וּבְהֵמָה — Man and Beast

1. אָדָם וּבְהֵמָה — *Man and beast*.

אָדָם, here translated *Man*, may also be rendered *Adam*, the first man, whose vast, all-encompassing, intellectual stature is completely unimaginable to us. Indeed, before Adam's initial sin the very angels of heaven thought him divine and wished to sing praises to him. [The greatness of Adam is the subject of an Overview in the ArtScroll edition of *Genesis* (pp. 13-16).]

אָדָם וּבְהֵמָה תּוֹשִׁיעַ ה׳, *Man and beast You save, HASHEM* (*Psalms* 36:7). Though man is the intellectual equal of Adam, God will save him only if he humbles himself like an animal (*Rashi*, based on *Chullin* 5b).

3. קַרְמָה — *Skin*.

The translation follows most commentators and is based on the verse וְקָרַמְתִּי עֲלֵיכֶם עוֹר, *I shall envelop you in skin* (*Ezekiel* 37:6). The word is related to קְרוּם, *membrane*.

A variant reading וְקוֹמָה, *and stature*, appears in some texts, notably *Rashi*.

4. דְּמוּת וְצֶלֶם — *Likeness and image*.

In announcing his intention to create Adam, God said: *Let us make man* בְּצַלְמֵנוּ, *in our image*, כִּדְמוּתֵנוּ, *after our likeness* (*Genesis* 1:27). צֶלֶם, *image*, refers to external appearance; דְּמוּת, *likeness*, refers to the resemblance of that appearance to something or someone else. Man's soul resembles the higher beings which are unseen yet eternal, while his body resembles the lower beings and the earth from which both he and they were taken (*Ramban* citing R' Yosef Kimchi).

[Please save *Man*, who resembles both the beasts of the earth (*flesh, sinew, bone and skin*) and the heavenly angels (*spirit and soul*).]

וְרִקְמָה — *A tapestry*.

All the elements mentioned above are embroidered into one great tapestry Man, by the master Artisan, God (based on *Radak* and *Ibn Ezra* to *Psalms* 139:15).

5. הוֹד לַהֶבֶל דָּמָה — *Splendor resembling futility*.

Despite all his trappings of splendor and majesty, *Man resembles futility, his days are like the passing shadow* (*Psalms* 144:4). This refers to the person who does not strive to fulfill the demands of his Divine image (*Sforno*).

6. וְנִמְשַׁל כַּבְּהֵמוֹת נִדְמָה — *Compared to the likeness of beasts*.

The words נִמְשַׁל [related to מָשָׁל, *parable*] and נִדְמָה [related to דְּמוּת, *likeness*] have the same meaning — *it is compared to* or *it resembles*. Man's splendor is so futile that it is not even compared to living beasts, but to a mere wall-painting of animals (*Iggeres HaTiyul, Psalms* 49:13).

◈§ Man and Beast

**5
1-12**
¹**M**an and beast:
  ² Flesh, spirit and soul, ³ sinew, bone and skin,
  ⁴ likeness and image — a tapestry.
  ⁵ Splendor resembling futility,
    ⁶ compared to the likeness of beasts —
    ⁷ luster, figure and stature.
  ⁸ Renew the face of the earth —
    ⁹ planting trees in desolate lands,
    ¹⁰ winepresses and stands of grain,
    ¹¹ vineyards and sycamores.
  ¹² To the demarcated land —

7. זִיו וְתֹאַר וְקוֹמָה — *Luster, figure, and stature.*

Continuing the thought of the preceding two stiches — as Man's splendor is futile and beast-like, so are his luster, figure and stature *(Kol Bo)*.

[Alternatively, a new thought begins here: Please save Man whom You have endowed with a unique luster, figure, and erect posture, which sets him above all Your other creatures.]

8. חִדּוּשׁ פְּנֵי אֲדָמָה — *Renew the face of the earth.*

You send forth Your spirit, they are created; You renew the face of the earth (Psalms 104:30). This expresses the concept that life is in a constant state of renewal — an old man expires, a baby is born; one life ends, another begins. *A generation goes and a generation comes, but the earth endures forever* (Ecclesiastes 1:4). Although individuals die, the species endures *(Radak)*.

9. טִיעַת עֵצִי נְשַׁמָּה — *Planting trees in desolate land.*

The prophet declares: *This very land which is desolate* (הַנְשַׁמָּה) [i.e., Eretz Yisrael after the destruction of the Temple and exile of the people] *has become a Garden of Eden* (Ezekiel 36:35).

Alternatively, נְשַׁמָּה, *desolate*, modifies עֲצֵי, *trees,* and alludes to barren trees. The stich is a request that even these trees be granted power to produce fruit *(Shaar HaShamayim)*.

Ramban (Genesis 1:11) wonders at the omission of barren trees from the account of Creation. He surmises that in their pristine state all trees bore edible fruit. Only after Adam and Eve ate the forbidden fruit of the Tree of Knowledge was the ground cursed (*Genesis* 3:17), and certain species of trees became incapable of bearing fruit.

10-11. יְקָבִים ... וְשִׁקְמָה — *Winepresses ... and sycamore.*

After mentioning barren trees our thoughts turn to fruit trees *(Shaar HaShamayim)*.

שִׁקְמָה — *Sycamore.*

This is a species of fig tree which grows in valleys *(Metzudos,* to *I Chronicles* 27:28). [It is usually identified as *Ficus Sycomorus* which grows in the Near East, and should not be confused with either the American sycamore which is chiefly a timber tree, or with the British sycamore which is chiefly grown as a shade tree.]

12. לְתֵבֵל הַמְסֻיָּמָה — *To the demarcated land.*

The extent to which Man may use the soil is demarcated by the many land-related *mitzvos* — e.g., כִּלְאַיִם, *forbidden mixtures* (Leviticus 19:19); שְׁמִיטָה, *Sabbatical Year* (ibid. 25:1-7); בַּל תַּשְׁחִית, *destruction of fruit trees* (Deuteronomy 20:19-20).

*Hoshanos/***Man and Beast**

ה מִטְרוֹת עֹז לְסַמְּמָה. נְשִׁיָּה לְקַיְּמָה. שִׂיחִים לְקוֹמְמָה.
יג-כב עֲדָנִים לְעָצְמָה. פְּרָחִים לְהַעֲצִימָה. צְמָחִים לְגָשְׁמָה.
קָרִים לְזָרְמָה. רְבִיבִים לְשַׁלְּמָה. שְׁתִיָּה לְרוֹמְמָה. תְּלוּיָה
עַל־בְּלִימָה:

During the first six days of Succos turn to page 84. On Hoshana Rabbah continue:

יהוה אֲדֹנֵינוּ מָה־אַדִּיר שִׁמְךָ בְּכָל־הָאָרֶץ, אֲשֶׁר תְּנָה הוֹדְךָ עַל־הַשָּׁמָיִם:
(עֲנָנָא בִּזְכוּתָא דְּאַהֲרֹן כַּהֲנָא עֲנָנָא:)

אדמה מארר

ו אֲדָמָה מֵאֵרֶר. בְּהֵמָה מְמַשְׁכֶּלֶת. גֹּרֶן מִגִּזָּם. דָּגָן
א-ד

13. מִטְרוֹת עֹז — *Powerful rains.*
Targum (Job 37:6) renders this phrase *heavy winter rains which cause herbage to sprout.*

לְסַמְּמָה — *To heal.*
This word is derived from סַם, *drug* (Beis Yaakov).
Alternatively, the word is related to סַמָּנִים, *herbs,* and the stich reads: *Powerful rains to cloak the earth with herbage* (Iyun Tefillah).

14. נְשִׁיָּה — *Forsaken wastes.*
Metzudos (Psalms 88:13) renders אֶרֶץ נְשִׁיָּה as *forgotten land.* Targum translates *thirsty and desolate.*

15-17. שִׂיחִים לְקוֹמְמָה ... פְּרָחִים לְהַעֲצִימָה — *To sustain with vegetation ... to invigorate with flowers.*
Tehillas HaShem reads שִׂיחִים לְהַעֲצִימָה ... פְּרָחִים לְקוֹמְמָה, which the English translation of that *siddur* renders: *To strengthen it with vegetation ... to restore it with flowers.*

19-20. לְזָרְמָה ... רְבִיבִים — *To pour a stream ... droplets.*
זֶרֶם is identified as a *stream of flowing water* (Rashi to Habbakuk 3:10) and רְבִיבִים as *droplets of rain.* The latter are so called because like the arrows of a skilled bowsman [רֹבֶה], they always strike their mark (Rashi to Deuteronomy 32:2).

לְשַׁלְּמָה — *To cloak.*
The text and translation follow *Beis Yaakov* and *Shaar HaShamayim.* Many other *siddurim* read לְשַׁלְּמָה, *to perfect.*

21. שְׁתִיָּה — *Thirsty earth.*
[This word is derived from שתה, *to drink.* It appears in Scripture only once: וְהַשְּׁתִיָּה כַדָּת, *And the drinking was according to the law* (Esther 1:8), where it refers to a banquet at which more wine was served than food. Thus, the *paytan* follows his earlier references to streaming, raining water with a prayer for the thirsty.
Many commentators render this as an allusion to the אֶבֶן שְׁתִיָּה, *foundation stone,* the focal point of the Holy Temple (see commentary to *hoshana* 2, stich 1). This interpretation, however, is totally out of context with the rest of the *hoshana.* This difficulty might be remedied by interpreting stiches 8 and 12 (*the face of the earth ... the demarcated land*), along with the modifying stiches which follow them, to refer to *Eretz Yisrael,* the Land *par excellence.*]

22. תְּלוּיָה עַל־בְּלִימָה — [*Which is*] *suspended upon silence.*
בְּלִימָה is a composite of two words בְּלִי, *without,* and מָה, *anything* (Ibn Ezra and Metzudos to Job 26:7).
Midrashically, בְּלִימָה may be interpreted *the peaceful one,* i.e., one who seeks peace by remaining silent in the face of argument. The Talmud cites the teaching of R' Elazar: The world exists in the merit of one who seals his lips (שֶׁבּוֹלֵם עַצְמוֹ) in time of dispute, as Scripture states: תֹּלֶה אֶרֶץ עַל בְּלִימָה, *He*

5
13-22

¹³ *to heal with powerful rains,*
¹⁴ *to give life to forsaken wastes,*
¹⁵ *to sustain with vegetation,*
¹⁶ *to enhance with sweet fruits,*
¹⁷ *to invigorate with flowers.*
¹⁸ *To rain on the sproutings —*
¹⁹ *to pour a stream of cool waters,*
²⁰ *to cloak with droplets,*
²¹ *to elevate the thirsty earth*
²² *which is suspended upon silence.*

During the first six days of Succos turn to page 84. On Hoshana Rabbah continue:

HASHEM, our Lord, how mighty is Your Name throughout the earth; for it were fit that You place Your splendor above the heavens. *(Answer us in the merit of Aaron the Kohen, answer us.)*

⚜ Ground from Accursedness

6
1-5

¹**G**round *from accursedness,* ² *beast from aborting,* ³ *granary from gazam,* ⁴ *grain from scorch,* ⁵ *wealth from*

---

suspends the earth upon the silent one (Job 26:7; Chullin 89a).

... הֹ׳ אֲדֹנֵינוּ — *HASHEM, our Lord* ...

For the *Talmud's* interpretation of this verse from *Psalms* (8:2) see comm. to *hoshana* 7, st. 5.

⚜ אֲדָמָה מֵאָרֵר — Ground from Accursedness

The holy tongue has but one word for blessing — בְּרָכָה. Implicit in this term are both inner, spiritual blessing and outer, material blessing. Thus, the same וַיְבָרֶךְ, *and He blessed,* is used regarding fish, Man and the Sabbath. The fish received an external blessing — *be fruitful and multiply* (Genesis 1:22); the Sabbath, an inherent sanctity — *God blessed the seventh day and hallowed it* (ibid. 2:3). But Man's blessing was two-pronged — *be fruitful and multiply, fill the earth and subdue it* (ibid. 1:28) [i.e., use your ingenuity to dominate the earth and its produce, and transform both for human purposes].

The antonym of blessing, on the other hand, may be expressed in either of two ways — קְלָלָה (see st. 19) or אָרֵר. The former, קְלָלָה (related to קַל, *light*), refers to a reduction of material means. Such a reduction diminishes one's resources, while his inner person re-

mains unchanged. Although his external loss may be considerable and extensive, his inner resources and potential are not affected by the קְלָלָה, *curse.*

אָרֵר alludes to the sapping of inner worthiness and energies. No longer is the accursed one capable of fulfilling his former potential; no longer can the accursed earth bring forth its crops in great abundance. This אָרֵר, *curse,* is internal and intensive (R' S.R. Hirsch to Genesis 1:28 and 12:3).

When Adam sinned, his punishment was indirect: אֲרוּרָה הָאֲדָמָה בַּעֲבוּרֶךָ, *accursed is the ground because of you; through suffering shall you eat* (Genesis 3:17). No longer will you, Adam, be nurtured by the bosom of your mother, the earth from which you were created. *Accursed is the ground because it bore you.* Henceforth, seed shall no longer sprout, and trees shall no longer bear fruit on the day they are planted *(Tan-*

[63]   *Hoshanos /* **Ground from Accursedness**

ו מַדְלֶקֶת. הוֹן מִמְּאֵרָה. וְאֹכֶל מִמְּהוּמָה. זַיִת מְנַשֵּׁל. חִטָּה
ה-טו מֵחָגָב. טֶרֶף מְגוֹבַי. יֶקֶב מְיֶלֶק. כֶּרֶם מִתּוֹלַעַת. לֶקֶשׁ
מֵאַרְבֶּה. מֶגֶד מִצְּלָצַל. נֶפֶשׁ מִבֶּהָלָה. שֹׂבַע מִסַּלְעָם.

chuma). *By the sweat of your brow shall you get bread to eat* (Genesis 3:19). No longer will the earth's produce nourish you immediately and directly. Before you can partake of your bread you must till, sow, and reap. But still the harvest will be in scant measure *(Ibn Ezra)*. All sorts of destructive, accursed insects will spring forth from the earth *(Rashi)*.

What hope has Man? How can he hope to relieve the accursedness which he brought to the earth? The Torah reveals the way:

> And it shall come to pass, when you will heed all of these laws, observe them and fulfill them, that HASHEM, your God, will ... love you, bless you, increase your number. He will bless the fruit of your womb, the produce of your earth, your grain, your wine and your oil, the offspring of your cattle and the flocks of your sheep, עַל הָאֲדָמָה, *upon the ground* ... *There shall be neither a sterile male nor a barren female among you and among your flocks* ... (Deuteronomy 7:12-14).

Fulfillment of God's will as expressed in His Torah is the redemption and salvation of Man. Such service can ameliorate the accursedness of the earth. On Hoshana Rabbah, and during this entire festival period, The Jew proclaims to God: We have used the produce of the earth in the ways prescribed by Your Torah — we have dwelt in the *succah* with its covering *(s'chach)* of plant material; we have taken the Four Species (lulav, esrog, myrtle and willow); we have read from the Torah which is written on animal skin; we have blown the shofar made from the ram's horn. We have heeded Your laws, fulfilled Your commands. Now, our God, may You fulfill the second part of the verse — undo the curse which You pronounced upon the earth.

3. גָּזָם — *Gazam.*

The accursedness caused by Adam's sin caused the earth to give forth various destructive insects *(Rashi to Genesis 3:17).* For this reason the poet mentions no less than eight insects in this *hoshana: gazam, chagav* (st. 8), *govai* (st. 9), *yelek* (st. 10), *arbeh* (st. 12), *tzlatzal* (st. 13), *salam* (st. 15) and *chasil* (st. 22). All are species of locusts (see *Rashi* to *Leviticus* 11:21-22 and *Deuteronomy* 28:42; *Metzudos* to *Joel* 1:4 and *Nachum* 3:17). Identification of each individual species however, is impossible *(Rashi to Leviticus* 11:21), and we have therefore left the names untranslated.

Perhaps each variety attacks the particular crop with which the *paytan* associates it *(Kol Bo).*

5. הוֹן — *Wealth.*

The difference between הוֹן, *wealth,* and עֹשֶׁר, *riches,* is not merely a difference in degree. The truly wealthy man is the one who is satisfied with his share *(Avos* 4:1). Indeed, the word הוֹן has the additional meaning of *it is sufficient* (see *Proverbs* 30:14-15; *R' Hirsch* to *Psalms* 112:3). We do not plead for protection of riches beyond what we need, only for our *wealth,* i.e., that which is necessary and sufficient for our sustenance.

מְאֵרָה — *Affliction.*

Among the castigations addressed to the wayward nation is the passage: *HASHEM shall send the* מְאֵרָה *against you (Deuteronomy* 28:20). *Rashi* relates מְאֵרָה to מַמְאֶרֶת *(Leviticus* 13:51) and מַמְאִיר *(Ezekiel* 28:24) which he renders הַכְאָבָה, *pain* or *affliction.* *Targum Yonason* translates *a curse upon your money.*

6. וְאֹכֶל מִמְּהוּמָה — *Food from confusion.*

Rashi renders מְהוּמָה as the *sound of confusion (Deuteronomy* 28:20). This

6 affliction, **6** food from confusion, **7** olives from dropping, **8** wheat from chagav, **9** nourishment from govai, **10** wine-press from yelek, **11** vineyard from worms, **12** late crop from arbeh, **13** fruit from tzlatzal, **14** soul from panic, **15** satiety from salam,

is an allusion to the tumult and panic caused by the sounds of an attacking army. During times of war foodstuffs become scarce, inflation sets in, and food prices soar *(Beis Avraham).*

[Alternatively, this refers to gluttonous repasts eaten in vast banquet halls among throngs of people. Invariably there is insurmountable difficulty in accommodating the entire assemblage. The resulting confusion causes ill will and physical discomfort. King Solomon taught: *Better to have little with fear of HASHEM, than a vast treasure accompanied by confusion. Better a meal of vegetables in a place of love, than a fatted ox, imbued with hatred (Proverbs 15:16-17).*]

7. נָשָׁל — *Dropping.*
The root נשל refers to unripe fruit dropping prematurely from its tree *(R' Hirsch to Deuteronomy 7:1; Beis Yaakov).*

8-10. חָגָב ... גּוֹבַי ... יֶלֶק — *Chagav ... govai ... yelek.*
These are all species of locusts (see comm. to st. 3).
Our spelling of גּוֹבַי is based on *Amos* 7:1 and *Nachum* 3:17. An alternative spelling גּוֹבַאי is the Aramaic form (see *Onkelos* to *Leviticus* 11:22).

9. טֶרֶף — *Nourishment.*
Give me neither poverty nor riches; הַטְרִיפֵנִי, *nourish me with my daily allotment of bread (Proverbs 30:8).*

11. כֶּרֶם מִתּוֹלַעַת — *Vineyard from worm(s).*
On a superficial level this stich is merely a request for protection of the grape crop against an infestation of worms. On a deeper plane the vineyard may be understood as an allusion to the Sages of Israel. [The academy at Yavneh was called כֶּרֶם בְּיַבְנֶה, *'vineyard' of Yavneh,* because the benches upon which the scholars sat in study were arranged in rows, like grapevines in a vineyard *(Yerushalmi, Berachos* 4:1).]

Kabbalistically, תּוֹלַע, *worm,* is used as a description of the טוּמְאָה, *contamination,* which seeks to undermine and destroy all that is holy. The עוֹלַת תָּמִיד, *daily* [lit., *continual*] *burnt offering,* is brought to counteract and repair the effects of that contamination. The letters of עוֹלַת, *burnt offering,* being the same as those of תּוֹלַע, *worm,* allude to the offering's task of undoing the effects of the contamination. Thus this stich is a prayer that the Torah scholars [*vineyard*] be protected from contamination [the *worm*] *(Shaar Yisas'char).*

[Perhaps because of this allusion some texts (e.g., *Tehillas Hashem*) read the synonymous תּוֹלַע in place of תּוֹלַעַת.]

12. לֶקֶשׁ — *Late crops.*
The root לקש means *to retard* or *hold back.* Thus מַלְקוֹשׁ are the *late rains (Rashi* to *Deuteronomy* 11:14) and לֶקֶשׁ are the *last crops* to sprout *(Radak* to *Amos* 7:1).

אַרְבֶּה — *Arbeh.*
[See comm. to st. 3.]

13. צְלָצַל — *Tzlatzal.*
A species of locust (see *commentary* to st. 3). [Perhaps this refers to a locust such as the cicada which produces a distinctive rasping, metallic sound. If so, the word צְלָצַל is related to צְלְצְלִים, *cymbals.*]

14. נֶפֶשׁ מִבֶּהָלָה — *Soul from panic.*
May man's soul not become panic-stricken when he sees the poor condition of his crops *(Kol Bo).*

15. שֹׂבַע — *Satiety.*
Because abundant, healthy crops cause man to be sated, such crops may be called שֹׂבַע, *satiety (Kol Bo).*

עֲדָרִים מְדֻלּוֹת. פָּרוֹת מְשֻׁדָּפוֹן. צֹאן מִצְמִיתוּת. קָצִיר מְקֻלָּלָה. רֹב מֵרָזוֹן. שִׁבֹּלֶת מִצִּנָּמוֹן. תְּבוּאָה מֵחָסִיל:

טז-כב

ו

During the first six days of Succos turn to page 84. On Hoshana Rabbah continue:

צַדִּיק יהוה בְּכָל־דְּרָכָיו, וְחָסִיד בְּכָל־מַעֲשָׂיו:
(עֲנָנָא בִּזְכוּתָא דְּיוֹסֵף צַדִּיקָא עֲנָנָא):

⚜️ לְמַעַן אֵיתָן

לְמַעַן אֵיתָן הַנִּזְרָק בְּלַהַב

א
ז

אֵשׁ.

סָלָם — Salam.
[See comm. to st. 3.]

16. עֲדָרִים מְדֻלּוֹת — Flocks from leanness [lit. *poverty*].
Flocks alludes to the nation of Israel which is often referred to in this way [e.g., *Psalms* 78:52] (*Kol Bo*). [דַּלּוּת is then taken in its literal sense, *poverty*: Save Israel (the *flocks*) from poverty.]

17. שִׁדָּפוֹן — The east wind.
Rashi to *Deuteronomy* 28:22 identifies שִׁדָּפוֹן as *the east wind*. The east wind is the strongest of all winds; it is the wind with which God punishes the wicked (*Rashi to Exodus* 14:21).

18. צֹאן — Sheep.
This is another allusion to Israel [e.g., *Now you My sheep, sheep of My pasture* (*Ezekiel* 34:31)] (*Kol Bo*; see commentary to st. 16 and hosh. 3, st. 18).

19. קְלָלָה — Curse.
See prefatory remarks.

20. רֹב — Abundance [lit., *many; much*].
Various interpretations of this obscure phrase are offered:
Isaac, in his blessing of Jacob, refers to grain and wine as 'abundant' (וְרֹב דָּגָן וְתִירֹשׁ; *Genesis* 27:28; *Tefillah Yesharah*).

For לְהַצְמִיחַ, *to sprout* (*Job* 38:27), *Targum* has לְמַרְבְּיָא. Based on this רֹב may be translated *sproutings* (*Avodas Yisrael*).
Although the crop may be abundant, with each ear of grain containing many kernels, the total amount of flour produced will be meager if the kernels are lean and emaciated (*Shaar HaShamayim*).

22. חָסִיל — Chasil.
[See comm. to st. 3.]

... צַדִּיק ה' — HASHEM is righteous ...
[As the sixth *hoshana*, this one represents the sixth *Sefirah*-emanation which is יְסוֹד, *Foundation*. The connection between this verse (*Psalms* 145:17) and the attribute of יְסוֹד, *Foundation*, becomes apparent when we realize that צַדִּיק יְסוֹד עוֹלָם, *the righteous one is the foundation of the world* (*Proverbs* 10:25).]
Both by example and by public discourse the righteous *tzaddik* teaches those around him proper behavior towards one another. His lessons preserve law and order and prevent anarchy. Thus he is truly *the foundation of the world* (based on *Gittin* 61a; *Rashi*).

⚜️ לְמַעַן אֵיתָן — In the Merit of the Courageous One

Who planted the seeds of superhuman fortitude and dignity with which millennia of Jews have endured hardship and privation? From whom did Israel inherit the ability to remain holy even amid holocaust?
Ramban provides the answer: כָּל מַה שֶּׁאֵירַע לָאָבוֹת סִימָן לַבָּנִים, *all that hap-*

**6
16-22** ¹⁶ *flocks from leanness,* ¹⁷ *fruits from the east wind,* ¹⁸ *sheep from extermination,* ¹⁹ *harvest from curse,* ²⁰ *abundance from emaciation,* ²¹ *grain spikes from withering,* ²² *crops from chasil.*

During the first six days of Succos turn to page 84. On Hoshana Rabbah continue:

HASHEM is righteous in all His ways; virtuous in all His deeds. (Answer us in the merit of the righteous Joseph, answer us.)

◂§ In the Merit of the Courageous One

**7
1** ¹ *In the merit of the courageous one who was hurled into flaming fire.*

pened to the Patriarchs is of prophetic significance to their descendants. For this reason, too, the Torah often relates seemingly unimportant events in the lives of our forebears. For this reason, too, the prophets were Divinely ordered to act out their prophecies (*Ramban* to Genesis 12:6; see ArtScroll *Bereishis,* overview p. 379, footnote p. 436).

Not only did the deeds of the Patriarchs insure the posterity of Israel, but they also inculcated the traits which engendered those deeds into the nation's fiber. The Talmudic dictum teaches: תָּמָה זְכוּת אָבוֹת, *the merits of the Patriarchs have expired* (*Shabbos* 55a; see comm. *hoshana* 1, st. 2), nevertheless, the qualities of character with which their merits have imbued their offspring have not expired. Because we still exhibit Abraham's loving-kindness, Isaac's courage, and Jacob's adherence to truth, because we follow the trails blazed by Moses and Aaron, Joshua and Samuel, David and Solomon, because we maintain and display the unwavering faith of Daniel and his companions, we are able to pray for salvation.

This *hoshana* traces the achievements of our spiritual models, and appeals for salvation in the merit of their indelible imprint upon Israel's national character.

1. לְמַעַן — *In the merit of.*

Although in *hoshana* 1 we translated לְמַעַן, *for the sake of,* we have followed the majority of commentators who here render *in the merit of.* This latter term is apropos to the deeds and attributes of the Patriarchs mentioned in this *hoshana,* but not to the attributes of God spoken of in *hoshana* 1.

אֵיתָן — *The courageous one* [i.e., Abraham].

Based on *Isaiah* 41:2 (see *Rashi* there), the Talmud (*Bava Basra* 15a) identifies אֵיתָן הָאֶזְרָחִי, *Eisan* [lit. *the strong one*] *the Easterner* (*I Kings* 5:11), as Abraham who was born and raised to the east of Canaan.

[The *paytan's* selection of the rare name *Eisan,* instead of his true name Abraham, is puzzling. Apparently the intention of the *paytan* in the entire *hoshana* is not to give names, but to list the primary characteristics of those who will be described. Since the *hoshana* goes on to describe Abraham's steadfast faith in God, despite the threat of violent death, the term אֵיתָן, *the courageous one,* is most apt.]

הַנִּזְרָק בְּלַהַב אֵשׁ — *Who was hurled into flaming fire.*

Abraham allowed himself to be thrown into a flaming furnace rather than deny his faith in Hashem.[1]

---

1. Terach was a manufacturer of idols. One day when he was not at home, his son Abraham smashed all the idols except for the largest one. Abraham then placed an axe in this idol's

וָאֵשׁ.	לְמַעַן בֵּן הַנֶּעֱקַד עַל עֵצִים	ז
אֵשׁ.	לְמַעַן גִּבּוֹר הַנֶּאֱבָק עִם שַׂר	ב־ו
אֵשׁ.	לְמַעַן דְּגָלִים נָחִיתָ בְּאוֹר וַעֲנָן	
אֵשׁ.	לְמַעַן הֹעֲלָה לַמָּרוֹם וְנִתְעַלָּה כְּמַלְאֲכֵי־	
אֵשׁ.	לְמַעַן וְהוּא לָךְ כְּסֶגֶן בְּאֶרְאֶלֵי־	

2. בֵּן הַנֶּעֱקַד — *The son* [i.e., Isaac] *who was bound.*

[The binding of Isaac as a sacrifice is related in *Genesis* 22:1-19. In those nineteen verses Isaac is referred to as בֵּן, *son*, no less than ten times, underscoring over and over that Abraham's desire to fulfill God's commandments took precedence not only over his own life (st. 1) but even over his love for his son. Although he personified in human form the Divine attribute of Lovingkindness, Abraham was able, at all times and in all situations, to subordinate that trait in the carrying out of God's will.]

עַל עֵצִים וָאֵשׁ — *Upon the wood near the fire.*

[The word עַל usually means *upon* but occasionally means *alongside* or *near* (see *Targum* to *Numbers* 2:5).Our use of *upon* in reference to the wood and *near* in conjunction with the fire is based on the verse: *He bound Isaac, his son, and placed him on the altar atop the wood* (*Genesis* 22:9) Atop the wood, but not atop the fire, for as long as Isaac was still alive, Abraham did not kindle the wood.]

3. גִּבּוֹר הַנֶּאֱבָק עִם שַׂר אֵשׁ — *The strong one* [i.e., Jacob] *who wrestled with a prince of fire.*

The "man" with whom Jacob wrestled (*Genesis* 32:25) is identified as שָׂרוֹ שֶׁל עֵשָׂו, *the guardian angel* [lit. *prince*] *of Esau* (*Bereishis Rabbah* 77:3). [Since angels appear as beings of fire (e.g., *Exodus* 3:2; *Judges* 13:20; *Isaiah* 6:2), the *paytan* describes Esau's guardian angel as *a prince created of fire*.]

4. דְּגָלִים — *The* [*tribal*] *banners.*

While traveling through the Wilderness, each tribe had a banner. It was the same color as its stone in the *Kohen Gadol's* breastplate and was embroidered with a picture depicting an animal or other object symbolic of that tribe.

hands and, when his father returned, blamed the destruction on it. When Terach rejoined that mere statues are incapable of such actions, Abraham argued that if Terach had no faith in the capability of the idols, he should not worship them.

To punish him for destroying the 'gods', Terach turned his son over to King Nimrod. The king commanded, 'Bow to the fire which I worship!'

'But,' Abraham replied, 'why not bow to water which has the power to quench fire?'

'All right then, bow to the water!' ordered Nimrod.

'Perhaps I should bow to the clouds which are strong enough to carry the water?' asked Abraham.

'So bow to the clouds.'

'But the wind pushes around the clouds!'

'Then bow to the wind.'

'If so, then I should bow to the people, who carry wind in their lungs.

Exasperated, the king declared, 'You are trying to influence me with your words. I bow only to the fire, and I shall throw you into it. Let the God to whom you bow come and save you from it.'

At this point, the angel Gabriel requested of the Holy One Blessed be He, 'Master of the World, let me descend and cool the fire, I shall then save the righteous Abraham from the fiery furnace.'

'I am Unique in My world,' replied the Holy One Blessed be He, 'and Abraham is unique in his. It is fitting that the Unique shall personally save the unique' (*Bereishis Rabbah* 38:18; *Pesachim* 118a).

**7
2-6**

² *In the merit of the son who was bound upon the wood near the fire.*

³ *In the merit of the strong one who wrestled with a prince of fire.*

⁴ *In the merit of the tribal banners which You guided with a light — and a cloud — of fire.*

⁵ *In the merit of him who was raised to the heavens and became as exalted as angels of fire.*

⁶ *In the merit of him who was to You like a deputy at the altars of fire.*

(See *Bamidbar Rabbah* 2:7 where the color and symbol of each tribe are enumerated). Hence the word דְּגָלִים, *banners*, is an allusion to the twelve tribes of Israel.

נָחִיתָ בְּאוֹר וְעָנָן אֵשׁ — *Which You guided with a light — and a cloud — of fire.*

And HASHEM went before them — by day in a pillar of cloud, to guide them on the way; and at night in a pillar of fire, to give light for them — that they might travel day and night (Exodus 13:21). The verse makes clear that the daytime cloud contained no fire, therefore the term וְעָנָן, *and a cloud*, must be taken as parenthetical. Indeed, in some liturgies (e.g., *Avodas Yisroel*) the stich reads: בְּעָנָן וְאוֹר אֵשׁ, *with a cloud and the light of a fire*. This latter reading finds support in *Psalms* (78:14): *He led them* בֶּעָנָן, *with a cloud by day, and all night long* בְּאוֹר אֵשׁ, *with the light of a fire* (*Iyun Tefillah*).

A third version is found in *Rashi* who omits the reference to עָנָן, *cloud*, entirely.

5. הֶעֱלָה לַמָּרוֹם — *Him* [i.e., Moses] *who was raised to the heavens* [lit. on high].

Moses ascended to God (*Exodus* 19:3) to accept the Tablets upon which were written the Ten Commandments. When the angels learned that Moses had entered the heavenly realm to accept the Torah and bring it down to Israel, they protested:

What is the frail human that You should remember him? And what is the son of mortal man that You should be mindful of him? HASHEM, our Lord, how mighty is Your Name throughout the earth, for it were fit that You place Your splendor above the heavens (*Psalms* 8:5,2).

God instructed Moses to refute the angels. Moses proved that the Torah laws cannot apply to the celestial beings, but must be meant for humankind, particularly Israel. When they finally accepted defeat, the angels befriended Moses and each of them presented him with a special gift (*Shabbos* 88b, 89a; see footnote to st. 11).

וַנִּתְעַלָּה כְּמַלְאֲכֵי־אֵשׁ — *And (he) became as exalted as angels of fire.*

During the forty days that Moses was in heaven he neither ate nor drank (*Deuteronomy* 9:9). Thus, his physical nature was elevated to such a degree that like the angels he needed neither food nor drink (*Tefillah Yesharah*).

A variant reading has בְּמַלְאֲכֵי אֵשׁ, *by angels of fire*. The angels exalted Moses by presenting him with gifts (*Shaar HaShamayim*).

Alternatively, Moses proved himself exalted by overpowering the angels in their debate (*Beis Yaakov*).

6. וְהוּא לְךָ כִּסְגָן — *Him* [i.e., Aaron] *who was to You like a deputy.*

Just as the ministering angels above are dedicated strictly to the service of God, so are the *Kohanim*-priests and particularly the *Kohen Gadol* [high priest]. Thus, Aaron the first *Kohen*

ז	לְמַעַן זֶכֶד דִּבְּרוֹת הַנְּתוּנוֹת	מֵאֵשׁ.
ז-יב	לְמַעַן חִפּוּי יְרִיעוֹת עֲנַן-	אֵשׁ.
	לְמַעַן טֶכֶס הַר יָרַדְתָּ עָלָיו	בָּאֵשׁ.
	לְמַעַן יְדִידוּת בַּיִת אֲשֶׁר אָהַבְתָּ מִשְּׁמֵי-	אֵשׁ.
	לְמַעַן כַּמָּה עַד שָׁקְעָה	הָאֵשׁ.
	לְמַעַן לָקַח מַחְתַּת־אֵשׁ וְהֵסִיר חֲרוֹן	אֵשׁ.

Gadol is alluded to here as the deputy of the chief ministering angel *(Shaar HaShamayim; Kol Bo)*.

[The translation of סְגָן, *deputy*, is based upon the Mishnaic use of the word, where it refers to the סְגָן כֹּהֲנִים, *Deputy Kohen Gadol* (e.g., *Yoma* 4:1).]

בְּאֶרְאֶלֵּי־אֵשׁ — *At the altars of fire.*

אֲרִיאֵל, lit. *lion of God*, is used by the prophets as a metaphor for the Temple altar, because fire rested upon it like a crouching lion (see ArtScroll *Ezekiel* 43:15). *Rashi (Isaiah* 33:7) translates אֶרְאֶלָּם as *their altar*.

Tefillah Yesharah offers a radically different interpretation: Although the word סְגָן does not appear in Scripture, its plural form, סְגָנִים, appears more than a dozen times, almost always as part of a roster of government officials (e.g., *Ezekiel* 23:12; *Nehemiah* 2:16). Thus, סְגָן means *ruler*.

Unlike *Rashi, Radak* translates אֶרְאֶלָּם as *angels*, a usage also found in the Talmud [e.g., *Kesubos* 104a, the אֶרְאֵלִים, *angels*, have vanquished the righteous pillars of Israel.]

Based on these two translations our stich becomes a continuation of the preceding one: Moses *became as exalted as angels of fire, and he became a ruler among the angels of fire* (see comm. to st. 5).

7. דִּבְּרוֹת הַנְּתוּנוֹת מֵאֵשׁ — *Commandments presented from a fire.*

Moses began his final blessing to Israel by describing the receiving of the Torah: *HASHEM appeared from Sinai...from His right he gave them a mandate of fire (Deuteronomy* 33:2). Originally, the commandments had been written in the spiritual realms 'with letters of white fire on a background of black fire,' as it were. God then engraved them onto tablets for presentation to Israel. Alternatively, when God presented the Ten Commandments to the nation, He descended upon Mount Sinai in a fiery cloud *(Rashi;* see *Exodus* 19:18).

8. חִפּוּי יְרִיעוֹת עֲנַן־אֵשׁ — *The canopy of curtains — a cloud of fire.*

The reference is to the Tabernacle built in the Wilderness, whose roof was made of several curtains.

[The absence of the conjunction וְ, *and*, before *a cloud of fire* indicates that the stich is based upon *Exodus* 40:38: *For* עֲנַן ה׳, *HASHEM's cloud, will be upon the Tabernacle by day,* וְאֵשׁ, *and a fire, will be there at night.* The "curtains" may refer figuratively to the cloud and fire which lay upon the Tabernacle.]

Some *siddurim*, however, read: וְעָנָן, *and a cloud*. The Tabernacle was covered with curtains *(Exodus* 26:1-14) and a cloud of fire *(Kol Bo)*.

9. טֶכֶס — *Array.*

[Although טכס usually refers to the ordering of troops in battle formation, it is used here to describe the orderly encampment of Israel at the foot of Mount Sinai (see *Rashi* to *Exodus* 19:2).]

Alternatively: The mountain was טָכַס, *prepared*, for God to descend upon it *(Shaar HaShamayim)*.

[טֶכֶס sometimes means *crown* (e.g., Yom Kippur *Musaf* liturgy: כְּטֶכֶס עַל רֹאשׁ מֶלֶךְ, *as a crown on a king's head).*

Its use here may be an allusion to the Talmudic statement: When the Jews at

7
7-12

⁷ In the merit of the gift of Commandments presented from a fire.

⁸ In the merit of the canopy of curtains — a cloud of fire.

⁹ In the merit of the array at the mountain upon which You descended in fire.

¹⁰ In the merit of the love of the Temple which You adored beyond heavens made of fire.

¹¹ In the merit of him who yearned until the sinking of the fire.

¹² In the merit of him who took a fire pan and removed an anger burning like fire.

Mount Sinai cried, 'We shall do, and we shall listen' (Exodus 24:7), placing action (do) before understanding (listen), 600,000 angels descended from heaven and placed two crowns upon the head of each Jew, one as a reward for 'we shall do', the other for 'we shall listen' (Shabbos 88a). Thus, the stich reads: In the merit of the crown we received at Mount Sinai when You descended...]

10. יְדִידוּת בַּיִת — *The love of the Temple* [lit. *house*].

The Tabernacle and Temple are both alluded to in the verse מַה יְדִידוֹת מִשְׁכְּנוֹתֶיךָ, *how beloved are Your dwelling places* (Psalms 84:2).

אֲשֶׁר אָהַבְתָּ מִשְּׁמֵי — *Which You adored beyond heavens.*

After building the Temple, King Solomon proclaimed: *Has God really preferred to dwell upon the earth; behold the heavens, and the very highest heavens cannot contain You, certainly this Temple, which I have built* (I Kings 8:27).

שְׁמֵי־אֵשׁ — *Heavens made of fire.*

The heavens are called שָׁמַיִם because the Holy One Blessed be He, combined אֵשׁ וּמַיִם, *fire with water*, to create heaven [שָׁמַיִם=אֵשׁ מַיִם] (*Chagigah* 12a).

An alternative reading, found in both *Rashi* and *Avodas Yisrael* omits the word בַּיִת, *Temple*. The stich, nevertheless, alludes to the *Beis HaMikdash*.[1]

11. כַּמָּה עַד שָׁקְעָה הָאֵשׁ — *Him* [i.e., Moses] *who yearned* [*for forgiveness*], *until the sinking of the fire.*

During the Wilderness wanderings, many Israelites chose to complain about imagined future difficulties. *HASHEM heard and His anger was kindled. The fire of HASHEM burned within them and consumed the lowly ones of the camp ... Moses prayed to HASHEM* וַתִּשְׁקַע הָאֵשׁ, *and the fire sank* [it was swallowed up by the ground (*Rashi*)] (Numbers 11:1-2; *Ramban; Rashi; Beis Yaakov*).

12. לָקַח מַחְתַּת־אֵשׁ וְהֵסִיר חֲרוֹן אַשׁ — *Him* [i.e., Aaron] *who took a fire pan and removed an anger burning like fire.*

Korach and his two hundred and fifty followers rebelled against the leadership of Moses, accusing him of nepotism in

---

1. This omission allows for a much broader interpretation of the stich. The Talmud (*Menachos* 53a,b) states: Let the beloved, descendant of the beloved, come and build the beloved, for the Beloved in the portion of the beloved, that the beloved may be forgiven therein.
 Let the beloved — Solomon, also called יְדִידְיָה, *Yedidyah* [lit. *beloved of God*] (II Samuel 12:25); **descendant of the beloved** — Abraham, whom God called יְדִידִי, *My beloved* (Jeremiah 11:15); **come and build the beloved** — Temple (Psalms 84:2); **for the beloved** — God, whom the prophet calls יְדִידִי, *my Beloved* (Isaiah 5:1); **in the portion of the beloved** — Benjamin; the *Beis HaMikdash* was built in the portion of Benjamin, called יְדִיד ה׳, *beloved of HASHEM* (Deuteronomy 33:12); **that the beloved** — Israel, called יְדִידוּת נַפְשִׁי, *My soul's beloved* (Jeremiah 12:7); **may be forgiven therein** (*Iyun Tefillah*).

בָּאֵשׁ.	ז לְמַעַן מְקַנֵּא קִנְאָה גְדוֹלָה
אֵשׁ.	יג־יז לְמַעַן נָף יָדוֹ וְיָרְדוּ אַבְנֵי־
אֵשׁ.	לְמַעַן שָׁם טָלֶה חָלָב כְּלִיל
בָּאֵשׁ.	לְמַעַן עָמַד בַּגֹּרֶן וְנִתְרַצָּה
הָאֵשׁ.	לְמַעַן פִּלֵּל בַּעֲזָרָה וְיָרְדָה

appointing his brother Aaron as *Kohen Gadol*. Moses proposed a test which would prove whether Aaron's position was a usurpation or ordained by God. Aaron, Korach, and each of the rebels were to take a pan of burning incense and present it in the Tabernacle as an offering to God, Who would then choose the offering of the righteous one. Aaron's priesthood was verified when Heaven sent down a fire which consumed the two hundred and fifty rebels, and the earth swallowed Korach and the families of the rebels (*Numbers* ch. 16).

In sympathy with the dead upstarts, the people turned upon Moses and Aaron, accusing them of 'murdering God's nation'. When God told the two righteous brothers to step aside so that He might destroy their opponents, Moses ordered Aaron, *'Take a pan, place upon it fire from the altar and incense. Go quickly to the congregation — that it shall cause them to be forgiven — for anger has gone forth from before HASHEM, the plague has started.*

Aaron followed the instructions *and the plague ended (Numbers 17:6-15).*[1]

13. מְקַנֵּא קִנְאָה גְדוֹלָה בָּאֵשׁ — *Him* [i.e., Elijah] *who zealously took great vengeance with fire.*

Ahab, the wicked king of the Ten Tribes, and Jezebel, his even more wicked queen, had long led the nation along the road to idolatry. But Elijah knew that the people inwardly resented the alien culture being pressed upon them. He challenged Ahab and the prophets of Baal into invoking their god to send a heavenly fire which would consume their offering to him. Elijah would offer an animal to the true God of Israel, and summon a fire from heaven to consume it.

When the priests of Baal were unsuccessful after an entire day's efforts, Elijah flooded his offering and altar with barrels of water and called out, *'Answer me, HASHEM, answer me.'* A fire descended, consumed the animal, the wood, the stones, the earth and even the water which had been poured over them.

The people subsequently carried the false prophets to the stream of Kishon where they were executed for practicing idolatry — the 'zealous vengeance' for which Elijah was responsible (see *I Kings* ch. 18; *Kol Bo*).

Alternatively, this stich refers to the zeal of פִּנְחָס, *Phineas*, who killed Zimri, prince of the tribe of Simeon, and the Midianite princess Kozbi, when the pair publicly committed adulterous acts. By his zeal, Phineas brought an end to the plague which had killed twenty-four thousand Israelites who had committed adultery with Midianite women *(Numbers* 25:1-15; *Beis Yaakov; Tefillah Yesharah).*

[It is noteworthy that Phineas and Elijah are identified in the *Midrash* as one and the same person *(Shir HaShirim Rabbah* 2).]

14. נָף יָדוֹ וְיָרְדוּ אַבְנֵי־אֵשׁ — *Him* [i.e., Joshua] *who raised his hand [in prayer] — and down came stones of fire.*

---

1. How did Moses know the secret of halting the plague with an incense offering?

After Moses proved that the Torah was meant not for the angels but for Israel, each angel presented Moses with a special gift. Even the Angel of Death gave him a gift — namely, the knowledge that incense offerings have the power to halt a plague (*Shabbos* 89a; see comm. to st. 5).

**7
13-17**

13 In the merit of him who zealously took great vengeance with fire.
14 In the merit of him who raised his hand in prayer—and down came stones of fire.
15 In the merit of him who offered a nursing ewe to be completely consumed by fire.
16 In the merit of him who stood in the granary and was shown favor with fire.
17 In the merit of him who prayed in the Courtyard and down came fire.

All the commentators understand this stich as a reference to the incident recorded in *Joshua* 10:11: *As they fled before the Israelites ... HASHEM threw huge stones upon them.*

[Two questions arise: a) No mention is made of Joshua raising his hand to cause the stones to descend; and b) the verse refers to אֲבָנִים גְּדֹלוֹת, *huge stones*, but not stones of fire. The explanation may be found in the *Midrash*.

When the plague of hail ended in Egypt we are taught: *The thunder ceased, the hail and rain did not reach the ground (Exodus 9:33).* But what happened to the hail that had already begun falling? It remained suspended in the air until the time of Joshua when *HASHEM threw huge stones ... (Shmos Rabbah 12:7).*

But the hailstones were brought upon the Egyptians only after Moses raised his hand to the heavens. Moreover, those stones were composed of *fire burning within the hail (Exodus 9:22-24).* Since the same hail stones which Moses brought down upon the Egyptians, were brought down upon the Emorites by Joshua, these two conditions must have applied there also.]

15. שָׂם טָלֶה חָלָב כְּלִיל אֵשׁ — *Him* [i.e., Samuel] *who offered* [lit., *placed*] *a nursing ewe to be completely consumed by fire.*

When the Philistines prepared for an attack upon the Israelites gathered in Mizpah, *Samuel took a* טָלֶה חָלָב, *nursing ewe, and brought it as a burnt-offering, to be completely consumed* [כָּלִיל], *before HASHEM. Then Samuel cried in prayer to HASHEM on behalf of Israel, and HASHEM answered him (I Samuel 7:9).*

The translation *nursing ewe* for טָלֶה חָלָב follows *Rashi (Avodah Zarah 24b). Radak* and *Metzudos* both render *suckling lamb.*

16. עָמַד בַּגֹּרֶן וְנִתְרַצָּה בָאֵשׁ — *Him* [i.e., David] *who stood in the granary and was shown favor with fire.*

When David bought the granary from Aravnah [=Arnan; see comm. to *hoshana* 2, st. 3] as the site of the future Temple, *Aravnah blessed the king, 'May HASHEM Your God find you[r offerings] acceptable' ... David erected an altar there and brought burnt-offerings and peace-offerings. Then HASHEM heeded the prayers of [those who dwelled in] the land ... (II Samuel 24:23,25;* brackets are interpolations of *Targum).*

17. פִּלֵּל בָּעֲזָרָה וְיָרְדָה הָאֵשׁ — *Him* [i.e., Solomon] *who prayed in the Courtyard and down came fire.*

Solomon fashioned a platform of copper and placed it in the Courtyard [of the newly completed Temple] ... *He ascended it, kneeled, and spread his palms heavenward ... When Solomon ceased to pray, a fire descended from heaven ... (II Chronicles 6:13, 7:1).*

ז לְמַעַן צִיר עָלָה וְנִתְעֲלָה בְּרֶכֶב וְסוּסֵי־ אֵשׁ.
יח-כב לְמַעַן קְדוֹשִׁים מֻשְׁלָכִים בָּאֵשׁ.
לְמַעַן רִבּוֹ רִבְבָן חָז וְנַהֲרֵי אֵשׁ.
לְמַעַן שַׁמּוֹת עִירְךָ הַשְּׂרוּפָה בָּאֵשׁ.
לְמַעַן תּוֹלְדוֹת אַלּוּפֵי יְהוּדָה תָּשִׂים כְּכִיּוֹר אֵשׁ:

During the first six days of Succos turn to page 84. On Hoshana Rabbah continue:

לְךָ יהוה הַגְּדֻלָּה וְהַגְּבוּרָה וְהַתִּפְאֶרֶת וְהַנֵּצַח וְהַהוֹד כִּי־כֹל בַּשָּׁמַיִם וּבָאָרֶץ לְךָ יהוה הַמַּמְלָכָה וְהַמִּתְנַשֵּׂא לְכֹל לְרֹאשׁ: וְהָיָה יהוה לְמֶלֶךְ עַל־כָּל־הָאָרֶץ בַּיּוֹם הַהוּא יִהְיֶה יהוה אֶחָד וּשְׁמוֹ אֶחָד: וּבְתוֹרָתְךָ כָּתוּב לֵאמֹר שְׁמַע יִשְׂרָאֵל יהוה אֱלֹהֵינוּ יהוה אֶחָד: בָּרוּךְ שֵׁם כְּבוֹד מַלְכוּתוֹ לְעוֹלָם וָעֶד:
(עֲנָנָא בִּזְכוּתָא דְּדָוִד מַלְכָּא מְשִׁיחָא עֲנָנָא:)

On Hoshana Rabbah turn to page 84.

18. צִיר עָלָה .... — *The agent* [of God, i.e., Elijah] *who ascended [to heaven] and was exalted, through a chariot and horses of fire.*

Elijah and his disciple Elisha were taking their final leave of each other before the master would be summoned to his heavenly abode. *Suddenly, a fiery chariot with fiery horses separated the two of them and Elijah ascended to the heavens in a storm wind* (II King 2:11).

19. קְדוֹשִׁים מֻשְׁלָכִים בָּאֵשׁ — *Holy ones* [i.e., Chananyah, Mishael and Azaryah] *who were cast into the fire.*

Three young Jewish servants of Nebuchadnezzar refused to bow to his idol. 'Now ... prostrate yourself before the image I made,' commanded the king, '...or you will instantly be thrown into a flaming kiln...' (Daniel 3:15). The entire story of their refusal to bow before the idol and their subsequent deliverance from the kiln appears in chapter 3 of *Daniel*.

Rashi substitutes קְטַנִּים, *youngsters*, for קְדוֹשִׁים, *holy ones*. This is based on *Daniel* 1:4 which identifies the trio as יְלָדִים, *lads*. Ibn Ezra surmises that they were no more than fifteen years old.

Kol Bo offers an alternative interpretation of קְדוֹשִׁים, *holy ones*. No specific person or people are referred to. The term includes the countless martyrs through the centuries who accepted torture and death. עַל קִידּוּשׁ הַשֵּׁם, *in sanctification of God's Holy Name*, rather than forsake Him for the idols of their oppressors.

20. רִבּוֹ רִבְבָן חָז וְנַהֲרֵי אֵשׁ — *Him* [i.e., Daniel] *who saw myriad myriads* [of angels] *and streams of fire.*

Daniel's prophetic vision of the four beasts symbolizing the kingdoms which would persecute Israel, ends with their judgment before the Heavenly Tribunal. Daniel describes the courtroom: *I watched till thrones were set up, and the Ancient of Days sat ...* נְהַר דִּי־נוּר, *a stream of fire flowing forth from before Him, a thousand thousands serving Him and* רִבּוֹ רִבְבָן, *myriad myriads standing before Him ...* (Daniel 7:9-10).

21. שַׁמּוֹת עִירְךָ הַשְּׂרוּפָה בָּאֵשׁ — *The ruins of your city* [i.e., Jerusalem] *which was devoured in fire.*

If a fire break out ... he who kindled the fire shall surely pay (Exodus 22:5). The Holy One Blessed be He, said, 'I am responsible to pay for the fire which I have kindled! I set the fire in Zion' — as the verse says: *He kindled a fire in Zion which consumed its foundations* (Lamentations 4:11). 'I shall some day rebuild it out of fire ' — as it is written: *And I shall be unto her ... a surrounding wall of fire ...* (Zechariah 2:9; Bava Kama 60b).

22. תּוֹלְדוֹת אַלּוּפֵי יְהוּדָה תָּשִׂים כְּכִיּוֹר אֵשׁ

7
18-22

18 *In the merit of the agent who ascended to heaven and was exalted, through a chariot and horses of fire.*
19 *In the merit of holy ones who were cast into the fire.*
20 *In the merit of him who saw myriad myriads and streams of fire.*
21 *In the merit of the ruins of Your city which was devoured in fire.*
22 *In the merit of the descendants of Judah's princes whom You will set as a flaming fire.*

During the first six days of Succos turn to page 84. On Hoshana Rabbah continue:

To You, HASHEM, is the Greatness and the Power and the Glory and the Eternality and the Splendor, even all that is in the heavens and the earth; to You HASHEM, is the Kingdom and the sovereignty over every ruler. HASHEM will be recognized as King over all the earth, on that day HASHEM will be One and His Name will be One. And in Your Torah it is written as follows: Listen, Israel, HASHEM is our God, HASHEM is One.

Blessed is the name of His glorious Kingdom forever and ever.

(Answer us in the merit of David the anointed king, answer us.)

On Hoshana Rabbah turn to page 84.

— **The descendants of Judah's princes whom You will set as a flaming fire.**
In that day [when Jerusalem will be redeemed and rebuilt] *I shall set* אַלּוּפֵי יְהוּדָה, *Judah's princes,* כְּכִיוֹר אֵשׁ, *as a flaming fire, among the trees ... and they shall consume to the right and to the left all the nations round about. Then Jerusalem will return to its place* (Zechariah 12:6).

Based on *Obadiah* 1:18, *Rashi* reads: לְמַעַן תּוֹלְדוֹת בֵּית יַעֲקֹב וּבֵית יוֹסֵף תָּשִׂים אֲלָפִים כְּכִיוֹר אֵשׁ, *In the merit of the descendants of the House of Jacob and the House of Joseph, set the princes as flames of fire.*

Judah's princes is a metaphor which includes all those Patriarchs and martyrs mentioned in this *hoshana* (*Kol Bo*). In their combined merit, and in the merit of the seeds of devotion to our God which they have sown within us, we beseech You, save us!

לְךָ ה׳ — *To You, HASHEM ...*
[II Chronicles 29:11; see comm. to *hoshana* 1, sts. 3,5,13,14.]

וְהָיָה ה׳ — *HASHEM will be ...*
[Zechariah 14:9; see comm. to *hoshana* 1, sts. 6,7,13.]

שְׁמַע יִשְׂרָאֵל — *Listen, Israel ...*
[Deuteronomy 6:4; see comm. to introductory *hoshana*.]

בָּרוּךְ שֵׁם — *Blessed is the name ...*
This verse is not of Scriptural origin but is appended to the verse שְׁמַע יִשְׂרָאֵל, *Listen, O Israel,* when it is recited during the daily morning and evening prayers. It is based upon the Talmud's narration of Jacob's deathbed dialogue with his sons. Jacob had summoned his sons, intending to reveal their lot at the End of Days. But the *Shechinah* and prophecy departed from him. Jacob feared that one of his sons lacked complete faith in God and was thus unworthy of being privy to such Divine secrets — perhaps he had a flawed son just as Abraham had his Ishmael and Isaac his Esau. His twelve sons responded as one, '*Listen, Israel* [i.e., Jacob], *HASHEM is our God, HASHEM is One.* Just as there is no duplicity in your heart, so is there no duplicity in our hearts.'

Being thus reassured, Jacob cried, '*Blessed is the name of His glorious kingdom forever and ever* (*Pesachim* 56a).

אֶעֱרוֹךְ שׁוּעִי

ח אֶעֱרוֹךְ שׁוּעִי. בְּבֵית שׁוְעִי. גִּלִּיתִי בַצוֹם פִּשְׁעִי.
א־יב דְּרַשְׁתִּיךָ בּוֹ לְהוֹשִׁיעִי. הַקְשִׁיבָה לְקוֹל שַׁוְעִי. וְקוּמָה
וְהוֹשִׁיעֵנִי. זְכֹר וְרַחֵם מוֹשִׁיעִי. חַי כֵּן תְּשַׁעְשְׁעֵנִי. טוֹב
בְּאֹנֶק שַׁעִי. יָחִישׁ מוֹשִׁיעִי. כַּלֵּה מַרְשִׁיעִי. לְבַל עוֹד

אֶעֱרוֹךְ שׁוּעִי — I Shall Arrange My Prayer

One must always anticipate troublesome situations and pray for salvation before oppressive times arrive. R' Elazar understood this lesson from the admonition of Job's friends (Job 36:19): הֲיַעֲרֹךְ שׁוּעֲךָ, *Have you arranged your prayer* [beforehand in order] *that oppression not overtake you? (Sanhedrin 44b)*.

When is the opportune time for such prayer?

Seek [דִּרְשׁוּ] *HASHEM when He may be found; call to Him when He is near (Isaiah 55:6).* The Talmud asks: When may He be found? When is He near? And answers: During the Ten Days [of Awe] beginning with Rosh HaShanah and culminating with Yom Kippur *(Rosh HaShanah 18a)*.

Now Israel prays that God recall its repentance during the period when God called for it. In response to my having *bared my transgression* before You on Yom Kippur, may You *pardon the iniquity of my wickedness* and *overlook my transgression*. Just as *I sought You* on that day, for salvation, You, in turn *arise* ... *remember and be merciful, my Savior*.

1. אֶעֱרוֹךְ שׁוּעִי — *I shall arrange my prayer.*

[Stiches 1 (based on *Job 36:19;* see pref.) and 2 serve as an introductory verse to this *hoshana* in much the same way that the verse, *My Lord, open my lips, that my mouth may tell Your praises (Psalms 51:17)*, is used to introduce the *Shemoneh Esrei* prayer.]

3. גִּלִּיתִי ... פִּשְׁעִי — *I have bared ... my transgression.*

He that hides his transgression shall not succeed; but he that admits and forsakes [his sins] *shall find mercy [Proverbs 28:13]; (Tefillah Yesharah).*

בַצוֹם — *On the fast day.*

This refers to Yom Kippur, when וִדּוּי, *confession,* highlights each of the prayers. Indeed, in the Temple the confession was an integral part of the sacrificial service: *And Aaron...shall confess...all the iniquities of the Children of Israel (Leviticus 16:21).*

4. דְּרַשְׁתִּיךָ — *I have sought You.*

[This is a further allusion to Yom Kippur, *when He may be found ... when He is near* (see pref.).]

5. הַקְשִׁיבָה לְקוֹל שַׁוְעִי — *Harken to the sound of my outcry.*

This stich is taken verbatim from *Psalms (5:3). Malbim* explains the difference between two almost synonymous expressions — הַאֲזִינָה, *give ear (ibid. v. 2)* and הַקְשִׁיבָה, *harken*. The former is used when the listener is close to the speaker, the latter implies a distance between the two.

[Perhaps the intent of the *paytan* is to contrast the Yom Kippur prayers, when He was still near (see comm. to sts. 3-4), to today's prayers, one week later. Although it is after the period of בְּהִיוֹתוֹ, *when He is found ...* בְּהִמָּצְאוֹ ... קָרוֹב *when he is near,* nevertheless, we ask God *to harken to the sound of my outcry,* even though we are far from Him.]

◆§ I Shall Arrange My Prayer

**8
1-12**

¹ *I shall arrange my prayer*
² *in the house of prayer:*
³ *I have bared, on the fast day, my transgression;*
⁴ *I have sought You on that day for salvation.*
⁵ *Harken to the sound of my outcry;* ⁶ *arise and save me;*
⁷ *remember and be merciful, my Savior.*
⁸ *Living God — in Your faithfulness let me rejoice.*
⁹ *Goodly One — turn to my groan,*
¹⁰ *may my savior hasten.*
¹¹ *Destroy the one who tempts me to sin,*
¹² *that he may no longer incriminate me.*

---

6. וְקוּמָה וְהוֹשִׁיעִי — *Arise and save me.*
The Psalmist cried: קוּמָה ה׳ הוֹשִׁיעֵנִי, *Arise, HASHEM, save me!* (Psalms 3:8; see comm. to *hoshana* 4, st. 4). To fit the rhythm of this *hoshana*, the *paytan* has elided the letter נ, *nun*, from the suffix. Accordingly, the word וְהוֹשִׁיעִי should be translated as if it read וְהוֹשִׁיעֵנִי, *and save me.* Similar license is taken by the *paytan* in stiches 4 (לְהוֹשִׁיעִי instead of לְהוֹשִׁיעֵנִי) and 8 (תְּשַׁעְשְׁעִי in place of תְּשַׁעַשְׁעֵנִי). *Elazar HaKalir*, author of the *hoshana* prayers, often takes such poetic liberties with Hebrew grammar (*Iyun Tefillah*).

7. זְכוֹר וְרַחֵם מוֹשִׁיעִי — *Remember and be merciful, my Savior.*
Remember the merits of Abraham, and for his sake *be merciful.* The *gematria* [numerical-value] of אַבְרָהָם, *Abraham*, is 248, as is the *gematria* of רַחֵם, *be merciful (Rashi).* [In conjunction with this interpretation, we have translated מוֹשִׁיעִי as a direct address to God — *my Savior.*]
Alternatively, *Remember* Your nation, and *be merciful* unto them by bringing מוֹשִׁיעִי, *my savior*, i.e., the Messiah *(Beis Avraham).*

8. ... חַי — *Living God* [lit., *Life* or *Life-giver*] ...
An alternative rendering of stiches 7 and 8 is based upon Jeremiah 31:19: *Is Ephraim not a beloved son* [בֵּן] *unto Me, or a child of rejoicing* [שַׁעֲשׁוּעִים]*? For whenever I speak of him, I shall surely remember him* [זָכֹר אֶזְכְּרֶנּוּ] *again ... I shall surely be merciful with him* [רַחֵם אֲרַחֲמֶנּוּ]. Thus, st. 8 continues the thought of the previous stich. There the words זְכוֹר וְרַחֵם, *remember and be merciful*, allude to the twin promises God made regarding Ephraim. This stich continues with the prayer: חַי, *Living God*, בֵּן, similarly, as You rejoiced with Ephraim, תְּשַׁעְשְׁעִי, *let me rejoice.* Accordingly, it is possible that the word בֵּן should read כְּבֵן, *like the son*, i.e., Ephraim *(Tefillah Yesharah).*

10. יָחִישׁ מוֹשִׁיעִי — *May my savior hasten.*
Many *siddurim* (Beis Yaakov, Shaar HaShamayim, Tefillah Yesharah) have יוֹחֵשׁ מוֹשִׁיעִי, *cause my savior to hasten.*
According to either version, the reference is to the Messiah *(Kol Bo; Beis Yaakov).*

11-12. כַּלֵּה מַרְשִׁיעִי לְבַל עוֹד תַּרְשִׁיעִי — *Destroy the one who tempts me to sin, that he may no longer incriminate me.*
The evil inclination who causes one to sin is the very Satan who prosecutes the sinner before the Heavenly Tribunal *(Rashi).*

ח תַּרְשִׁיעִי. מַהֵר אֱלֹהֵי יִשְׁעִי. נֶצַח לְהוֹשִׁיעִי. שָׂא־נָא עָוֹן
יג-כב רִשְׁעִי. עֲבוֹר עַל פִּשְׁעִי. פְּנֵה־נָא לְהוֹשִׁיעִי. צוּר צַדִּיק
מוֹשִׁיעִי. קַבֶּל־נָא שַׁוְעִי. רוֹמֵם קֶרֶן יִשְׁעִי. שַׁדַּי מוֹשִׁיעִי.
תּוֹפִיעַ וְתוֹשִׁיעִי:

Turn to page 84.

אל למושעות

ט
א-ג אֵל לְמוֹשָׁעוֹת. בְּאַרְבַּע שְׁבֻעוֹת. גְּשָׁמִים בִּשְׁוָעוֹת.

13. מַהֵר אֱלֹהֵי יִשְׁעִי — *Hasten, God of my salvation.*

The *paytan* bases himself on a longer passage in *Psalms* (79:8-9): מַהֵר, *Hasten, let Your mercy come to meet us for we have fallen very low. Assist us,* אֱלֹהֵי יִשְׁעֵנוּ, *God of our salvation, for the sake of Your Name's glory* (*Tefillah Yesharah*).

14. נֶצַח — *Eternally.*

Or, perhaps, *Eternal One* (see comm. to *hoshana* 1, st. 14).

15-16. שָׂא ... עָוֹן ... עֲבוֹר עַל פִּשְׁעִי — *Pardon the iniquity...overlook my transgression.*

נֹשֵׂא עָוֹן *Who, O God, is like You,* וְעֹבֵר עַל פֶּשַׁע *Who pardons iniquity, and overlooks transgression* (*Micah* 7:18).

Whoever commits a sin creates a prosecuting angel for himself (*Avos* 4:11). But who sustains this angel? What is the source of its life? God could say to the sinner, 'You created this angel — now you feed him. Let him become a parasite, feeding on you, sapping you of your vitality.' But God in His great mercy does not say this, Instead he is נֹשֵׂא, literally, *carries* or *supports* the עָוֹן, angel created through iniquity. Thus man remains healthy enough to repent, despite the fact that an angel came into existence through him.

Furthermore, *with You [God] is forgiveness* (*Psalms* 130:4). Not with an angel, not with a messenger, not with an agent — but with God — lies forgiveness. He Himself washes away the soil of sin. He Himself overlooks transgressions (*Tomer Devorah*).

18. צוּר צַדִּיק מוֹשִׁיעִי — *Rock, Righteous One, Who is my Savior.*

[צוּר, *Rock*, referring to God, is an allusion to His immutable strength, His omnipotence and His eternality. As a metaphor for God the word appears frequently in Scripture, almost always in conjunction with יְשׁוּעָה, *salvation* (e.g., *II Samuel* 22:47; *Psalms* 62:3). צַדִּיק, *Righteous One*, is also commonly used as an epithet for God (e.g., *Exodus* 9:27; *Psalms* 145:17), however, it rarely appears together with salvation (perhaps *Psalms* 115:5-6 is an exception). Only once do צוּר, *Rock*, and צַדִּיק, *Righteous One*, appear in the same verse as epithets for God: הַצּוּר, *The Rock, His works are perfect ...* צַדִּיק, *a Righteous One, and a Just One is He* (*Deuteronomy* 32:4). Since no mention of salvation is made in that verse, the *paytan's* combination of these words with reference to God as Savior remains obscure. Perhaps the present text is a merger of two versions of the *hoshana* which were once extant — one reading צוּר, *Rock*, the other, צַדִּיק, *Righteous One.*]

20. רוֹמֵם קֶרֶן יִשְׁעִי — *Elevate the horn of my salvation.*

Tefillah Yesharah cites *Psalms* 89:19: *According to Your will You elevate our horns.* Radak and Metzudos to that verse understand *horn* as a reference to the kings of Israel.

Kol Bo, on the other hand, cites *Psalms* 18:3, where the term קֶרֶן יִשְׁעִי, *Horn of my salvation*, is one of many expressions alluding to God. Radak explains that just as the horned animal uses its horns to push its enemy or any

8
13-22

¹³ *Hasten, God of my salvation,*
¹⁴ *eternally to save me.*
¹⁵ *Please, pardon the iniquity of my wickedness,*
¹⁶ *overlook my transgression,*
¹⁷ *turn, now, and save me.*
¹⁸ *Rock, Righteous One, Who is my Savior —*
¹⁹ *accept now my prayer,*
²⁰ *elevate the horn of my salvation.*
²¹ *Shaddai — my Savior,*
²² *shine Your countenance upon me and save me.*

Turn to page 84.

◦§ O God! Bring About Salvations

9
1-3

¹ *O God! Bring about salvations*
² *because of the four oaths*
³ *of those who approach with pleas.*

other obstacle from its path, so does God push aside the enemies of Israel.

21. שַׁדַּי — *Shaddai.*
Usually translated *Almighty* or *Omnipotent, Shaddai* is one of the Holy Names of God. Midrashically, this Name is a contraction of שֶׁאָמַרְתִּי לְעוֹלָמִי דַּי, *I have said to My world, 'Enough!'* For had God not cried 'Enough' to the heavens and the earth, they would still be spreading out, even to this very day (*Bereishis Rabbah* 5:8; 46:3).

◦§ אֵל לְמוֹשָׁעוֹת — O God! Bring About Salvations

1. אֵל לְמוֹשָׁעוֹת — *O God! Bring about salvations.*
King David sang: *God is for us* אֵל לְמוֹשָׁעוֹת, *a God of salvations, though* ... [*He*] *has many avenues toward death* (*Psalms* 68:21). For us, Israel, He is a God of salvations, but for our enemies, He has many avenues which will lead to destruction (*Radak*).
Although the *paytan* borrowed this phrase from Scripture, he uses it in a different context. Instead of drawing the Psalmist's contrast between the salvation of Israel and the destruction of its enemies, the *paytan* connects it to the next stich — *O God! Bring about salvations, because of the four oaths* (see comm. to st. 2; *Rashi* as interpreted by *Iyun Tefillah*).

2. בְּאַרְבַּע שְׁבֻעוֹת — *Because of [the] four oaths.*

Four times God turned to Israel and adjured them — as indicated by the four times *Song of Songs* uses the expression הִשְׁבַּעְתִּי אֶתְכֶם בְּנוֹת יְרוּשָׁלִָם, *I have adjured you, O daughters of Jerusalem* (2:7; 3:5; 5:8; 8:4).

R' Chelbo taught that God demanded four oaths of Israel regarding their exile: a) That they not rebel against the governments [of the lands in which they are dispersed]; b) that they not delay the end [i.e., by their sins (*Rashi*)]; c) that they not reveal the mysteries [i.e., the depths of Torah knowledge (*Rashi*)] to the nations; and d) that they not seek to end their exile by armed force or great masses. [The reason God adjured them is that] otherwise why should the Messiah come to gather Israel in from the Diaspora?

R' Onia taught that the four oaths

ט **דּוֹפְקֵי עֶרֶךְ שׁוּעוֹת. הוֹגֵי שַׁעֲשׁוּעוֹת. וְחִידָתָם**
ד־טו **מְשַׁתַּעְשְׁעוֹת. זֹעֲקִים לְהַשְׁעוֹת. חוֹכֵי יְשׁוּעוֹת. טְפוּלִים
בָּךְ שָׁעוֹת. יוֹדְעֵי בִין שָׁעוֹת. כּוֹרְעֶיךָ בְּשַׁוְעוֹת. לְהָבִין
שְׁמוּעוֹת. מִפִּיךְ נִשְׁמָעוֹת. נוֹתֵן תְּשׁוּעוֹת. סְפוּרוֹת**

correspond to four generations which attempted to force the end [before the advent of the Messiah] and came to sorrow ... They gathered and armed for war but many of them fell in battle. Why? *For they had no faith in God, and trusted not in "His" salvation* (Psalms 78:22) [but instead took their fate in their own hands] (*Shir HaShirim Rabbah* 2:7; Rashi to *Kesubos* 111a where R' Chelbo's proem appears with minor variations).

We, however, rely on You alone: *O God! Bring about salvations because of the four oaths* which You adjured us (Rashi).

A variant reading is בְּאַרְבָּעָה שָׁבוּעוֹת, *in four weeks*, and is a reference to the four weeks of Tishrei during which the world is judged (*Kol Bo; Iyun Tefillah*). To be more precise, the week before Rosh HaShanah, during which סְלִיחוֹת, *prayers for forgiveness*, are said each morning before daybreak, along with the first three weeks of Tishrei which end on Hoshana Rabbah, the day the final seal is placed on the verdict which had been written on Rosh HaShanah (see pref. remarks to *hoshana* 1; *Shaar Yisas'char*).

3. גָּשִׁים בְּשַׁוְעוֹת — *[Of] those who approach with pleas.*

During Israel's very first exile, in Egypt, וַתַּעַל שַׁוְעָתָם, *their pleas rose to God* (Exodus 2:23; Rashi).

4. דּוֹפְקֵי עֶרֶךְ שׁוּעוֹת — *They knock [on the doors] where prayers are arranged.*

Based upon Job 36:19 [see comm. to *hoshana* 8, st. 1], the synagogue is called the place *where prayers are arranged* (Rashi).

Alternatively, *they knock* on the heavenly gates of Mercy *with the order of their prayers* (*Tefillah Yesharah*).

5. הוֹגֵי שַׁעֲשׁוּעוֹת — *They meditate upon the beloved* [*Torah*].

Israel studies the Torah — which says of itself, '*I was nurtured by Him, and I was* שַׁעֲשׁוּעִים, *beloved, to Him each day'* (Proverbs 8:30) — at all times. Thus they fulfill that which God bade Joshua (1:8): וְהָגִיתָ, *and you shall meditate upon it* [i.e., Torah] *day and night* (*Tefillah Yesharah*).

6. וְחִידָתָם — *And their riddles.*

Stich 5 alludes to the Written Torah — Scripture — while riddles [see *Proverbs* 1:6] refers to the Oral Torah — the Talmud and its commentaries. Many of the teachings of the Talmudic Sages are terse and cryptic, requiring intense study to decipher them (*Dover Shalom*).

7. זֹעֲקִים — *They cry.*
[See comm. to *hoshana* 4, st. 7.]

לְהַשְׁעוֹת — *For attention* [lit. *to cause to turn toward*].

וַיִּשַׁע ה', *HASHEM turned to Abel ... but to Cain* — לֹא שָׁעָה, *He did not turn* (Genesis 4:4-5; see alternative translation of the word הוֹשַׁעְנָא, comm. to introductory *hoshana*).

8. חוֹכֵי — *They yearn.*
[See comm. to *hoshana* 4, st. 8.]

9. טְפוּלִים בָּךְ שָׁעוֹת — *They cling to You, to You they turn.*

בָּךְ, *to You,* is read as if it were written twice — טְפוּלִים בָּךְ, *they cling to You,* בָּךְ שָׁעוֹת, *to You they turn* (based on *Beis Yaakov* and *Kol Bo*).

Alternatively, *they cling to You* — *please turn to them* (*Beis Avraham*).

10. יוֹדְעֵי בִין שָׁעוֹת — *They know the understanding of the hours.*

From the offspring of Yisachar came יוֹדְעֵי בִינָה לָעִתִּים, *those who know the*

9
4-15

⁴ *They knock on the doors where prayers are arranged;*
⁵ *they meditate upon the beloved Torah*
⁶ *and their riddles are beloved;*
⁷ *They cry for attention;* ⁸ *they yearn for salvation;*
⁹ *they cling to You, to You they turn.*
¹⁰ *They know the understanding of the hours,*
¹¹ *yet they kneel before You pleading*
¹² *That they may understand the lessons*
¹³ *which were heard from Your mouth.*
¹⁴ *O Grantor of salvations,* ¹⁵ *gather the counters*

---

understanding of the times, to know how Israel should act (I Chronicles 12:32).

The Midrash asks: What is *the understanding of the times?* R' Tanchuma explains this as a reference to those *mitzvos* which are dependent upon time [e.g., the Sabbath; recitation of *Shema*]. Yisachar's children study the Torah and are familiar with its laws. With the approach of each season, they teach the laws pertaining to that period, so that *Israel should know how to act.*

R' Yosi ben Kitzri understands the verse as an allusion to the intricate knowledge of time and its function which is necessary to establish the calendar. Not only must the judges know the time when the new moon can be sighted, they must be familiar with the phases of the sun and numerous astronomical and agricultural calculations taken into account in determining the calendar.

Although the *paytan* adapted the verse to fit the rhyme scheme by substituting שָׁעוֹת, *hours*, for עִתִּים, *times*, nevertheless, either of the Midrashic interpretations is valid here *(Iyun Tefillah).*

Alternatively, they know which hours and times are propitious for prayer. They know that the Ten Days of Awe are the days when HASHEM may be found, when He is near to respond to prayers. [See pref. remarks to *hoshana* 8] *(Beis Avraham).*

10⁻13. Although they are well learned and wise in the intricacies of Halachah, nevertheless, they turn to You praying that You grant them an even deeper understanding of the Torah that they heard directly from Your mouth at Sinai *(Kol Bo).*

14. נוֹתֵן ... — *O Grantor ...*

This stich (paraphrased from *Psalms* 144:10: הַנּוֹתֵן תְּשׁוּעָה לַמְּלָכִים, *He Who grants salvation to kings ...*) refers back to מִפִּיךָ, *from Your mouth,* You,*Grantor of salvations (Iyun Tefillah).*

15. סְפוּרוֹת מַשְׁמָעוֹת — *Gather the counters.*

The sages are referred to as סוֹפְרִים, *counters* for various reasons:

— They arrange the laws of the Torah into mnemonic groupings which are identified by number, e.g., there are four classification of damage (*Bava Kama* 1:1), fifteen women free their counterparts from the obligation of levirate marriage (*Yevamos* 1:1; *Iyun Tefillah* citing *Yerushalmi Shekalim* 5:1).

— They study the verses which speak of the End of Days and attempt to calculate the date of Messiah's coming *(Rashi).*

— They count every letter of the Torah [and explain its purpose and the lessons to be derived from it] *(Kiddushin* 30a).

מַשְׁמָעוֹת — *Gather.*

ט מַשְׁמָעוֹת. עֵדוּת מַשְׁמִיעוֹת. פּוֹעֵל יְשׁוּעוֹת. צַדִּיק
טז־כב נוֹשָׁעוֹת. קִרְיַת תְּשׁוּעוֹת. רֶגֶשׁ תְּשָׁאוֹת. שָׁלֹשׁ שָׁעוֹת.
תָּחִישׁ לִתְשׁוּעוֹת:

This rare usage of the root שמע, to hear, may be found in Scripture: וַיְשַׁמַּע שָׁאוּל אֶת־הָעָם, Saul gathered the nation (I Samuel 15:4).

Rashi explains that they were gathered by the voice of a crier, thus, וַיְשַׁמַּע, he called together. [Perhaps the paytan used this root to allude to the מְבַשֵּׂר, herald, who will announce Messiah's coming (see comm. to קוֹל מְבַשֵּׂר, the voice of the herald, p. 142).]

An alternative reading has סְפוּרוֹת נִשְׁמָעוֹת and is based on the verse: God, with our ears we have heard (שָׁמַעְנוּ) our fathers have recounted (סִפְּרוּ) to us, the deeds which You performed in their days, in days of old (Psalms 44:2). Thus: סְפוּרוֹת נִשְׁמָעוֹת, The recountings which are heard (Beis Yaakov).

16. עֵדוּת מַשְׁמִיעוֹת — (They) that teach [lit., make heard] the testimony.

The *mitzvos* of the Torah are referred to as עֵדוּת ה׳, *the testimonies of HASHEM* (Psalms 19:8). Performance of the *mitzvos* bears witness to the performer's belief and faith in God (Metzudos). In particular, the tablets upon which the Ten Commandments were inscribed are called שְׁנֵי לֻחֹת הָעֵדֻת, *two tablets of testimony* (Exodus 31:18).

17-18. פּוֹעֵל יְשׁוּעוֹת צַדִּיק נוֹשָׁע — O Worker of salvations, [send] the righteous one who will find salvation.

Rashi explains that stich 17 alludes to God, Who is called *Worker of salvations in the midst of the earth* (Psalms 74:12). Stich 18 refers to the Messiah and paraphrases the prophet's description: *Behold your king shall come to you; צַדִּיק וְנוֹשָׁע הוּא, he is righteous and will find salvation* [in God (Rashi)] (Zechariah 9:9).

19. קִרְיַת תְּשׁוּעוֹת — [For the] city of salvations.

Both according to our reading and an alternative reading, קָרֵב תְּשׁוּעוֹת, *bring salvations near*, this stich refers to the salvation of Jerusalem and is connected to stich 20 (Iyun Tefillah).

20. רֶגֶשׁ תְּשָׁאוֹת — Swarming with masses.

Isaiah (22:2) describes Jerusalem as תְּשֻׁאוֹת מְלֵאָה, *filled with masses, city of tumultous crowds*.

21. שָׁלֹשׁ שָׁעוֹת — [During the] three hours.

The Holy One Blessed be He, divided the twelve hours of daytime into four periods of three hours each. During the first of these periods, He sits and engages Himself in Torah study. Another three hours He spends judging the world; should He see that strict justice demands the destruction of the world, He [so to speak] rises from the Throne of Justice and sits on the Throne of Mercy. For three more hours He supplies the entire universe with sustenance ... (Avodah Zarah 3:2).

We beseech God to hasten salvations during the three hours in which He judges His world (Rashi), and to support us during the three hours that he provides our means of sustenance (Kol Bo).

Alternatively, the three hours refers

הושענות/אל למושעות [82]

9
16-22
¹⁶ *that teach the testimony.*
¹⁷ *O Worker of salvations,*
¹⁸ *send the righteous one who will find salvation.*
¹⁹ *For the city of salvations* ²⁰ *swarming with masses,*
²¹ *during the three hours*
²² *hasten the time of salvations.*

to the three hours during which God will exact retribution from Esau's descendants. These hours are hinted to by Isaiah (33:10): 'עַתָּה, *Now, I shall rise,*' says HASHEM. 'עַתָּה, *Now, I shall be exalted;* עַתָּה, *now, I shall be elevated*' [i.e., because of the increasing measure of evil dealt by the enemy of My nation, I shall no longer tarry. *Now, I shall act (Rashi)*]. The word עַתָּה, *now,* may be read עִתָּה, *its hour,* the three-fold use of the word implying three hours (*Yalkut Shimoni* II, 988). The *paytan* refers to these three hours and asks that God hasten their coming *(Rashi; Tefillah Yesharah).*

Alternatively, the *three hours* refer to the three prayers of the day, *Shacharis, Minchah* and *Maariv.* The Talmud (*Berachos* 32b) relates that the righteous of a bygone era would spend one hour in the recitation of *Shemoneh Esrei* at each service. Thus three hours of each day were spent in direct communication of prayer to God. During these three hours we pray for salvation *(Beis Yaakov).*

22. תָּחִישׁ לִתְשׁוּעוֹת — *Hasten the time of salvations.*

After describing life in Messianic times, the prophet gives a time frame for this final redemption: בְּעִתָּהּ אֲחִישֶׁנָּה, *In its proper time shall I hasten it (Isaiah 60:22).*[1]

The Talmud asks: If it is the proper time, then it has not been hastened; if it has been hastened, then it is before the proper time? And answers: If Israel proves worthy of redemption before the pre-ordained time, then *I shall hasten it* and the Messiah will arrive in the merit of the nation. If, however, they prove unworthy of his coming, he will, nevertheless, come at the appointed time *(Sanhedrin 98a).*

---

1. R' Alexandri said that R' Yehoshua ben Levi noted a contradictory passage. Scripture says [that the redemption will occur] בְּעִתָּהּ, *in its appointed time.* Then it says אֲחִישֶׁנָּה, *I will hasten it (Isaiah 60:22).*

[The explanation is] if they are deserving: *I will hasten it.* If they are not deserving: *in its appointed time (Sanhedrin 98a).*

This seminal passage sheds light on the great body of Messianic literature. There *is* an appointed time, but there can also be ways to hasten his coming.

On that same page, the Talmud relates how R' Yehoshua ben Levi was dispatched by the prophet Elijah to inquire directly of the Messiah as to when he would arrive. The holy *Tanna* did so and the Messiah greeted him warmly. In answer to his question, the redeemer said הַיּוֹם, [*I will come*] *today.* R' Yehoshua complained to Elijah that the Messiah had deceived him — that day was over, but the Exile still endured. Elijah answered that R' Yehoshua had misunderstood. The Messiah had meant to say הַיּוֹם־אִם בְּקֹלוֹ תִשְׁמָעוּ, [*I will come*] *today — if you but heed His voice (Psalms 95:7),* i.e., if Israel would but obey the word of God!

כהושעת אלים

[*After each day's* hakafah-*circuit (except on the Sabbath),
the following* hoshana *is said*]:

י
א־ד

אֲנִי וָהוּ הוֹשִׁיעָה נָּא:

כְּהוֹשַׁעְתָּ אֵלִים בְּלוּד עִמָּךְ.
בְּצֵאתְךָ לְיֵשַׁע עַמָּךְ. כֵּן הוֹשַׁעֲנָא:

כְּהוֹשַׁעְתָּ גּוֹי וֵאלֹהִים.
דְּרוּשִׁים לְיֵשַׁע אֱלֹהִים. כֵּן הוֹשַׁעֲנָא:

כְּהוֹשַׁעְתָּ אֵלִים — As You Saved the Terebinths

אֲנִי וָהוּ הוֹשִׁיעָה נָּא — *ANI VAHO, bring salvation now.*
Every day [of the Succos festival] they would circle the altar one time saying: אָנָּא ה' הוֹשִׁיעָה נָּא, *Please, HASHEM, bring salvation now;* אָנָּא ה' הַצְלִיחָה נָּא, *please HASHEM, bring success now* (Psalms 118:25). Rabbi Yehuda maintains [that they used the formula] אֲנִי וָהוּ הוֹשִׁיעָה נָּא, *ANI VAHO, bring salvation now.*
On that day [i.e., Hoshana Rabbah] they would circle the altar seven times (Succah 45a).

The obscure terms אֲנִי וָהוּ, *ANI VAHO, are identified by Rashi as two in a series of seventy-two Names of God, each containing three letters. The complete series is composed of the letters which make up three consecutive verses of Exodus* (14:19-21), *each of which contains exactly seventy-two letters. In the mystical formula by which these names are formed, vs.* 19 *and* 21 *are read in their proper order, while v.* 20 *is read backwards. A table showing these groups of 72 letters is given below. The first letter of v.* 19, *the last of v.* 20, *and the first of v.* 21, *gives the name* וְהוּ.

Taking the thirty-seventh letters in the table yields the name אֲנִי.

The particular aptness of these two Names stems from their *gematria* [*numerical value*], 78, which is equal to that of אָנָּא ה', *please, HASHEM (Rashi).*

Tosafos explains that the formula *ANI VAHO bring salvation now* is a prayer for the return of the *Shechinah* manifestation from its exile to *Eretz Yisrael* [see comm. beginning of Introductory Hoshana, p. 36]. This interpretation is based on the following *Midrash*:

Homiletically, the pronouns אֲנִי, *I,* and הוּא, *He,* of the two verses, *And I,* [וַאֲנִי], *was among the exiles (Ezekiel* 1:1), *and And He* [וְהוּא] *was bound in chains (Jeremiah* 40:1) *both refer to the Shechinah in exile (Introduction to Eichah Rabbasi* 74).

According to this Midrashic view that the word *VAHO* is derived from וְהוּא, *and he,* the vocalization should be אֲנִי וְהוּ (a reading retained in *Siddur Tehillas Hashem*), or as the *Yerushalmi* has it אֲנִי וְהוּא, *I and He,* with no reference to the three-letter Names (*Yerushalmi Succah* 4:3).

```
 ו י ס ע מ ל א כ ה א ל ה י מ ה ה ל ך ל פ נ י מ ח נ ה י ש ר א ל ו י ל כ מ א ח ר י ה מ ו י ס ע ע מ ו ד ה ע נ נ מ פ נ י ה מ ו י ע מ ד מ א ח ר י ה מ
 ה ל י ל ה ל כ ה ז ה א ה ז ב ר ק א ל ו ה ל י ל ה ת א ר א י ו כ ש ח ח ו נ נ ה י ה י ו ל א ר ש י ת ה נ ח מ נ י ב ו מ י ר צ מ ח נ מ נ י ב א ב י ו
 ו י ט מ ש ה א ת י ד ו ע ל ה י מ ו י ו ל כ י ה ו ה א ת ה י מ ב ר ו ח ק ד י מ ע ז ה כ ל ה ל י ל ה ו י ש מ א ת ה י מ ל ח ר ב ה ו י ב ק ע ו ה מ י מ
```

הושענות/כהושעת אלים [84]

◆§ As You Saved the Terebinths

10
1-4

[After each day's *hakafah*-circuit (except on the Sabbath),
the following *hoshana* is said]:

ANI VAHO, bring salvation now.

¹ **A**s You saved the terebinths in Lud along with Yourself
² when You went forth to save the nation — so save now.

³ As You saved   a nation and its leaders
⁴ who sought the salvations of God —   so save now.

The verse עִמּוֹ־אָנֹכִי בְצָרָה, *I [God] am with him [Israel] in times of trouble* (Psalms 91:15), teaches that the *Shechinah* is in exile along with Israel, and the *Shechinah* will be redeemed together with the nation. This theme recurs throughout the *hoshana* (e.g., stiches 10-14).

A final interpretation of the term אֲנִי וָהוּ, ANI VAHO, is based on Abba Shaul's understanding of the verse: זֶה אֵלִי וְאַנְוֵהוּ, *this is my God and I shall beautify Him* (Exodus 15:2). The word וְאַנְוֵהוּ is interpreted homiletically as אֲנִי וָהוּא, *I and He;* it teaches that one must seek to emulate his Creator by always saying 'I and He, I should be like Him — just as He is merciful, so shall I be merciful; just as He is gracious, so shall I be gracious' (*Shabbos* 133b).

1. אֵלִים — *Terebinths.*

Israel, staunch and firm in its faith in God, is compared to the oak-like terebinth tree: *And they [those who return to Jerusalem] will be called terebinths of righteousness, planted by HASHEM to be glorified* (Isaiah 61:3; Rashi).

Alternatively, אֵלִים may be translated *powerful ones* (as in *Psalms* 29:1), and refers to the Patriarchs who were *powerful in their faith* (*Tefillah Yesharah*).

לוּד — *Lud.*

A reference to Egypt. The Ludim descended from *Mitzrayim*, founder of Egypt (see *Genesis* 10:13).

עִמָּךְ — *Along with Yourself.*

As long as Israel was enslaved in Egypt, God kept a brick under His feet [so to speak] as a constant reminder of the bricks that the enslaved Jews were forced to produce. When He redeemed them the brick turned to sapphire and emitted a joyful glow (*Rashi* to *Exodus* 24:10).

2. בְּצֵאתְךָ — *When You went forth.*

This stich is a paraphrase of *Habbakuk* 3:13, יָצָאתָ לְיֵשַׁע עַמֶּךָ, *You have gone forth to save Your nation,* which *Mahari Kara* sees as a reference to *Exodus* 11:4: *So says HASHEM, 'At midnight I shall go forth ...'*

3. גוֹי וֵאלֹהִים — *A nation and [its] leaders.*

The translation follows *Rashi* who cites *Exodus* 7:1: HASHEM *said to Moses: See, I have made you a lord* (אֱלֹהִים) *over Pharaoh.* Thus *a nation and its leaders* means Israel, Moses and Aaron.

Alternatively, the stich refers to God and is another case of the recurring theme that God is exiled together with His people (*Kol Bo*).

4. דְּרוּשִׁים — *Who sought* [lit., *who seek*].

[See pref. remarks to *hoshana* 8.]

י כְּהוֹשַׁעְתָּ הֲמוֹן צְבָאוֹת.
ה״י וְעִמָּם מַלְאֲכֵי צְבָאוֹת. כֵּן הוֹשַׁעְנָא:

כְּהוֹשַׁעְתָּ זַכִּים מִבֵּית עֲבָדִים.
חַנּוּן בְּיָדָם מַעֲבִידִים. כֵּן הוֹשַׁעְנָא:

כְּהוֹשַׁעְתָּ טְבוּעִים בְּצוּל גְּזָרִים.
יְקָרְךָ עִמָּם מַעֲבִירִים. כֵּן הוֹשַׁעְנָא:

5. הֲמוֹן — *Multitude.*

When God changed Abram's name, He explained the implication of the new name אַבְרָהָם, Abraham: 'I have made you the father [אָב] of a multitude [הֲמוֹן] of nations' (Genesis 17:5). Thus, Abraham's descendants are called הֲמוֹן, *multitude (Rashi).* The word *nations* in this sense means *the tribes of Israel,* a usage also found elsewhere in Scripture (e.g., Genesis 35:11; *Iyun Tefillah*).

צְבָאוֹת — *Hosts.*

A צְבָא, *host,* is an organized force, disciplined to achieve an end defined by its commander. Thus an army is a *host,* as is the heavenly *host.* In this stich, the term refers to the tribes which left Egypt as we find *I shall bring forth My hosts* [צִבְאֹתַי]*, My people, the Children of Israel (Exodus 7:4; Rashi).*

6. וְעִמָּם מַלְאֲכֵי צְבָאוֹת — *And with them the hosts of angels.*

For on this very day I brought your hosts [צִבְאוֹתֵיכֶם] *forth from the land of Egypt (Exodus 12:17).*

Mechilta explains *your hosts* as alluding to the multitudes of Israel. However, when the verse is reiterated a slight change of terminology occurs: *On this very day all of the hosts of HASHEM* [צִבְאוֹת ה׳] *went forth from the land of Egypt* (ibid. v. 41). Not your hosts but hosts of HASHEM — this refers to the hosts of angels. [*Malbim* explains that the angels were sent to protect the Israelites during their Egyptian exile. When Israel left Egypt these guardian angels left with them] (*Iyun Tefillah*).

Alternatively, מַלְאֲכֵי צְבָאוֹת refers to Moses and Aaron who delivered the nation from Egypt as מַלְאֲכֵי ה׳ צְבָאוֹת, *messengers of HASHEM of hosts (Shaar HaShamayim; Kol Bo).*

Beis Yaakov cites a *Midrash* which teaches that 900 million angels of destruction descended upon Egypt. All of them left together with Israel.

7. זַכִּים — *Pure ones.*

Those who were redeemed from Egypt were pure from sin *(Rashi).* When the time came for Israel to be redeemed from Egypt, many Jews were loath to leave. They preferred their lives of slavery to the responsibility they would bear as a kingdom of priests and a holy nation. They died and were buried during the plague of darkness (*Rashi* to *Exodus* 10:22). Thus, after the death of the sinful ones, only the pure of heart were redeemed (*Rashi* as interpreted by *Iyun Tefillah*).

8. חַנּוּן — *Gracious One.*

An alternative reading here is חִנָּם, *without pay.* The Israelites were forced to work without receiving any remuneration *(Beis Efraim).*

בְּיָדָם מַעֲבִידִים — *From* [lit. *with* or *in*] *those who forced manual labor upon them.*

The translation of *manual* for בְּיָדָם follows *Rashi.*

Dover Sholom renders: *The Gracious One gave into their hands those who forced labor upon them.*

In keeping with the theme of this *hoshana* (see pref.), *Beis Yaakov* translates: *With their hands they enslaved* (so to speak) *the Gracious One,* for He was in Exile alongside His nation.

הושענות/כהושעת אלים [86]

10   ⁵ *As You saved the multitude of hosts*
5-10   ⁶ *and with them the hosts of angels —*   *so save now.*
        ⁷ *As You saved pure ones from the house of slavery,*
         ⁸ *Gracious One, from those who forced*
          manual labor upon them —   *so save now.*
        ⁹ *As You saved those sinking in the depths of the rifts,*
         ¹⁰ *Your honor was with them*
          when they crossed —   *so save now.*

[Indeed, the brick which God used as a footstool (see comm. to st. 1) symbolized His manufacturing bricks together with them (see *Exodus* 4:7-19; *Tefillah Yesharah*).]

9. טְבוּעִים בְּצוּל גְזָרִים — *Those sinking in the depths of the rifts.*

The stich alludes to the Israelites, who were apprehensive that they might be drowned in the Sea of Reeds (*Kol Bo*); alternatively, the Egyptians *thought* the Israelites had drowned (*Shaar HaShamayim*).

Alternatively this may refer to the danger related in *Sanhedrin* 103b (see *Rashi*). The *Midrash* teaches that Moses strove to keep the promise made to Joseph that his remains would be removed from Egypt when the Exodus took place. Although it was known that Joseph's coffin was at the bottom of the Nile, it was not known where. On a piece of parchment, Moses wrote the words עֲלִי שׁוֹר, *Rise up, O ox!,* a reference to the ox-like strength with which Moses was later to bless the tribe of Joseph (*Deuteronomy* 33:17). He threw the parchment into the river, and immediately the coffin rose to the surface. Michah, a sinful Jew, retrieved the parchment with the intention of using it for his own ends. Indeed, during the period of Judges, Michah used the supernatural powers of the parchment to give the appearance of legitimacy to an idol. When Michah went through the Sea of Reeds with his parchment, the angel of the sea was angered that it had to be split miraculously to save the life of a sinner. Enraged, the angel wished to bring the seas' waters crashing down on Israel. The nation was saved in the merit of two precepts — Torah, which it was preparing to accept, and tefillin, about which it had already been commanded. Accordingly, our stich refers to the Israelite nation which was saved from sinking into the depths of the split sea.[1]

10. יְקָרְךָ — *Your honor.*

This is another allusion to the redemption of the *Shechinah* along with the redemption of Israel [see comm. to ANI VAHO] (*Rashi; Kol Bo*).

Alternatively, יְקָרְךָ is synonymous with יָדְךָ, *Your hand,* meaning the hand of God which was evident at the splitting of the Sea of Reeds [see *Exodus* 14:31]. This translation is based upon *Onkelos* (to *Exodus* 33:23) who renders יְקָרִי for כַּפִּי, *My palm* (*Rashi*).

Alternatively, יְקָרְךָ refers to Joseph whose coffin crossed the sea [see comm. to st. 9] together with the Israelites. Joseph, like his son Ephraim, was called יַקִּיר, *beloved,* of God [*Jeremiah* 31:19; see comm. to *hoshana* 8, st. 8] (*Rashi*).

---

1. The commandment of tefillin is found in the Torah for the first time in *Exodus* 13:1-10. That chapter, given after the first *Pesach* lamb had been eaten but before the Exodus, reviews the laws of Pesach and goes on to give the precept of tefillin. Upon hearing this *mitzvah*, the people used the skins and sinews of the lamb to make tefillin, which they wore as they left Egypt and as they advanced between the waters of the Sea of Reeds. This allusion to tefillin may be found in stich 10 as well, for the word יְקָר is interpreted by *Megillah* 16b as a reference to tefillin (R' Yehoshua Leib Diskin cited by *Iyun Tefillah*).

יא-כ	י	כְּהוֹשַׁעְתָּ כַּנָּה מְשׁוֹרֶרֶת וַיּוֹשַׁע.	
		לְגוֹחָהּ מְצֻיֶּנֶת וַיִּוָּשַׁע.	כֵּן הוֹשַׁעְנָא:
		כְּהוֹשַׁעְתָּ מַאֲמַר וְהוֹצֵאתִי אֶתְכֶם.	
		נָקוּב וְהוֹצֵאתִי אִתְּכֶם.	כֵּן הוֹשַׁעְנָא:
		כְּהוֹשַׁעְתָּ סוֹבְבֵי מִזְבֵּחַ.	
		עוֹמְסֵי עֲרָבָה לְהַקִּיף מִזְבֵּחַ.	כֵּן הוֹשַׁעְנָא:
		כְּהוֹשַׁעְתָּ פִּלְאֵי אָרוֹן כְּהֻפְשַׁע.	
		צַעַר פְּלֶשֶׁת בַּחֲרוֹן אַף וְנוֹשַׁע.	כֵּן הוֹשַׁעְנָא:
		כְּהוֹשַׁעְתָּ קְהִלּוֹת בָּבֶלָה שִׁלַּחְתָּ.	
		רַחוּם לְמַעֲנָם שִׁלַּחְתָּ.	כֵּן הוֹשַׁעְנָא:

11-14. Torah scrolls are written without the use of vowel points. The proper vowelization of each word has been handed down from generation to generation, dating from our teacher Moses who heard the words pronounced by God Himself. For midrashic, homiletic, and exegetical purposes, other pronunciations may be utilized, with the guidelines set by the Tradition. Two examples of this license form the basis of the next four stiches.

שִׁירַת הַיָּם, *The Song of the Sea*, in which Moses led the nation after crossing the Sea of Reeds is introduced in Scripture with two verses [*Exodus* 14:30-31] beginning with the words וַיּוֹשַׁע ה׳, *HASHEM delivered* (or, *saved*). But with different vowels, these words could be read וַיִּוָּשַׁע ה׳, *HASHEM was delivered*, indicating the deliverance of the *Shechinah* from its Egyptian exile alongside of Israel.

In commanding Moses to appear before Pharaoh to demand the release of Israel from bondage, God said: *I am HASHEM — I shall bring you forth* [וְהוֹצֵאתִי אֶתְכֶם] *from the Egyptian oppression (Exodus 6:6).* The vowels of this phrase, too, can be changed to yield an allusion to the redemption of God Himself. For וְהוֹצֵאתִי read וְהוּצֵאתִי, *I shall be brought forth*, and for אֶתְכֶם read אִתְּכֶם, *with you*. (*Minchas Shai* to *Isaiah* 43:14, where a full discussion of the topic of dual meanings based on changed vowel arrangements is offered).

11. כַּנָּה — *The garden.*
Psalms 80:9 refers to Israel as *the vine You caused to journey out of Egypt*; v. 16 speaks of וְכַנָּה, *and the garden* (see *Radak*) *which Your right hand planted* (*Rashi*).

12. גוֹחָהּ — *He Who draws forth.*
This description of the Creator is found in *Psalms* 22:10: *Because You drew me forth* (גֹחִי) *from the womb* (*Rashi*).

15. סוֹבְבֵי מִזְבֵּחַ — *Those who went roundabout with the altar.*
When Joshua led the nation in the capture of Jericho, they circled the city one time on each of six consecutive days. On the seventh day they circled Jericho seven times after which its walls miraculously were destroyed, allowing Israel to enter [see *Joshua* chap. 6] (*Rashi*). [Although Scripture mentions only that the Ark of the Covenant led the encircling procession, *Rashi* probably assumes that the other appurtenances of the Sanctuary, such as the altar, followed behind the Ark.]

10
11-20

¹¹ *As You saved the garden which sang 'He delivered,'*
¹² *regarding Him Who draws forth it is pronounced*
'He was delivered' — so save now.
¹³ *As You saved with the declaration*
'I shall bring you forth,'
¹⁴ *which may be interpreted,*
'I shall be brought forth with you' — so save now.
¹⁵ *As You saved those who went roundabout with the altar,*
¹⁶ *those who carry the willow to encircle the altar —*
so save now.
¹⁷ *As You saved the Ark of the Name,*
captured as a result of sin,
¹⁸ *When You punished Philistia with flaming anger,*
and it was saved — so save now.
¹⁹ *As You saved the congregations which*
You had sent to Babylon,
²⁰ *Merciful One, for their sake*
were You also sent — so save now.

---

16. מִזְבֵּחַ — *The altar.*

During the time of the Holy Temple the *hakafah*-circuits went around the sacrificial altar. Today, the *bimah*, *reading platform*, is encircled as a reminder of those days [see overview] *(Kol Bo).*

17-18. While still smarting from defeat by the Philistines, the elders of Israel took the Ark of the Covenant to lead their troops to battle. They were certain that the merit of the Ark and the Tablets and Torah it contained would protect them, but God willed otherwise and the Ark was captured by the Philistines. However, each city to which the Ark was brought was visited by a plague. Finally the elders of Philistia decided to return it to Israel *(I Samuel chap. 5). The Ark of HASHEM was in Philistine fields for seven months (I Samuel 6:1).*

The Midrash *(Bereishis Rabbah 54:4)* teaches that the seven-month exile of the Ark was in punishment for the seven ewes which Abraham gave Abimelech, king of Philistia, as evidence of the treaty between them *(Genesis 21:22-34)* — a treaty which displeased God.

17. פְּלָאֵי אֲרוֹן — *The Ark of the Name* [lit. *wonders of the Ark*].

The word פְּלָאֵי, literally, *wonders*, refers to the Ineffable Name, as when the angel replied to Manoach: *Why do you ask my name, it is* פֶּלִאי [Peli] *(Judges 13:18).* The intent of the angel's response was that his own name is not important. Only by utilizing פְּלָאֵי, *the wondrous Name of my Creator*, do I perform my heavenly duties *(Rashi).*

R' Shimon bar Yochai taught: The Ineffable Name of God and all His descriptive Names were placed into the Ark *(Bava Basra 14b).*

Alternatively, פְּלָאֵי אֲרוֹן, *the wonders of the Ark*, is a reference to the awesome plagues visited upon the Philistines during the time they kept the Ark *(Kol Bo).*

כְּהִפְשֵׁע — *As a result of sin.*

An allusion to Abraham's treaty with Abimelech which was displeasing to God, hence, sinful *(Rashi).*

Alternatively, this refers to Israel's

יּ כְּהוֹשַׁעְתָּ שְׁבוּת שִׁבְטֵי יַעֲקֹב.
כא-כג תָּשׁוּב וְתָשִׁיב שְׁבוּת אָהֳלֵי יַעֲקֹב. וְהוֹשִׁיעָה נָא:

(כְּהוֹשַׁעְתָּ שׁוֹמְרֵי מִצְוֹת. וְחוֹכֵי יְשׁוּעוֹת. אֵל לַמּוֹשָׁעוֹת. וְהוֹשִׁיעָה נָא):

On Hoshana Rabbah turn to page 106. During the first six days of Succos continue:

אֲנִי וָהוֹ הוֹשִׁיעָה נָּא:

הוֹשִׁיעָה אֶת־עַמֶּךָ, וּבָרֵךְ אֶת־נַחֲלָתֶךָ וּרְעֵם וְנַשְּׂאֵם עַד־הָעוֹלָם: וְיִהְיוּ דְבָרַי אֵלֶּה אֲשֶׁר הִתְחַנַּנְתִּי לִפְנֵי יהוה, קְרֹבִים אֶל־יהוה אֱלֹהֵינוּ יוֹמָם וָלָיְלָה, לַעֲשׂוֹת מִשְׁפַּט עַבְדּוֹ וּמִשְׁפַּט עַמּוֹ יִשְׂרָאֵל דְּבַר־יוֹם בְּיוֹמוֹ: לְמַעַן דַּעַת כָּל־עַמֵּי הָאָרֶץ, כִּי יהוה הוּא הָאֱלֹהִים, אֵין עוֹד:

The Torah Scroll is returned to the Ark and the chazzan says Kaddish, p. 148.

sin of bringing the Ark to the battlefield without asking Samuel's consent. This lack of respect for the prophet allowed the Ark to be captured *(Beis Avraham)*.

20. לְמַעַנְכֶם שִׁלָּחְתִּי — *For their sake were You also sent.*

Thus says HASHEM, Your Redeemer, Holy One of Israel: לְמַעַנְכֶם שִׁלַּחְתִּי בָבֶלָה, *For your sake I have sent you to Babylon* (Isaiah 43:14). In line with the Midrashic method of revowelization for exegetic purposes mentioned in commentary to sts. 11-14, the *paytan* reads שֻׁלַּחְתִּי, *I have been sent*, for שִׁלַּחְתִּי, *I have sent (Minchas Shai)*.

21-22. Continuing from the previous stich: *As You saved the ... tribes of Jacob* from their Babylonian exile, so may You *return Yourself, and restore ... the tents of Jacob* along with You *(Beis Avraham)*.

22. אָהֳלֵי יַעֲקֹב — *The tents of Jacob.*

מַה־טֹּבוּ אֹהָלֶיךָ יַעֲקֹב, *How goodly are your tents, Jacob* (Numbers 24:5). This verse refers to the *Beis HaMikdash* [see *Shmos Rabbah* 31:10] and the synagogues and study halls [see *Sanhedrin* 105b]. We ask for the rebuilding of the Holy Temple in Jerusalem, and for the restoration of all desecrated synagogues and study halls of the Diaspora *(Kol Bo)*.

[We pray that all these holy buildings be relocated in *Eretz Yisrael* in accordance with the Talmudic dictum: In future times the synagogues and study halls of Babylon will be re-established in *Eretz Yisrael* (*Megillah* 29a). And in fulfillment of the prophecy: *So says HASHEM: See, I shall return* שְׁבוּת אָהֳלֵי יַעֲקֹב, *the captivity of the tents of Jacob; and the city shall be built upon its hill and the Temple will sit in its place* (Jeremiah 30:18).]

23. Although the *hoshana* verses are generally attributed to R' Elazar HaKalir, this line was added at a later date by a *paytan* named שְׁמוּאֵל, *Shmuel*, as the acrostic clearly shows. That *Rashi*, who comments on virtually every stich of the *hoshana* prayers, omits this stich from his *siddur* indicates that it was not yet written in *Rashi's* time [4800/1040 C.E. — 4865/1105 C.E.] *(Iyun Tefillah)*.

[It is possible that observance of *mitzvos* and longing for the Messiah

10
21-23

²¹ *As You saved the captivity of the tribes of Jacob,*
²² *return and restore the captivity of the tents of Jacob,*
  and bring salvation now.
(²³ *As You saved those observant of mitzvos,*
  and hopeful for salvation —
O God Who brings about salvation, bring salvation now.)

On Hoshana Rabbah turn to page 106. During the first six days of Succos continue:

ANI VAHO, bring salvation now.

Save Your nation and bless Your heritage, tend them and elevate them forever. May these words of mine, which I have supplicated before HASHEM, be near to HASHEM, our God, by day and by night; that He bring about justice for His servant and justice for His people, Israel, each day's need in its day; that all the peoples of the earth shall know that HASHEM is God, there is no other.

The Torah Scroll is returned to the Ark and the chazzan says Kaddish, p. 148

---

had ebbed during the time of the *paytan* Shmuel. Therefore, he found it necessary to strengthen these two basic tenets of Judaism by reminding his generation that all salvation comes in their merit.]

אֵל לְמוֹשָׁעוֹת — *O God Who brings about salvation.*

[See comm. to *hoshana* 9, st. 1.]

•⇨ הוֹשִׁיעָה אֶת־עַמֶּךָ — **Save Your Nation**

Each day's *hoshana* service closes with three verses. The first (Psalms 28:9) is by King David; the other two (I Kings 8:59-60) are by his son, King Solomon.

הוֹשִׁיעָה... — *Save...*

Throughout Psalms 27 and 28 King David pleads with God to release him from his temporal duties as king and shepherd of the nation, that he might be enabled to spend more time on perfecting his personal service of God (Radak). [At the end of his plea he asks that God, Himself, assume the duties which until now had been David's. *Save Your nation, bless them, tend them,* You, God, personally.]

[But the formulation of this prayer was not original with the Psalmist, for it dates back to Moses. It had reached David through the tradition of oral transmission, father to son, teacher to disciple, until David committed it to writing.] When Moses wished to bless the Israelites, the angel of death blocked his way. Moses grabbed the angel and flung him to the earth. He then blessed the nation in the very presence of the one who would prevent such blessings. Thus Scripture testifies: *This is the blessing with which Moses ... blessed the Children of Israel before his death* (Deut. 31:3). What is the implication of the phrase 'before his death?' Would one think that Moses blessed Israel after his death? *Before his death* is to be taken literally — in the presence of the angel sent to bring about his death. And what blessing did he give the nation at that time? He invoked God's direct Providence, saying; *Save Your nation* and *bless Your heritage ...* (Yalkut Shimoni I, 951).

וְיִהְיוּ דְבָרַי אֵלֶּה — *May these words of mine.*

At the dedication of the Holy Temple, King Solomon invoked God to cause his *Shechinah* to rest in the newly built edifice and hearken to all the prayers directed there by the nation. His prayer is recorded in *I Kings* 8:22-54.

After praying, Solomon blessed the

אום נצורה

On Shabbos the following hoshana is said:

יא
א-ז אוֹם נְצוּרָה כְּבָבַת. בּוֹנֶנֶת בְּדַת נֶפֶשׁ מְשִׁיבַת. גּוֹמֶרֶת הִלְכוֹת שַׁבָּת. דּוֹרֶשֶׁת מַשְׂאַת שַׁבָּת. הַקּוֹבַעַת אֲלָפִים תְּחוּם שַׁבָּת. וּמְשִׁיבַת רֶגֶל מְשַׁבָּת. זָכוֹר וְשָׁמוֹר מְקַיֶּמֶת

nation. Part of the blessing was an expression of the hope that the prayer he had just uttered would be acceptable to God: *May these words of mine, which I have supplicated before HASHEM ...* (see *Metzudos* to *I Kings* 8:59).

מִשְׁפָּט — *Justice.*
In this verse the term מִשְׁפָּט, *justice,* refers to avenging the wrong inflicted by our enemies (*Rashi*).
Alternatively, it is a request for the necessities of life which are our due (*Radak*).

עַבְדּוֹ ... עַמּוֹ — *His servant ... His people.*
We ask that God provide both the private needs of each individual and the public needs of the community (*Metzudos*).

אוֹם נְצוּרָה ... — Nation Protected

The Four Species, *lulav, esrog,* myrtle and willow, are not taken on the Sabbath, because the Sages declare them to be מֻקְצָה, *set apart,* thereby forbidding their use, or even moving them from place to place. This decree was issued to prevent an unlearned man from bringing his *lulav* and *esrog* to a learned neighbor's home for instruction in their use. Such carrying through a public thoroughfare would constitute a desecration of the Sabbath (*Succah* 42b, 43a).

Since the Four Species are not taken on the Sabbath, *hakafah*-circuits are omitted on that day (*Rashi,* responsum cited by *Tur* 660).

Whether the *Hoshana* prayers are also omitted on the Sabbath is discussed in *Tur* (*Orach Chaim* 660):

R' Sherira Gaon would cancel the prayers lest the children, having heard the recital of those prayers in the synagogue, return home to get the Four Species with usually accompany these prayers.

Tur, however, is of the opinion that since no *hakafah*-circuit is made, even children will realize that this day is different and will not be misled into taking the *lulav.*

Present day custom is divided between Ashkenazic and Sephardic communities. The Sephardic liturgy (which incidentally is totally different from the one presented in this volume) follows *R' Sherira Gaon* and omits the *Hoshana* service on the Sabbath. All Ashkenazic liturgies (with the exception of *Chabad-Lubavitch*) contain a special Sabbath *hoshana*. The Ark is opened but no Torah scroll is removed, and the *bimah* is not circled during the recital of this *hoshana*. As would be expected, the theme of this *hoshana* is the observance of the various *mitzvos* related to the Sabbath.

1. נְצוּרָה כְּבָבַת — *Protected like the pupil [of the eye].*

The expression בָּבַת עַיִן, *pupil of the eye,* is frequently used as a metaphor for a delicate, treasured, loved one zealously protected from harm. God's protection of Israel, therefore, is likened to a person's concern lest his eye be harmed. Although the link between the nation's position as pupil of the eye and the observance of the Sabbath is obscure, the two are often found together in the liturgy [e.g., in the *zemiros Dror Yikra* and *Shabbos HaYom*].

☙ Nation Protected

**11
1-6**

On Shabbos the following hoshana is said:

¹ **N**ation protected like the pupil of the eye —
² she seeks understanding of the law
   which restores the soul:
³ She studies the laws of the Sabbath,
⁴ explicates the burdens of the Sabbath,
⁵ Establishes two thousand as the boundary of the Sabbath,
⁶ and restrains her foot because of the Sabbath.

---

2. בּוֹנֶנֶת — *She seeks understanding.*

Derived from בִּינָה, *understanding* (Rashi). Alternatively, *she builds,* from בנה, *to build,* i.e., Israel constructs palaces of novellae on Torah *(Beis Avraham).*

בְּדָת — *Of the law* [i.e., the Torah].

[See commentary to hoshana 1, st. 4.]

נֶפֶשׁ מְשִׁיבַת — *Which restores the soul.*

The Torah of HASHEM is perfect, מְשִׁיבַת נָפֶשׁ, *it restores the soul* (Psalms 19:8). Torah study leads one from the pathway to death and sets him on the pathway to life *(Rashi).*

3-6. [The list of thirty-nine forbidden labor of the Sabbath *(Shabbos 73a)* concludes with the prohibition against transporting objects from one domain to another (see commentary to st. 17). By specifying only this final labor, the *paytan* implies that all the others have been studied also, for one does not begin at the end. Even those prohibitions enacted by the Rabbis, such as תְּחוּם שַׁבָּת, *Sabbatical boundaries,* are diligently studied. Moreover, they are not merely considered food for academic discussion but are strictly obeyed.]

4. מַשְׂאַת שַׁבָּת — *The burdens of the Sabbath.*

Transporting objects on the Sabbath is culpable under Torah law only if the item transported has a minimum value or utility. Accordingly, the dimensions may vary from object to object. The principles involved in determining these laws of *the burdens of the Sabbath* are discussed at length in the Talmud, primarily in *Shabbos 76a-82a.*

The expression מַשְׂאַת שַׁבָּת, *the burdens of the Sabbath,* is taken from Jeremiah (17:21): וְאַל־תִּשְׂאוּ מַשָּׂא בְּיוֹם הַשַּׁבָּת, *You shall not bear burdens on the day of Sabbath* (Rashi).

5. אַלְפַּיִם תְּחוּם — *Two thousand as the boundary.*

Although the enactment of תְּחוּם שַׁבָּת, *Sabbatical boundaries,* is of Rabbinic origin, nevertheless, support [אַסְמַכְתָּא] for such a limitation is found in Scripture. אַל־יֵצֵא אִישׁ מִמְּקֹמוֹ בַּיוֹם הַשְּׁבִיעִי, *Let no man leave his place on the seventh day* (Exodus 16:29), alludes to the two thousand cubit limit past an inhabited area beyond which it is forbidden to walk on the Sabbath. *His place* refers to the city or town in which one lives, and includes a two thousand cubit wide belt around it. That a surrounding area of that size is considered part of the city is derived from *Numbers 35:5* where a two thousand cubit wide belt is provided for each of the Levite cities *(Eruvin 51a).*

6. וּמְשִׁיבַת רֶגֶל — *And restrains her* [lit. *a] foot.*

This is a continuation of the previous stich — after establishing the two thousand cubit limit, the people scrupulous-

יא
ח־כ

בַּשַׁבָּת. **חָשָׁה** לְמַהֵר בִּיאַת שַׁבָּת. **טוֹרַחַת** כֹּל מִשְׁשָׁה לַשַׁבָּת. **יוֹשֶׁבֶת** וּמַמְתֶּנֶת עַד כְּלוֹת שַׁבָּת. **כָּבוֹד וָעֹנֶג** קוֹרְאָה לַשַׁבָּת. **לְבוּשׁ** וּכְסוּת מְחַלֶּפֶת בַּשַׁבָּת. **מַאֲכָל** וּמִשְׁתֶּה מְכִינָה לַשַׁבָּת. **נֹעַם** מְגָדִים מַנְעֶמֶת לַשַׁבָּת. **סְעוּדוֹת שָׁלֹשׁ** מְקַיֶּמֶת בַּשַׁבָּת. **עַל־שְׁתֵּי** כִּכָּרוֹת בּוֹצַעַת בַּשַׁבָּת. **פּוֹרֶטֶת** אַרְבַּע רְשֻׁיּוֹת בַּשַׁבָּת. **צִוּוּי** הַדְלָקַת נֵר מַדְלֶקֶת בַּשַׁבָּת. **קִדּוּשׁ** הַיּוֹם מְקַדֶּשֶׁת בַּשַׁבָּת. **רֹנֶן** שֶׁבַע

ly adhere to it, restraining their feet from overstepping the boundary (based on *Radak* to *Isaiah 58:13*, אִם־תָּשִׁיב מִשַׁבָּת רַגְלֶךָ, *if you restrain, because of the Sabbath, your feet*).

7-10. There are minor variations between the first and second versions of the Ten Commandments (*Exodus 20:1-14* and *Deuteronomy 5:5-18*). The Sages explain that God spoke both versions simultaneously — a feat impossible for the human mouth to duplicate (*Shevuos* 20b) and that both versions are authoritative sources of halachic exegesis. The differences between the two are explicated and expounded upon. The *mitzvah* of Sabbath is expressed in the first Commandments as זָכוֹר אֶת־יוֹם הַשַׁבָּת, 'Remember' the day of Sabbath (*Exodus 20:8*), while in the second Commandments it reads שָׁמוֹר אֶת־יוֹם הַשַׁבָּת, 'Safeguard' the day of Sabbath (*Deuteronomy 5:12*). In Mechilta, many lessons are derived from this change of verb. Among them are those referred to in the following stiches: One must hasten the arrival of the Sabbath — 'remember' it before its onset [st. 8]; and delay its departure — 'safeguard' the Sabbath when it leaves [st. 10].

Also, 'Remember' the day of Sabbath throughout the week. Whenever a goodly portion comes your way, set it aside, 'safeguard' it, for the Sabbath [st. 9; see also *Beitzah 16a*] (*Rashi; Shaar HaShamayim*).

8. חָשָׁה לְמַהֵר בִּיאַת שַׁבָּת — *By rushing* [lit. she rushes] *to hasten the onset of the Sabbath*.

This stich coupled with stich 10 is similar to a line found in the Friday evening *zemer 'Kol Mekadesh'*: הַמְאַחֲרִים לָצֵאת מִן הַשַׁבָּת וּמְמַהֲרִים לָבוֹא, *Who delay departing from the Sabbath and rush to enter* [see ArtScroll Zemiroth p. 82] (*Iyun Tefillah*).

Alternatively, *she rushes and hastens to complete her work before the onset of the Sabbath* (*Beis Avraham*).

11-16. וְקָרָאתָ לַשַׁבָּת עֹנֶג, *if you proclaim the Sabbath 'a delight'*, לִקְדוֹשׁ ה' מְכֻבָּד, *the holy [day] of HASHEM 'honored one'*, ... *then you shall be granted pleasure with HASHEM* ... (*Isaiah 58:13-14*).

11. כָּבוֹד — *Honor*.

This refers to the בִּגְדֵי שַׁבָּת, *Sabbath clothing*, worn in honor of the day, as mentioned in the next stich.

עֹנֶג — *Delight*.

This refers to the food, drink and meals mentioned in stiches 13-16 (*Beis Avraham*).

13. מְכִינָה לַשַׁבָּת — *She prepares for the Sabbath*.

Not בַּשַׁבָּת, 'on' the Sabbath, but לַשַׁבָּת, 'for' the Sabbath. The preparation must take place during the six days of the work week (*Kol Bo*). One who toils before the Sabbath shall eat on the Sabbath; but if one does not toil before the Sabbath, whence shall he eat on the Sabbath? (*Avodah Zarah 3a*).

15. סְעוּדוֹת שָׁלֹשׁ — *Three meals*.

Three times in one sentence, Moses used the word הַיּוֹם, *today*, referring to the Sabbath *manna* portion: *And Moses said, 'Eat of it today* (הַיּוֹם) *for today*

⁷ *'Remember' and 'Safeguard', she fulfills on the Sabbath*
⁸ *by rushing to hasten the onset of the Sabbath;*
⁹ *By toiling throughout the six for the Sabbath;*
¹⁰ *by sitting, patiently waiting until
the end of the Sabbath;*
¹¹ *'Honor' and 'Delight' she proclaims the Sabbath:*
¹² *clothing and raiment she changes for the Sabbath;*
¹³ *Food and drink she prepares for the Sabbath;*
¹⁴ *of the sweetness of delicate fruits she partakes
on the Sabbath;*
¹⁵ *Three meals she fulfills on the Sabbath;*
¹⁶ *over two loaves she breaks bread on the Sabbath.*
¹⁷ *She distinguishes four domains on the Sabbath.*
¹⁸ *The command of kindling the light she fulfills
for the Sabbath.*
¹⁹ *The Sanctification of the day she recites on the Sabbath.*
²⁰ *A seven-part prayer she prays on the Sabbath.*

(הַיּוֹם) *is the Sabbath of HASHEM, today* (הַיּוֹם) *you will not find it in the field* (*Exodus* 16:25). This triple mention alludes to three meals which should be eaten each Sabbath day, one in the evening, two in the daytime (*Shabbos* 117b).

16. שְׁתֵּי כִכָּרוֹת — *Two loaves.*
When the Israelites gathered their portions of *manna* on the first Friday that it fell, they were surprised to find לֶחֶם מִשְׁנֶה, *double [portions of] food* — i.e., twice the usual allotment (*Exodus* 16:22). To remember the 'double food' which fell in honor of the Sabbath, we honor the Sabbath with two loaves (*Shabbos* 117b).

17. אַרְבַּע רְשׁוּיוֹת — *Four domains.*
Regarding the prohibitions against transporting objects from private to public (or public to private) property, four distinct domains are recognized (the definitions offered here are incomplete, as a comprehensive listing would be cumbersome and outside the scope of this work):

רְשׁוּת הָרַבִּים, *Public domain* — a non-enclosed area, sixteen or more cubits wide, used daily by vast numbers of people.

רְשׁוּת הַיָּחִיד, *Private domain* — an area enclosed for purposes of habitation.

כַּרְמְלִית, *Median domain* — public property not meeting the halachic requirements of a public domain; or private property not meeting the enclosure requirements of a private domain.

מְקוֹם פְּטוּר, *Free space* — certain well-defined areas which fall into none of the above categories.

Torah law forbids transport of objects between a public and a private domain, or for a distance of four cubits or more within a public domain. The movement of items between either of these locations and a median domain, or over a four cubit distance within a median domain is forbidden by Rabbinic decree. Between any of these three domains and a free space, objects may be carried, providing four cubits are not traversed within a public or median domain. Within a private domain no restrictions exist.

20. רִנֶּן שֶׁבַע — *A seven-part prayer.*
The *Amidah* of the Sabbath contains only seven benedictions. The first three

יא מְפַלֶּלֶת בַּשַּׁבָּת. שִׁבְעָה בַדָּת קוֹרְאָה בַּשַּׁבָּת. תַּנְחִילֶנָּה
כא-כב לְיוֹם שֶׁכֻּלּוֹ שַׁבָּת:

◆§ כהושעת אדם

אֲנִי וָהוּ הוֹשִׁיעָה נָּא:

יב כְּהוֹשַׁעְתָּ אָדָם יְצִיר כַּפֶּיךָ לְגוֹנְנָה.
א-ד בְּשַׁבַּת־קֹדֶשׁ הִמְצֵאתוֹ כֹּפֶר וַחֲנִינָה. כֵּן הוֹשַׁעְנָא:

כְּהוֹשַׁעְתָּ גּוֹי מְצֻיָּן מְקַוִּים חֹפֶשׁ.
דֵּעָה כּוֹנְנוּ לָבוּר שְׁבִיעִי לָנֶפֶשׁ. כֵּן הוֹשַׁעְנָא:

and the last three blessings of the weekday *Shemoneh Esrei* are separated by one longer blessing relating to the sanctity of the day.

Alternatively, רֶנֶן שֶׁבַע means *seven prayers* and refers to the seven readings of the *Amidah* on the Sabbath — *Maariv*, *Shachris*, *Musaf* and *Minchah*, the last three being repeated by the *chazzan* for a total of seven (*Tefillah Yesharah*).

21. בַּדָּת — *Of the Torah.*
[See commentary to *hoshana* 1, st. 4.]
Shaar HaShamayim reads בַּדָּת, *according to the rule*. Each of the seven who reads from the Torah follows the same set of rules, namely pronouncing the correct blessings before and after.

22. תַּנְחִילֶנָּה לְיוֹם — *Cause her to inherit the day* [lit., *to a day*].
Grammatically the prefix לְ, *to*, seems out of place here. For this reason *Avodas Yisrael* omits it, reading תַּנְחִילֶנָּה יוֹם, *cause her to inherit a day*.
Tefillah Yesharah justifies our reading with an interpolation — *cause her to inherit that reward she deserves for observing the Sabbath, but defer such reward to a day ...*

יוֹם שֶׁכֻּלּוֹ שַׁבָּת — *The day which will be* [lit. *is*] *completely a Sabbath*.
Just as the Sabbath is described as מֵעֵין עוֹלָם הַבָּא, *a semblance of the World to Come* (Sabbath *Zemiroth*; see also *Berachos* 57b), so is The World to Come described as יוֹם שֶׁכֻּלּוֹ שַׁבָּת וּמְנוּחָה לְחַיֵּי הָעוֹלָמִים, *the day which will be completely a Sabbath and rest day for eternal life* (*Tamid* 7:4).

◆§ כְּהוֹשַׁעְתָּ אָדָם — As You Saved Adam

Unlike the other *hoshanos* which were composed by R' Elazar HaKalir this *hoshana* is by R' Menachem ben R' Machir, a student of Rashi. While the others just follow an alphabetical scheme, this *hoshana* continues with an acrostic of the author's name, מְנַחֵם בְּרַבִּי מָכִיר, with the blessing חֲזַק לָעַד אָמֵן, *may he be strengthened forever, amen*, in a style common to most *paytanim*. This *hoshana* was written specifically for the Sabbath and contains many

---

1. Interpreting this stich Kabbalistically שִׁבְעָה, *seven*, represents the seventh *sefirah*-emanation מַלְכוּת, *kingship* [see commentary end of *hoshana* 1]. בַּדָּת has a *gematria* value of 424, the same *gematria* as מָשִׁיחַ בֶּן דָּוִד, *Messiah, scion of David*. Thus this stich is a prayer for the advent of the King Messiah (*Shaar Yisas'char*).

11
21-22
²¹ *Seven portions of the Torah she reads on the Sabbath.*
²² *Cause her to inherit the day which will be completely a Sabbath.*

◈§ As You Saved Adam

ANI VAHO, bring salvation now.

12
1-4
¹ **A**s *You saved Adam, Your handiwork, to be his shield;*
² *on the holy Sabbath You brought forth for him forgiveness and grace —*   *so save now.*
³ *As You saved the distinctive nation which sought freedom;*
⁴ *With wisdom they anticipated the choice of the seventh for rest —*   *so save now.*

allusions to the *mitzvos* and customs of the day.

This *hoshana* is found in most Ashkenazic liturgies with the exception of *Tehillas Hashem* (which omits the entire *Hoshana* Service on the Sabbath) and *Avodas Yisrael* (which substitutes a different *hoshana*[1]).

1. אָדָם ... בְּשַׁבָּת ... הִמְצֵאתוֹ כֹּפֶר — *Adam ... on the Sabbath ... You brought forth for him forgiveness.*

When Adam sinned by eating from the Tree of Knowledge, he should have received the death sentence and been doomed to *Gehinnom* for eternity, as God Himself had forewarned him: *For on the day you eat of it you shall surely die* (Genesis 2:17). By what merit was he spared?

Adam committed his sin on Friday afternoon, a short while before the onset of the Sabbath. Before his sentence was carried out, the holiness of the Sabbath descended. So Adam's death would in no small measure have marred the peacefulness and sanctity of the day. The Sabbath itself came to Adam's defense and cried, 'Master of the World, during the first six days no one died in all the universe. Do You want death to begin with me? Is this a display of my sanctity? Is this a display of my blessing?' So Adam was saved from *Gehinnom* in the merit of the Sabbath (*Midrash Shocher Tov* 92:1).

3. גּוֹי מְצֻיָּן — *The distinctive nation.*

My father (Jacob) went down to Egypt ... וַיְהִי־שָׁם לְגוֹי, *and became there*

1. *Avodas Yisrael* has the following in place of כְּהוֹשַׁעְתָּ אָדָם, *As You Saved Adam:*

כְּהוֹשַׁעְתָּ אַב הֲמוֹן הִשְׁלִיךְ עָלֶיךָ יְהָב. בַּעֲרוֹ רָדַף וּמִלַּטְתּוֹ מִלַּהַב.	כֵּן הוֹשַׁע נָא:
כְּהוֹשַׁעְתָּ גִּזְעוֹ מָסַר יְחִידָתוֹ לַשֶּׁבַח. דִּבַּרְתָּ לְהוֹרוֹ יָדְךָ אַל תִּשְׁלַח.	כֵּן הוֹשַׁע נָא:
כְּהוֹשַׁעְתָּ הַנֶּאֱבָק עִם מַלְאָךְ קָדוֹשׁ וָעִיר. וּמִלַּטְתּוֹ מִשְׁטַם שֵׂעִיר.	כֵּן הוֹשַׁע נָא:
כְּהוֹשַׁעְתָּ זַרְעוֹ בְּבוֹאָם עַל הָעִיר בֶּטַח. חֲרַדְתָּ צְרִימוֹ בְּנָסְעָם וְהָלְכוּ לָבֶטַח.	כֵּן הוֹשַׁע נָא:
כְּהוֹשַׁעְתָּ טְהוֹרִים מִמַּפְרִיכֵמוֹ בְּמַדְלֵבָן. יָרְדוּ בִמְצוּלוֹת כְּמוֹ אֶבֶן.	כֵּן הוֹשַׁע נָא:
כְּהוֹשַׁעְתָּ כָּלִיל כְּנִתְעַלְּמָה בְּגֹמֶא צוּרָתוֹ. לְוִיָּתוֹ אֶל חֵיק הוֹרָתוֹ.	כֵּן הוֹשַׁע נָא:
כְּהוֹשַׁעְתָּ מְצֻנָּף בַּר כְּנִתְעַבָּר. נֶאֱמָן חָל בַּעֲדוֹ וְנִתְגַּבָּר.	כֵּן הוֹשַׁע נָא:
כְּהוֹשַׁעְתָּ סָגַר בְּיַד יִשְׁבִּי בְּנוֹב הַגִּתִּי. עָזְרוּ אֲבִישַׁי וַיִּךְ אֶת הַפְּלִשְׁתִּי.	כֵּן הוֹשַׁע נָא:
כְּהוֹשַׁעְתָּ פָּקִיד כְּנֶגֶד שֶׁבַע מִמְּעוֹנוֹ. צִפִּית לִישְׁעוֹ וְשׁוֹבַבְתּוֹ לִמְלוֹנוֹ.	כֵּן הוֹשַׁע נָא:
כְּהוֹשַׁעְתָּ קֶצֶב פָּר וְשָׁעְתוֹ לְמַעְלָה. רִשְׁפָּתוֹ הָאֵשׁ וְגַם הַמַּיִם אֲשֶׁר בַּתְּעָלָה.	כֵּן הוֹשַׁע נָא:
כְּהוֹשַׁעְתָּ שׁוּעַ לְךָ כִּי מֵת הַיֶּלֶד. תָּשָׁב רוּחוֹ אֵלָיו וַיַחַם בְּשַׂר הַיָּלֶד.	כֵּן הוֹשַׁע נָא:
כְּהוֹשַׁעְתָּ שׁוֹמְרֵי מִצְווֹת. וְחוֹכֵי יְשׁוּעוֹת. אֵל לְמוֹשָׁעוֹת.	וְהוֹשִׁיעָה נָא:

יב   כְּהוֹשַׁעְתָּ הָעָם נְהַגְתָּ כַּצֹּאן לְהַנְחוֹת.
ה"יב   וְחֹק שַׂמְתָּ בְּמָרָה עַל־מֵי מְנֻחוֹת.   כֵּן הוֹשַׁעְנָא:

כְּהוֹשַׁעְתָּ זְבוּדֶיךָ בְּמִדְבַּר־סִין בַּמַּחֲנֶה.
חָכְמוּ וְלָקְטוּ בַּשִּׁשִּׁי לֶחֶם מִשְׁנֶה.   כֵּן הוֹשַׁעְנָא:

כְּהוֹשַׁעְתָּ טְפוּלֶיךָ הוֹרוּ הֲכָנָה בְּמָדְעָם.
יָשָׁר כֹּחָם וְהוֹדָה לָמוֹ רוֹעָם.   כֵּן הוֹשַׁעְנָא:

כְּהוֹשַׁעְתָּ כִּלְכְּלוּ בְעֹנֶג מָן הַמְשֻׁמָּר.
לֹא הָפַךְ עֵינוֹ וְרֵיחוֹ לֹא נָמָר.   כֵּן הוֹשַׁעְנָא:

a nation (Deuteronomy 26:5). This verse teaches that the Jews were מְצֻיָּנִים שָׁם, distinctive there (Passover Haggadah).

Mechilta teaches that the Jews in Egypt were identifiable by their clothes, their names, and their language. This may not necessarily mean that they wore specific Jewish garb or spoke only Hebrew. Perhaps their distinctiveness lay in the fact that they wore only modest attire; when they talked, 'the name of God was regularly on their lips'; and they did not name their children after Egyptians deities (R' Joseph Elias, ArtScroll Haggadah).

4. כִּוְּנוּ לָבוֹר שְׁבִיעִי — *They anticipated the choice of the seventh.*

In those days when Moses matured and went forth among his brothers, he saw their burdens (Exodus 1:11). He saw that they were allowed no time for rest from their labors. To ease their burdens, Moses suggested to Pharaoh that a worker who never rests is sure to die. 'Yet, you, Pharaoh, have all these slaves working continuously. If they are not given one day's rest each week, they will not survive.'

'Go,' replied Pharaoh, 'and do as you suggest.' Moses went and ordained the seventh day as their day of rest, thus anticipating God's future commandment of Sabbath rest (Shmos Rabbah 1:28).

6. וְחֹק שַׂמְתָּ בְּמָרָה — *And You issued a statute at Marah.*

After the miraculous crossing of the Sea of Reeds, the Israelites *traveled for three days through the wilderness but found no water. They arrived at Marah but were unable to drink the water ... for it was bitter ... HASHEM showed Moses a stick which he cast into the waters and they became sweet. There* [in Marah] *He issued a statute and a law, ... and tested them* (Exodus 15:22-25). The statute and law refer to two commandments to observe the Sabbath and to honor parents, the *mitzvos* which would later be repeated in the Ten Commandments. That they were conveyed to Israel before they were given at Sinai is derived by the Sages from a phrase contained in each of these two commandments when they were issued at Sinai: כַּאֲשֶׁר צִוְּךָ ה' אֱלֹהֶיךָ, *as HASHEM, your God, has commanded you* (Deuteronomy 5:12,16), indicating that these particular laws had been taught previously (Sanhedrin 56b).

עַל־מֵי מְנֻחוֹת — *Beside tranquil waters.*

This phrase, borrowed from *Psalms* 23:2, alludes to the newly sweetened waters of Marah (Beis Yaakov).

7. זְבוּדֶיךָ — *Your portion.*

Israel is referred to as חֵלֶק ה', *HASHEM's portion* (Deuteronomy 32:9).

בְּמִדְבַּר־סִין — *At the Wilderness of Sin.*

This was the place where the manna first fell, in response to the nation's complaints about lack of food (see Exodus chapter 16).

12
5-12

⁵ As You saved the people whom You
  guided like a flock to contentment;
⁶ And You issued a statute at Marah
  beside tranquil waters —   *so save now.*
⁷ As You saved Your portion in the encampment
  at the Wilderness of Sin;
⁸ They acted wisely and gathered
  double bread on the sixth —   *so save now.*
⁹ As You saved those who clung to You,
  who derived the rules of preparation
  through their wisdom
¹⁰ Their shepherd blessed their talent
  and deferred to them —   *so save now.*
¹¹ As You saved those You sustained on the
  day of delight with the guarded manna
¹² whose appearance did not change
  and whose aroma did not sour —   *so save now.*

8. לֶחֶם מִשְׁנֶה — *Double bread.*

This refers to the two loaves over which one breaks bread for the Sabbath meals (see commentary to *hoshana* 11, st. 16).

9. הוֹרוּ הֲכָנָה בְּמַדָּעָם — *[Those] who derived the rules of preparation through their wisdom.*

When the manna fell on the sixth day, there was a double portion, and *the elders of the congregation came and told Moses* (*Exodus* 16:22). But why just the elders — were the others not interested in discovering the reason for the double portion? The people presented this question before the elders *who in their wisdom derived the rules of preparation* of food for the Sabbath. These rules (see *Eruvin* 38b) taught that food for the Sabbath must be prepared beforehand, and that no food may be prepared on a Sabbath or festival for another day. Although God had taught these laws to Moses (*Exodus* 16:5), he had not yet taught them to the nation. The *paytan* alludes to the elders' wisdom in deducing these rules before they were taught.

After deriving the rules of preparation, the elders presented their conclusions to Moses who admitted his error [st. 10] in not having taught the rules earlier, and he blessed them (*Iyun Tefillah*).

10. יִשַּׁר כֹּחָם — *Blessed their talent* [lit., *aligned their strengths*].

[Although the root יָשָׁר, *straight*, is never used in Scripture in this sense, the blessing יִשַּׁר כֹּחֲךָ (some read יְיַשֵּׁר), *may your strength be aligned*, is found often in Talmud, e.g., *Yevamos* 62a, in praise of one who has either fulfilled a *mitzvah* or performed a kindness and is commonly used today as an expression of thanks.]

רוֹעָם — *Their shepherd.*

I.e., Moses.

11. בְּעֹנֶג — *On the day of delight.*

[This reference to the Sabbath is based on *Isaiah* 58:13, see commentary to *hoshana* 11, sts. 11-16.]

מָן הַמִּשְׁמָר — *The guarded manna.*

Moses told the people to prepare the extra portion of *manna*, set it aside and 'guard' it until the next morning (*Exodus* 16:23).

12. לֹא הָפַךְ עֵינוֹ וְרֵיחוֹ לֹא נָמָר — *Whose appearance did not change and whose aroma did not sour.*

Of Friday's double portion of manna,

יב כְּהוֹשַׁעְתָּ **מִ**שְׁפְּטֵי מַשָּׂאוֹת שַׁבָּת גָּמָרוּ.
יג-כב
נָחוּ וְשָׁבְתוּ רְשֻׁיּוֹת וּתְחוּמִים שָׁמָרוּ.
כֵּן הוֹשַׁעְנָא:

כְּהוֹשַׁעְתָּ **סִ**ינַי הִשְׁמִיעוּ בְּדִבּוּר רְבִיעִי.
עִנְיַן זָכוֹר וְשָׁמוֹר לְקַדֵּשׁ שְׁבִיעִי.   כֵּן הוֹשַׁעְנָא:

כְּהוֹשַׁעְתָּ **פִּ**קְדוּ יְרִיחוֹ שֶׁבַע לְהַקֵּף.
צָרוּ עַד־רִדְתָּהּ בַּשַּׁבָּת לְתַקֵּף.   כֵּן הוֹשַׁעְנָא:

כְּהוֹשַׁעְתָּ **ק**ֹהֶלֶת וְעַמּוֹ בְּבֵית עוֹלָמִים.
רִצּוּךָ בְּחָגְגָם שִׁבְעָה וְשִׁבְעָה יָמִים.
כֵּן הוֹשַׁעְנָא:

כְּהוֹשַׁעְתָּ **שָׁ**בִים עוֹלֵי גוֹלָה לְפִדְיוֹם.
תּוֹרָתְךָ בְּקָרְאָם בַּחַג יוֹם יוֹם.   כֵּן הוֹשַׁעְנָא:

one half was to be set aside for the Sabbath. Unlike the manna of other days which *would become wormy and foul smelling (Exodus 16:20)* if it were left overnight, the Sabbath manna remained absolutely fresh.

13.-14. מַשָּׂאוֹת ... רְשֻׁיּוֹת וּתְחוּמִים — *Burdens ... domains and boundaries.*

[For the laws pertaining to limitations on carrying and traveling on the Sabbath see commentary to *hoshana* 11, sts. 4-6,17.]

15. בְּדִבּוּר רְבִיעִי — *The fourth pronouncement.*

[The fourth of the Ten Commandments contains the laws of the Sabbath.]

16. זָכוֹר וְשָׁמוֹר — *'Remember' and 'Safeguard'.*

[The Torah commands two varieties of Sabbath observance. See commentary to *hoshana* 11, sts. 7-10.]

17. יְרִיחוֹ שֶׁבַע לְהַקֵּף — *At Jericho to encircle seven times.*

Jericho was circled one time each day for six consecutive days. On the seventh day — the Sabbath — the city was circled seven times, after which the walls crumbled, allowing Jericho to be conquered by the Israelite army (see *Joshua* chap. 6 and *Rashi*; see also commentary to *hoshana* 10, st. 15).

The relationship between the encirclement of Jericho and the hakafah-circuits on Hoshana Rabbah is not coincidental. Twice the word וַאֲסוֹבְבָה, *I shall encircle*, appears in Scripture: *I shall encircle Your altar, HASHEM* (*Psalms* 26:6); and וַאֲסוֹבְבָה בָעִיר, *I shall encircle the city* (*Song of Songs* 3:2). The number of circuits *around the altar* on Hoshana Rabbah is derived from the number of circuits *around the city* of Jericho. Just as Jericho was circuited once on each of the first six days, so the altar is circuited once on each of the first six days of Succos. And just as Jericho was circuited seven times on the seventh day, so the altar is circuited seven times on Hoshana Rabbah (*Tefillah Yesharah* based on *Yalkut Shimoni* II, 703).

19. קֹהֶלֶת — *Koheles.*

The reference is to King Solomon. The word קֹהֶלֶת literally means *the one who assembles.* Solomon's words were spoken in public assembly and so he was called קֹהֶלֶת, *Koheles* (*Koheles Rabbah* 1:2. See ArtScroll *Koheles* 1:1).

12
13-22

¹³ As You saved those who study the laws
regarding the burdens of the Sabbath;
¹⁴ They are content and they rest,
guarding domains and boundaries — so save now.
¹⁵ As You saved those permitted to hear
the fourth pronouncement at Sinai;
¹⁶ the theme of 'Remember' and
'Safeguard' to sanctify the seventh — so save now.
¹⁷ As You saved those bidden at Jericho
to encircle seven times;
¹⁸ They besieged it until its downfall on the Sabbath,
to strengthen them — so save now.
¹⁹ As You saved Koheles and his nation
in the eternal Temple,
²⁰ They pleased You when they celebrated seven
and another seven days — so save now.
²¹ As You saved those who returned
arising from exile to redemption;
²² As they read Your Torah on the
festival, every day — so save now.

Alternatively, the name refers to the vast amount of wisdom which was 'assembled' within him *(Ibn Ezra)*, or because he 'assembled' much wisdom *(Rashi)*.

20. רְצוּךְ בְּחָגְגָם שִׁבְעָה וְשִׁבְעָה יָמִים — *They pleased You when they celebrated seven and another seven days.*

The dedication of the Temple of Solomon began on the eighth day of Tishrei, and continued for seven days. Even though the third day of their feasting was Yom Kippur, the celebration continued and the fast was not observed. The next day a worried nation feared that it would be punished with excision (כָּרֵת) for having desecrated the sanctity of Yom Kippur, when a heavenly voice proclaimed, 'You are all eligible for the World to Come!' *(Moed Katan* 9a).

That seven day celebration ended on the fourteenth of Tishrei, the eve of Succos. Instead of returning home, the nation celebrated for another seven days — their first pilgrimage festival in the Temple. Only after Succos did they take leave of Solomon and the Temple (see *I Kings* 8:65-66).

21-23. *Nehemiah* 8 relates that when the returnees from the Babylonian exile gathered before Ezra on the first day of the seventh month [Rosh HaShanah], he read the entire Torah to them. When they heard that the fifteenth day of that month would be Succos they diligently prepared the four species and erected Succos. *And he read in the Scroll of God's Torah each day, from the first day to the last (Nehemiah* 8:18). In that year, Succos was celebrated in an unusually grand style and was accompanied by שִׂמְחָה גְדוֹלָה מְאֹד, *very great joy (ibid. v. 17).*

24-32. The following stiches are based primarily on the narrative of the *aravah* ritual found in chapter 4 of *Succah* (see ArtScroll *Mishnah, Succah* 4:2-5): The *aravah* [willow] branches were used

יב כְּהוֹשַׁעְתָּ **מְ**שַׂמְּחֶיךָ בְּבִנְיַן שֵׁנִי הַמְחֻדָּשׁ.
כג-לד
נוֹטְלִין לוּלָב כָּל־שִׁבְעָה בַּמִּקְדָּשׁ. כֵּן הוֹשַׁעְנָא:

כְּהוֹשַׁעְתָּ **ח**ִבּוּט עֲרָבָה שַׁבָּת מַדְחִים.
מַרְבִּיּוֹת מוֹצָא לִיסוֹד מִזְבֵּחַ מַנִּיחִים.
כֵּן הוֹשַׁעְנָא:

כְּהוֹשַׁעְתָּ **בָּ**רַכּוֹת וַאֲרוּכוֹת וּגְבוֹהוֹת מְעַלְּסִים.
בִּפְטִירָתָן יֹפִי לְךָ מִזְבֵּחַ מְקַלְּסִים. כֵּן הוֹשַׁעְנָא:

כְּהוֹשַׁעְתָּ **מ**וֹדִים וּמְיַחֲלִים וְלֹא מְשַׁנִּים.
כֻּלָּנוּ אָנוּ לְיָהּ וְעֵינֵינוּ לְיָהּ שׁוֹנִים. כֵּן הוֹשַׁעְנָא:

כְּהוֹשַׁעְתָּ **יֶ**קֶב מַחֲצָבֶיךָ סוֹבְבִים בְּרַעֲנָנָה.
רוֹנְנִים אֲנִי וָהוֹ הוֹשִׁיעָה נָּא. כֵּן הוֹשַׁעְנָא:

כְּהוֹשַׁעְתָּ **ח**ֵיל זְרִיזִים מְשָׁרְתִים בִּמְנוּחָה.
קָרְבַּן שַׁבָּת כָּפוּל עוֹלָה וּמִנְחָה. כֵּן הוֹשַׁעְנָא:

every day in the Temple, and the ritual of beating it on the ground was observed even on the Sabbath. Willows grew in abundance in a place near Jerusalem known as Motza. The people would pick eleven cubit long willows from Motza and stand them up around the ten cubit high altar. They made their daily circuits around the altar and, as they completed the final circuit on Hoshana Rabbah, they would proclaim, 'Beauty becomes you, O Altar.'

26. מַרְבִּיּוֹת — *Branches.*

The translation follows *Sefer Ha-Aroch*. *Shaar HaShamayim* renders *plantings*.

מוֹצָא — *Motza.*

The *gemara* identifies Motza as Kolonia. But why does the Tanna call it *Motza*, literally, *removed* or *exempt*? Because the citizens of Kolonia were exempt from paying taxes (*Succah* 45a). This exemption was in return for the willows cut from their field (*R' Ovadiah MiBertinoro*).

[Perhaps מוֹצָא, *Motza*, which the Mishnah locates as 'just below Jerusalem,' is identical with מוֹצָה, *Motzah*, which was in Benjamin's portion (*Joshua* 18:26), for Jerusalem included portions of Benjamin and Judah.]

27. בְּרַכּוֹת וַאֲרוּכוֹת וּגְבוֹהוֹת — *With supple, long, and tall [willows].*

This description of the eleven cubit willow branches used in the Temple may be found in the glosses of R' Ronsburg to *Succah* 45a. The wording as it appears in the text however, is בְּרַבּוֹת, *with many*.

29. וְלֹא מְשַׁנִּים — *But never exchanged.*

Unlike the idol worshipers of the First Temple era (see *I Kings* 18:21), the people of the Second Temple *never exchanged* the God of their ancestors for the false gods of their neighbors (*Beis Yaakov*).

31. יֶקֶב מַחֲצָבֶיךָ — *The wine cellar of Your hewing.*

The altar is called a wine cellar. At the southwestern corner of the altar roof were two funnel-shaped pipes which led deep into the ground under the altar.

12
23-34

²³ As You saved those who brought You joy
    with the renewed Second Temple;
²⁴ Who took up the lulav all seven days
    in the Sanctuary —   so save now.
²⁵ As You saved those for whom the
    beating of the willow overrode the Sabbath;
²⁶ Those who placed Motza's branches
    at the base of the altar —   so save now.
²⁷ As You saved those who praised with
    supple, long, and tall willows;
²⁸ who departed while extolling,
    'Beauty becomes you, O Altar' —   so save now.
²⁹ As You saved those who thanked
    and hoped, but never exchanged;
³⁰ Like them we all cry out,
    'We are YAH's and our eyes are to YAH' — so save now.
³¹ As You saved those who encircled
    the wine cellar of Your hewing with greenery;
³² Singing, 'ANI VAHO
    bring salvation now' —   so save now.
³³ As You saved the army of speedy ones
    who serve on the day of contentment,
³⁴ With the doubled Sabbath offering,
    of burnt and meal offering —   so save now.

Into one were poured the wine libations which accompanied each burnt offering and each peace offering. Into the other were poured the water libations which were exclusive to the Succos festival.

With this in mind the Talmud explains a verse in *Isaiah* (5:1-2):

I shall sing now for my beloved, my beloved's song of his vineyard. My beloved had a vineyard atop a fertile hill. He fenced it, he stoned it, he planted in it a vine. He built a tower in its midst, and also hewed a wine cellar within it ...

He planted in it a vine refers to the Holy Temple, *and built a tower in its midst* — to the altar, *and also hewed a wine cellar within it* — to the pipes of the libations (*Succah* 49a).

33. חֵיל זְרִיזִים — *The army of speedy ones.*

This refers to the *Kohanim* who perform the Temple service with dispatch (see *Eruvin* 103a).

בִּמְנוּחָה — *On the day of* [lit. *with*] *contentment.*

The Sabbath is called the day of contentment (see *hoshana* 11, st. 22). The Temple service is performed even on the Sabbath, despite the many otherwise forbidden labors involved (*Sanhedrin* 35a).

34. קָרְבַּן שַׁבָּת כָּפוּל — *The doubled Sabbath offering.*

Unlike the additional [מוּסָף] offerings of the festivals, which comprised varying numbers of oxen, rams, lambs, and

יב כְּהוֹשַׁעְתָּ לְוִיֶּיךָ עַל־דּוּכָנָם לְהַרְבַּת.
לד-מא
אוֹמְרִים מִזְמוֹר שִׁיר לְיוֹם הַשַּׁבָּת. כֵּן הוֹשַׁעְנָא:

כְּהוֹשַׁעְתָּ נְחוּמֶיךָ בְּמִצְוֹתֶיךָ תָּמִיד יִשְׁתַּעְשְׁעוּן.
וּרְצֵם וְהַחֲלִיצֵם בְּשׁוּבָה וָנַחַת יִנָּשֵׁעוּן.
כֵּן הוֹשַׁעְנָא:

כְּהוֹשַׁעְתָּ שְׁבוּת שִׁבְטֵי יַעֲקֹב.
תָּשׁוּב וְתָשִׁיב שְׁבוּת אָהֳלֵי יַעֲקֹב. וְהוֹשִׁיעָה נָּא:

(כְּהוֹשַׁעְתָּ שׁוֹמְרֵי מִצְוֹת. וְחוֹכֵי יְשׁוּעוֹת.
אֵל לַמּוֹשָׁעוֹת. וְהוֹשִׁיעָה נָּא:)

אֲנִי וָהוּ הוֹשִׁיעָה נָּא:

הוֹשִׁיעָה אֶת־עַמֶּךָ, וּבָרֵךְ אֶת־נַחֲלָתֶךָ, וּרְעֵם וְנַשְּׂאֵם עַד־הָעוֹלָם: וְיִהְיוּ דְבָרַי אֵלֶּה אֲשֶׁר הִתְחַנַּנְתִּי לִפְנֵי יהוה, קְרוֹבִים אֶל־יהוה אֱלֹהֵינוּ יוֹמָם וָלָיְלָה, לַעֲשׂוֹת מִשְׁפַּט עַבְדּוֹ וּמִשְׁפַּט עַמּוֹ יִשְׂרָאֵל דְּבַר־יוֹם בְּיוֹמוֹ: לְמַעַן דַּעַת כָּל־עַמֵּי הָאָרֶץ, כִּי יהוה הוּא הָאֱלֹהִים, אֵין עוֹד:

The Ark is closed and the chazzan says Kaddish, p. 148

goats with their accompanying meal offerings (see chapters 28-29 of *Numbers*), the Sabbath offering consisted of two lambs accompanied by two *esronim* of flour. Hence this sacrifice is called 'doubled' *(Beis Yaakov).*

עוֹלָה וּמִנְחָה — *Burnt and meal offering.*
[Once again the *paytan* underscores the difference between the Sabbath and the festival. In addition to the burnt and meal offerings of the festival, a sin offering in the form of a he-goat was brought. On the Sabbath no such offering was brought.]

35-36. While the *Kohanim* were sacrificing the required daily offerings, a choir of *Levites* would mount a platform [דּוּכָן] standing in the Temple courtyard, and accompany the service with music and song. *Tamid* 7:4 lists the psalms which were designated for the respective days of the week. On the

12
35-41

³⁵ As You saved Your Levites who sang
upon their platform,
³⁶ Saying, 'A psalm, a song
for the Sabbath day' — so save now.
³⁷ As You saved those whom You comforted,
those who constantly find joy in Your mitzvos;
³⁸ So may You favor them and give them rest,
and tranquility, and contentedly may they
attain salvation — so save now.
³⁹ As You saved the captivity of the tribes of Jacob,
⁴⁰ return and restore the captivity of Jacob's tents
and bring salvation now.
(⁴¹ As You saved those observing mitzvos,
and hoping for salvation —
O God Who brings salvations bring salvation now.)

ANI VAHO, bring salvation now.

Save Your nation and bless Your heritage, tend them and elevate them forever. May these words of mine, which I have supplicated before HASHEM, be near to HASHEM, our God, by day and by night; that He bring about justice for His servant and justice for His people, Israel, each day's need in its day; that all the peoples of the earth shall know that HASHEM is God, there is no other.

The Ark is closed and the chazzan says Kaddish, p. 148

Sabbath they sang, מִזְמוֹר שִׁיר לְיוֹם הַשַּׁבָּת, A psalm, a song for the Sabbath day' (Psalms 92). The Mishnah interprets: A song ... to the time to come, to the day which will be completely a Sabbath and rest day for eternal life.

37. נִחוּמֶיךָ — Those whom You comforted.
It is I, it is I Who comforts you ... I am HASHEM, your God ... (Isaiah 51:12, 15).

38. וּרְצֵם וְהַחֲלִיצֵם — So may You favor them and give them rest.
This phrase is borrowed from the special paragraph added to בִּרְכַּת הַמָּזוֹן, Grace after Meals, on the Sabbath.

39-41. [These three stiches appear as sts. 21-23 of hoshana 10. See commentary there.]

הוֹשִׁיעָה אֶת־עַמֶּךָ — Save Your nation.
[These verses also follow hoshana 10. See commentary there.]

[105] Hoshanos / **As You Saved Adam**

∽§ תתננו

יג
א־יט

On Hoshana Rabbah continue here:

אֲנִי וָהוּ הוֹשִׁיעָה נָּא:

תִּתְּנֵנוּ לְשֵׁם וְלִתְהִלָּה. תְּשִׁיתֵנוּ אֶל־הַחֶבֶל וְאֶל־הַנַּחֲלָה. תְּרוֹמְמֵנוּ לְמַעְלָה לְמָעְלָה. תְּקַבְּצֵנוּ לְבֵית הַתְּפִלָּה. תַּצִּיבֵנוּ כְּעֵץ עַל־פַּלְגֵי־מַיִם שְׁתוּלָה. תִּפְדֵּנוּ מִכָּל־נֶגַע וּמַחֲלָה. תְּעַטְּרֵנוּ בְּאַהֲבָה כְלוּלָה. תְּשַׂמְּחֵנוּ בְּבֵית הַתְּפִלָּה. תְּנַחֲלֵנוּ עַל־מֵי מְנֻחוֹת סֶלָה. תְּמַלְּאֵנוּ חָכְמָה וְשִׂכְלָה. תַּלְבִּישֵׁנוּ עֹז וּגְדֻלָּה. תַּכְתִּירֵנוּ בְּכֶתֶר כְּלוּלָה. תְּיַשְּׁרֵנוּ בְּאְרַח סְלוּלָה. תַּטְעֵנוּ בִּישֶׁר מְסִלָּה. תְּחָנֵּנוּ בְּרַחֲמִים וּבְחֶמְלָה. תַּזְכִּירֵנוּ בְּמֵי זֹאת עוֹלָה. תּוֹשִׁיעֵנוּ לְקֵץ הַגְּאֻלָּה. תְּהַדְּרֵנוּ בְּזִיו הַמּוּלָה. תַּדְבִּיקֵנוּ

∽§ תִּתְּנֵנוּ — Establish Us

Although all the *hoshanos* (except *hoshana* 12) are attributed to R' Elazar HaKalir, only this *hoshana* bears his signature. Its acrostic contains the twenty-two letters of the *aleph-beis* in reverse order, followed by אֶלְעָזָר חֲזַק *Elazar Chazak* [lit. *Elazar, may he be strengthened.*]

In most liturgies תִּתְּנֵנוּ, *Establish us,* is the first in a series of additional *hoshanos* chanted on Hoshana Rabbah after the completion of the seven *hakafah*-circuits. *Avodas Yisrael,* however, has it as the *hoshana* for the seventh *hakafah*.

1. תִּתְּנֵנוּ לְשֵׁם וְלִתְהִלָּה — *Establish us for fame and renown.*

Fulfill Your words: *At that time I shall bring you in, and at that time I shall gather you; for* לְשֵׁם אֶתֵּן אֶתְכֶם וְלִתְהִלָּה, *I shall establish you for fame and renown among all the people of the earth, when I return your captivity before your very eyes; says HASHEM* (Zephaniah 3:20).

2. תְּשִׁיתֵנוּ — *Place us.*

Kol Bo and *Iyun Tefillah* read תְּשִׁיבֵנוּ, *return us.*

אֶל־הַחֶבֶל וְאֶל־הַנַּחֲלָה — *Upon our measured heritage* [lit. *our measuring rope and our heritage*].

Eretz Yisrael is thus described: *Then He drove away peoples* [the seven Canaanite nations *(Rashi)*] *before them* [the Israelites] *and apportioned them* בְּחֶבֶל נַחֲלָה, *a measured heritage* [lit. *a heritage with measure*] (Psalms 78:55).

3. לְמַעְלָה לְמָעְלָה — *Ever higher* [lit. *higher, higher*].

Raise us higher in the spiritual realm; raise us higher in the material realm (*Beis Avraham*).

4. בֵּית הַתְּפִלָּה — *House of Prayer.*

This title for the Holy Temple is found in *Isaiah* (56:7): *I shall bring them to My holy mountain, I shall cause the joy* בְּבֵית תְּפִלָּתִי, *in My House of Prayer...for My House shall be called* בֵּית תְּפִלָּה, *House of Prayer, for all peoples.*

Avodas Yisrael reads: תְּקוֹמְמֵנוּ לְכֶרֶם סְגֻלָּה, *establish us as a treasured vineyard. Isaiah* (5:7) calls the House of Israel כֶּרֶם ה׳, *HASHEM's vineyard*; God designated them [*Exodus* 19:5]: סְגֻלָּה

הושענות/תתננו [106]

⤳ Establish Us

13
1-18

On Hoshana Rabbah continue here:

ANI VAHO, bring salvation now.

¹ Establish us for fame and renown; ² place us upon our measured heritage; ³ raise us ever higher; ⁴ gather us to the House of Prayer; ⁵ stand us erect, like a tree embedded by streams of water; ⁶ redeem us from every plague and sickness; ⁷ envelop us with perfect love; ⁸ gladden us in the House of Prayer; ⁹ lead us beside tranquil waters, forever; ¹⁰ fill us with wisdom and sense; ¹¹ clothe us with strength and greatness; ¹² crown us with the perfect crown; ¹³ set us right on the level road; ¹⁴ plant us on the straight path; ¹⁵ grace us with mercy and pity; ¹⁶ remember us with 'How worthy is she!'; ¹⁷ save us for the final End of Redemption; ¹⁸ beautify

מִכָּל־הָעַמִּים, *most beloved of all the nations (Iyun Tefillah).*

5. פַּלְגֵי־מָיִם — *Streams of water.*
The root פלג means *to divide*. A flowing stream often separates into many branches (*Beis Yaakov*).

שְׁתוּלָה — *Embedded.*
The righteous man is *like a tree embedded* [שָׁתוּל] *by streams of water* (*Psalms* 1:3). The verse does not read נָטוּעַ, *planted*, but שָׁתוּל, *embedded*. Were all the winds to blow at it, they would be unable to budge it from its place (*Midrash Tehillim* 1:11).

7. אַהֲבָה כְּלוּלָה — *Perfect love.*
The translation follows *Iyun Tefillah* and the English edition of *Tehillos Hashem*. *Beis Avraham* renders *an all-encompassing love*, i.e., a love for each and every Jew.

8. [See commentary to st. 4.]

9. ...תְּנַהֲלֵנוּ — *Lead us...*
[This stich is based on *Psalms* 23:2. See commentary to *hoshana* 12, st. 6.]

סֶלָה — *Forever.*
One of the most obscure words in Scripture, סֶלָה, *Selah*, appears only in *Psalms* and *Habbakuk*. The word is variously translated *forever* (*Targum*; *Metzudos*), or *amen* (*Ibn Ezra*). A third possibility, given by both *Ibn Ezra* and *Radak* to *Psalms* 3:3, is that *Selah* is a musical instruction to the choir to raise its voices. This last interpretation obviously was not intended by the *paytan* here.

10. חָכְמָה וְשֵׂכֶל — *Wisdom and sense.*
...Torah *wisdom* and common *sense* (*Beis Avraham*).

12. כֶּתֶר כְּלוּלָה — *Perfect crown.*
I.e., perfectly beautiful crown (*Iyun Tefillah*).
Two alternative readings of the stich are: בְּכֶתֶר הַמְעוּלָה, *with the distinguished crown* (*Tehillas Hashem*); and כְּחָתָן וְכַלָּה, *like a groom and bride* (*Avodas Yisrael*).

16. מִי זֹאת עֹלָה — *How worthy is she!* [lit. *Who is this who rises?*].
The translation follows *Rashi* to *Song of Songs* 8:5 where these words are spoken by God and His Heavenly Tribunal with reference to the still exiled Community of Israel (*ArtScroll Song of Songs*, p. 193).

17. קֵץ — [*Final*] *End.*
Daniel (11:40) refers to the final

יג כְּאֵזוֹר חֲתוּלָה. תְּגַדְּלֵנוּ בְּיָד הַגְּדוֹלָה. תְּבִיאֵנוּ לְבֵיתְךָ
כב-כח בְּרִנָּה וְצָהֳלָה. תְּאַמְּצֵנוּ בְּרֶוַח וְהַצָּלָה. תְּאַדְּרֵנוּ בְּאֶבֶן
תְּלוּלָה. תְּלַבְּבֵנוּ בְּבִנְיַן עִירְךָ כְּבַתְּחִלָּה. תְּעוֹרְרֵנוּ לְצִיּוֹן
בִּשְׂכְלוּלָה. תִּזָּכְנוּ בִּנְבוּנְתָהּ הָעִיר עַל תִּלָּהּ. תַּרְבִּיצֵנוּ
בְּשָׂשׂוֹן וְגִילָה. תְּחַזְּקֵנוּ אֱלֹהֵי יַעֲקֹב סֶלָה:

◈§ אנא אזון

יד אָנָּא הוֹשִׁיעָה נָּא:
א-ו

אָנָּא אֱזוֹן חִין תָּאֲבֵי יִשְׁעָךְ.
בְּעַרְבֵי נַחַל לְשַׁעְשְׁעָךְ.   וְהוֹשִׁיעָה נָּא:

אָנָּא גְּאַל כַּנַּת נִטְעָךְ.
דּוּמָה בְּטַאטְאָךְ.   וְהוֹשִׁיעָה נָּא:

אָנָּא הַבֶּט לִבְרִית טִבְעָךְ.
וּמַחֲשַׁכֵּי־אֶרֶץ בְּהַטְבִּיעָךְ.   וְהוֹשִׁיעָה נָּא:

redemption as עֵת קֵץ, *the time of the End*, and (12:13) קֵץ הַיָּמִין, *the End of Days*.

Avodas Yisrael reads תּוֹשִׁיעֵנוּ בְּיָדְךָ הַגְּדוֹלָה, *Save us with Your great hand*.

18. הַמּוּלָה — *Angels* [lit. *words*].

The sound of the angelic choir, standing before the Heavenly Throne and singing praises of God is described by Ezekiel (1:24): *The sound of* הַמֻּלָּה, *the words, was like the sound of an encampment*. The *paytan* extends to the angels themselves the term הַמֻּלָּה, *words*, which the prophet used in reference to them (*Iyun Tefillah*).

20. Avodas Yisrael reads תַּגִּיעֵנוּ לְקֵץ הַגְּאֻלָּה, *Let us attain the End — the Redemption* (see commentary to st. 17).

23. אֶבֶן תְּלוּלָה — *The elevated stone*.

אֶבֶן, *stone*, refers to the Temple which contained the אֶבֶן שְׁתִיָּה, *foundation stone*, mentioned in *hoshana* 2, st. 1. תְּלוּלָה, an intensified form of תֵּל, *hill*, means a lofty mountain (see Ezekiel 17:22). Thus אֶבֶן תְּלוּלָה is *the Temple which stood on a lofty mount* (based on *Beis Avraham*)

An alternative text for sts. 22-23 has תְּאַדְּרֵנוּ בְּיֶשַׁע וְגִילָה, *Adorn us with salvation and gladness*, followed by תְּאַמְּצֵנוּ בְּרֶוַח וְהַצָּלָה, *Strengthen us with relief and rescue* (*Beis Yaakov*; *Avodas Yisrael*; *Iyun Tefillah*).

25. Avodas Yisrael reads: תַּעֲלֵנוּ עַל כָּל־אֹם לִתְהִלָּה, *elevate us over every nation for renown*.

26. הָעִיר עַל תִּלָּהּ — *The City on its hill*.

This reference to rebuilt Jerusalem is paraphrased from *Jeremiah* 30:18. *Metzudos* explains that תִּלָּהּ, *its hill*, refers both to its physical elevation and to its lofty spiritual position.

Avodas Yisrael reads: תַּזְכִּירֵנוּ בְּשָׂשׂוֹן וְגִילָה, *remember us with joy and gladness*.

27. Based on Ezekiel 34:14, *Avodas Yisrael* and *Iyun Tefillah* read: תַּרְבִּיצֵנוּ

13
19-28
us with the radiance of angels; ¹⁹ cause us to cleave to You like a tightly wrapped sash; ²⁰ make us great with Your great hand; ²¹ bring us to Your Temple with joyous song and cheer; ²² strengthen us with relief and rescue; ²³ adorn us with the elevated stone; ²⁴ hearten us with the rebuilding of Your city as of old; ²⁵ awaken us to Zion in its completeness; ²⁶ let us merit the rebuilding of the City on its hill; ²⁷ let us recline with joy and gladness; ²⁸ strengthen us, O God of Jacob, Selah.

◈§ Please Hearken

14
1-6

Please bring salvation now.

¹ Please hearken to the plea of those who long for
   Your salvation;
   ² with willows of the stream they bring You joy —
                                          and bring salvation now.

³ Please redeem the garden of Your planting,
   ⁴ as You sweep away Dumah —and bring salvation now.

⁵ Please gaze upon the covenant of Your signet ring,
   ⁶ even as You sink the ones who darken the earth —
                                          and bring salvation now.

בְּמִרְעֶה שָׁמֵן לְהַצִּילָה, *let us recline in rich pastures for deliverance.*

28. For translation of סֶלָה, *Selah*, see comm. to st. 9.

◈§ אָנָּא אֱזוֹן — Please Hearken

2. עַרְבֵי נָחַל — *Willows of the stream.*
Scripture describes one of the Four Species as עַרְבֵי נָחַל, *willows of the stream* (Leviticus 23:40). The Talmud offers two explanations of this term: 1) Willows which grow by the side of a stream; and 2) willows whose leaves are elongated like a stream. Although willows growing in the fields or on mountaintops are also acceptable for the fulfillment of this *mitzvah* (*Succah* 33b), it is preferable to use willows which grew alongside a stream (Rashi).

3. בְּנַת נִטְעָךְ — *The garden of Your planting.*
Psalms 80:16 refers to Israel as וְכַנָּה אֲשֶׁר־נָטְעָה יְמִינֶךָ, *the garden* (see *Radak*) *which Your right hand planted* (Rashi).

4. דּוּמָה — *Dumah.*
Isaiah 21:11 prophesies the doom of דּוּמָה, *Dumah*, a name which *Rashi* understands to be synonymous with אֱדוֹם, *Edom*. *Ibn Ezra* and *Radak* trace *Dumah* to the descendants of Ishmael (see Genesis 25:14).

5-6. הַבֵּט לַבְּרִית... — *Gaze upon the covenant...*
Paraphrased from Psalms 74:20, these stiches allude to the covenant of circumcision which is likened to the embossed image caused by a signet ring because it is indelibly inscribed, so to speak, in the flesh of each male Jew. He is thus 'stamped' with the King's signet ring.

טַבְעָךְ — *Your signet ring.*

יד	אָנָּא	זְכָר־לָנוּ אָב יְדָעָךְ.
ז־כ		חַסְדְּךָ לָמוֹ בְּהוֹדִיעָךְ. וְהוֹשִׁיעָה נָּא:
	אָנָּא	טְהוֹרֵי לֵב בְּהַפְלִיאָךְ.
		יֻוָּדַע כִּי הוּא פִלְאָךְ. וְהוֹשִׁיעָה נָּא:
	אָנָּא	כַּבִּיר כֹּחַ תֶּן־לָנוּ יִשְׁעָךְ.
		לַאֲבוֹתֵינוּ כְּהִשָּׁבְעָךְ. וְהוֹשִׁיעָה נָּא:
	אָנָּא	מַלֵּא מִשְׁאֲלוֹת עַם מְשַׁוְּעָךְ.
		נֶעֱקַד בְּהַר מוֹר כְּמוֹ שׁוְּעָךְ. וְהוֹשִׁיעָה נָּא:
	אָנָּא	סַגֵּב אֶשְׁלֵי נִטְעָךְ.
		עָרִיצִים בַּהֲנִיעָךְ. וְהוֹשִׁיעָה נָּא:
	אָנָּא	פְּתַח־לָנוּ אוֹצְרוֹת רִבְעָךְ.
		צִיָּה מֵהֶם בְּהַרְבִּיעָךְ. וְהוֹשִׁיעָה נָּא:
	אָנָּא	קוֹרְאֶיךָ אֶרֶץ בְּרוֹעֲךָ.
		רְעֵם בְּטוּב מִרְעָךְ. וְהוֹשִׁיעָה נָּא:

This word is cognate with טַבַּעַת, *ring* (Rashi). *Beis Yaakov* derives this word from מַטְבֵּעַ, *a coin*, into which a picture is engraved.

מַחֲשַׁכֵּי־אָרֶץ — *The ones who darken the earth*.

In *Psalms* 74:20 the commentators all translate *the dark 'places' of earth*. Here, however, Rashi renders *the idolators who darken the earth* with their sinfulness, and who will one day sink into *Gehinnom*.

Alternatively, stiches 5 and 6 refer to the following Midrash (*Aggados Bereishis* 17):

Gaze upon the covenant — although Israel's deeds may prove unworthy, He, nevertheless, redeems them in the merit of the covenant of circumcision. When the Israelites crossed the Sea of Reeds the guardian angel of the sea wanted to drown them. He argued, 'Until now both the Egyptians and the Israelites worshiped idols, why should these be saved and the others drowned? I shall destroy all the idolators.' But when the waters reached their hips, their robes began floating up, revealing to the sea that they were circumcised. Upon seeing this the angel fled.

Accordingly, מַחֲשַׁכֵּי־אָרֶץ, *the ones who darken the earth*, refers to the Egyptians who *were* drowned by the sea (*Tefillah Yesharah*).

7. אָב יְדָעָךְ — *The Patriarch who perceived You.*

Abraham recognized his Creator at the age of three (*Nedarim* 32).

8. חַסְדְּךָ — *Your loving-kindness.*

Loving-kindness is the attribute of Abraham (see commentary at end of *hoshana* 1). He spread the name of God by opening his home to wayfarers. They would bless him for his hospitality, to which he would respond, 'Have you eaten *my* food? I have fed you food belonging to the God of the universe. Thank, praise, and bless Him Who

14
7-20

⁷ *Please recall on our behalf the Patriarch who perceived You;* ⁸ *may Your loving-kindness be upon them, for he made You known —*   *and bring salvation now.*

⁹ *Please, when You set aside the pure of heart* ¹⁰ *it will be known that this is Your wonder —*
    and bring salvation now.

¹¹ *Please, Almighty One, grant us Your salvation,* ¹² *as You swore to our fathers —*
    and bring salvation now.

¹³ *Please fulfill the requests of Your entreating nation* ¹⁴ *as the bound one on the myrhh mountain entreated You —*   *and bring salvation now.*

¹⁵ *Please strengthen the tamarisks of Your planting* ¹⁶ *as You cause the idolators to wander —*
    and bring salvation now.

¹⁷ *Please open the treasure troves of Your rains for us* ¹⁸ *as You water the parched earth from them —*
    and bring salvation now.

¹⁹ *Please — those who call to You, when You bring the earth destruction,* ²⁰ *shepherd them in Your goodly pastures —*
    and bring salvation now.

---

spoke and the world came into being' (*Sotah* 10b).

14. ... נֶעֱקַד — *The bound one.*
When Isaac was bound as an offering (*Genesis* 22:1-19) he prayed that whenever his descendants would entreat God to save them in the merit of Isaac's willingness to sacrifice his life to God, God should hearken to their prayers (*Rashi*).

הַר מוֹר — *Myrrh mountain.*
Song of Songs 4:6 describes Mount Moriah [where Abraham bound Isaac, and where the Holy Temple stood] as: *mountain of myrrh, hill of frankincense. Targum* explains that the daily incense offering in the Holy Temple contained myrrh and frankincense. [The word מוֹרִיָּה, *Moriah*, may then be translated *God's myrrh*. See comm. to *hoshana* 2, st. 5.]

15. אֲשָׁלֵי — *Tamarisks.*
[For Israel as the planting of God see commentary to st. 3.]

17. [This stich is based on *Deuteronomy* 28:12. See commentary, end of יְהִי רָצוֹן, *May it be favorable*, p. 153.]

רְבִיעֲךָ — *Your rains.*
Cognate with רוֹבֵעַ, *impregnator*, רְבִיעַ means *rain*. Rain "impregnates" the earth enabling it to bear fruit. For this reason a field for which the rains are sufficient irrigation is called בֵּית הַבַּעַל, literally, *husband's house* (*Tefillah Yesharah*).

19. בְּרוֹעֲצָךְ — *When You bring...destruction.*
The translation follows *Rashi* and is

יד אָנָא שְׁעָרֶיךָ תַּעַל מִמְשׁוֹאָךְ.
כא-כב תֵּל תַּלְפִּיּוֹת בְּהַשִּׁיאָךְ.   וְהוֹשִׁיעָה נָּא:

﬩§ תעינו

טו אָנָא אֵל נָא הוֹשַׁעְנָא וְהוֹשִׁיעָה נָּא:
א-ח

אֵל נָא תָּעִינוּ כְּשֶׂה אֹבֵד.
שְׁמֵנוּ מִסִּפְרְךָ אַל תְּאַבֵּד.   הוֹשַׁעְנָא וְהוֹשִׁיעָה נָּא:

אֵל נָא רְעֵה אֶת־צֹאן הַהֲרֵגָה.
קְצוּפָה וְעָלֶיךָ הֲרוּגָה.   הוֹשַׁעְנָא וְהוֹשִׁיעָה נָּא:

אֵל נָא צֹאנְךָ וְצֹאן מַרְעִיתֶךָ.
פְּעֻלָּתְךָ וְרֵעִיתֶךָ.   הוֹשַׁעְנָא וְהוֹשִׁיעָה נָּא:

אֵל נָא עֲנִיֵּי הַצֹּאן.
שִׂיחָם עֲנֵה בְּעֵת רָצוֹן.   הוֹשַׁעְנָא וְהוֹשִׁיעָה נָּא:

based on *Isaiah* 24:19. *Avodas Yisrael* derives the word from רֵעָה, *friend*, and renders *when You befriend them.*

20. רְעֵם בְּטוּב מִרְעֶךָ — *Shepherd them in Your goodly pastures.*

Fulfill the words of Your prophet: בְּמִרְעֶה־טוֹב אֶרְעֶה אֹתָם, *Upon good pasture I will shepherd them* (*Ezekiel* 34:14).

21. שְׁעָרֶיךָ תַּעַל — *Raise Your gates.*

According to *Midrash Eichah* (2:9), the gates of the Holy Temple were not destroyed by the enemy along with the rest of the Temple. They miraculously sank into the ground. This was in reward to the gates for having honored the Ark by rising to allow it to enter (see *Shabbos* 30a).

22. תֵּל תַּלְפִּיּוֹת — *Hill of Talpios.*

[For various interpretations of this obscure reference to the Temple see commentary to *hoshana* 2, st. 22.]

﬩§ תָּעִינוּ — We Have Strayed

1-2. תָּעִינוּ... — *We have strayed...*

Because *we have strayed* from the paths of Your Torah, we feel *like lost sheep* who cannot find their way back to the flock without the shepherd's help. Therefore, do not punish us by excising our name from Your Book. Instead, *save us*, guide us along the road to repentance (*Rashi* to *Psalms* 119:176).

מִסִּפְרְךָ — *From Your Book.*

After the sin of the Golden Calf Moses pleaded: *If You forgive their sin* [then all is well]; *if not, please erase me from the Book which You have written.* God responded: [Only] *he who has sinned before Me shall I erase from My Book* (*Exodus* 32:32-33).

Ramban explains *Book* as a reference to the Book of Life (see comm. to בְּסֵפֶר חַיִּים טוֹבִים, *In the Book of Good Life*, p. 150).

[Thus, we pray that despite our lapses, may we nevertheless, be inscribed and sealed in the Book of Life.]

14
21-22
²¹ *Please raise Your gates in the wake of Your desolation*
²² *when You exalt the Hill of Talpios —*
and bring salvation now.

⋙ We have Strayed

15
1-8
Please God, please! Save now and bring salvation now.

¹ *Please God! We have strayed like lost sheep;*
² *do not cause our name to be lost from Your Book —*
save now and bring salvation now.

³ *Please God! Graze the sheep of the slaughter,*
⁴ *who are the victims of wrath and are killed for Your sake —*
save now and bring salvation now.

⁵ *Please God! Your sheep and the sheep of Your pasture,*
⁶ *Your accomplishment and Your beloved —*
save now and bring salvation now.

⁷ *Please God! The poorest of the sheep,*
⁸ *answer their prayers at an opportune time —*
save now and bring salvation now.

---

3. רְעֵה אֶת־צֹאן הַהֲרֵגָה — *Graze the sheep of the slaughter.*

Thus says HASHEM, my God: וְאֶרְעֶה אֶת צֹאן הַהֲרֵגָה..., *and I shall graze the sheep of the slaughter, they are truly* עֲנִיֵּי הַצֹּאן, *the poorest of the sheep ...* (Zechariah 11:7). Sheep which are barren or whose wool does not grow well will not be kept by the rancher. Their only value is for slaughter (*Metzudos*). Similarly, when the Jews who are God's flock [see stich 5] do not fulfill His *mitzvos*, they are considered worthless and are given over to be slaughtered at the hands of their enemies (*Kol Bo*). [See also commentary to *hoshana* 3, sts. 5-6.]

5. צֹאנְךָ וְצֹאן מַרְעִיתֶךָ — *Your sheep and the sheep of Your pasture.*

Based on *Ezekiel* 34:31, where God describes Israel as צֹאנִי צֹאן מַרְעִיתִי, *My sheep, the sheep of My pasture.*

Avodas Yisrael omits the conjunctive וְ, *and*, accordingly the interpretation would be *Your sheep [who are] the sheep...*

Iyun Tefillah defends the use of 'and.' He explains that *Your sheep* refers to Jews who do not follow God's will; they are 'His flock,' but they are not the sheep of His *pasture*, because He does not exercise personal supervision over them, as it were. *The sheep of Your pasture*, however, are those who fulfill the Divine will. They are tended by God Himself. [See also *Psalms* 79:13.]

7. עֲנִיֵּי הַצֹּאן — *The poorest of the sheep.*

[See commentary to st. 3.]

8. בְּעֵת רָצוֹן — *At an opportune time.*

When is *an opportune time*? Whenever the congregation prays together (*Berachos* 8a).

טו אֵל נָא **נוֹשְׂאֵי** לְךָ עַיִן.
מִתְקוֹמְמֵיהֶם יִהְיוּ כְאַיִן. הוֹשַׁעְנָא וְהוֹשִׁיעָה נָּא:

אֵל נָא לִמְנַסְּכֵי לְךָ מַיִם.
בְּמַעְיְנֵי הַיְשׁוּעָה יִשְׁאֲבוּן מָיִם.
הוֹשַׁעְנָא וְהוֹשִׁיעָה נָּא:

אֵל נָא **יַעֲלוּ** לְצִיּוֹן מוֹשִׁיעִים.
טְפוּלִים בְּךָ וּבְשִׁמְךָ נוֹשָׁעִים.
הוֹשַׁעְנָא וְהוֹשִׁיעָה נָּא:

אֵל נָא **חֲמוּץ** בְּגָדִים.
זְעוֹם לְנַעֵר כָּל־בּוֹגְדִים. הוֹשַׁעְנָא וְהוֹשִׁיעָה נָּא:

אֵל נָא **וְזָכוֹר** תִּזְכּוֹר.
הַבִּכּוּרֵי בִלְתְּךָ נָכוֹר. הוֹשַׁעְנָא וְהוֹשִׁיעָה נָּא:

אֵל נָא **דּוֹרְשֶׁיךָ** בְּעַנְפֵי עֲרָבוֹת.
גַּעְיָם שְׁעֵה מֵעֲרָבוֹת. הוֹשַׁעְנָא וְהוֹשִׁיעָה נָּא:

10. מִתְקוֹמְמֵיהֶם — *Those who rise against them.*

This is a prayer for the annihilation of Israel's enemies *(Rashi)*.

Some liturgies read מִתְקוֹמְמֶיךָ, *those who rise against You* [God] *(Avodas Yisrael, Kol Bo)*. [In either case, the enemy is one and the same, for the enemies of Israel are the enemies of God.]

11. לִמְנַסְּכֵי לְךָ מַיִם — *Those who pour water before You.*

On each day of Succos, a water libation would be offered on the altar in addition to the wine libation which accompanied the burnt offerings. [See *Succah* 48a ff. for a complete description of the libations and the festivities at the drawing of the water. See also commentary to *hoshana* 12, st. 31.]

12. בְּמַעְיְנֵי — *(As) from the springs.*

The prefix בְּ, *as*, is used here in an obscure manner. *Beis Yaakov* explains that this stich is a prayer for abundant water — may Israel joyously draw water as if from an inexhaustible spring, like one who joyously draws God's salvation from the endless springs of salvation.

13. מוֹשִׁיעִים — *Saviors.*

This stich is based upon *Obadiah 1:21*: *And saviors shall go up upon Mount Zion to punish Mount Esau, then, unto HASHEM shall be the kingdom.*

Saviors is variously explained as the princes of Israel *(Rashi)*, the judges of Israel *(Ibn Ezra)*, or the Messiah together with the seven shepherds and eight officers [see *Micah 5:4*; and comm. to *hoshana 18*, st.9] who will accompany him *(Radak)*.

15. חֲמוּץ בְּגָדִים — *With bloodied clothes.*

This stich is based on *Isaiah 63:1*, as interpreted by the Sages. When the proper time comes, God will avenge Himself against Edom for its outrages against Israel. In the manner common to prophecy, God is metaphorically portrayed as a warrior who becomes

15
9-20

⁹ *Please God! Those who raise their eyes to You,*
¹⁰ *may those who rise against them be as naught —*
   save now and bring salvation now.

¹¹ *Please God! Those who pour water before You,*
¹² *from the springs of salvation*
   may they draw water —
      save now and bring salvation now.

¹³ *Please God! May saviors arise from Zion;*
¹⁴ *those who cling to You and are saved in Your Name —*
      save now and bring salvation now.

¹⁵ *Please God! With bloodied clothes,*
¹⁶ *be enraged to shake out all the rebels —*
      save now and bring salvation now.

¹⁷ *Please God! Remember may You remember,*
¹⁸ *those purchased for a lesech and a kor —*
      save now and bring salvation now.

¹⁹ *Please God! Those who seek You with aravos branches,*
²⁰ *to their cries turn, from Aravos —*
      save now and bring salvation now.

---

soiled by the blood of his slain foe. The Sages teach that no nation can be defeated on earth until its heavenly guardian angel is stripped of his power above. When the End of Days comes, therefore, God will destroy the angel of Edom, which is also the angel of evil, and His clothing will become bloodied, as it were. (See *Rashi* to *Isaiah* 63:1 and *Makkos* 12a; ArtScroll *Zemiroth*, p. 178 ff).

17. וְזָכוֹר תִּזְכּוֹר — *Remember may You remember.*

The double expression of this stich is based upon *Leviticus* 26:42, *And I shall remember My covenant with Jacob, also My covenant with Isaac, also My covenant with Abraham* אֶזְכּוֹר, *I shall remember,* וְהָאָרֶץ אֶזְכּוֹר, *and the land I shall remember.* Thus the stich is a prayer that God remember — i.e., redeem — both Israel and its land (*Rashi*).

18. הַגְּבוּרֵי בְלֶתֶךְ וָכוֹר — *Those purchased for a lesech and a kor.*

I have bought her [=Israel] for Myself בַּחֲמִשָּׁה עָשָׂר כָּסֶף, *for fifteen pieces of silver, a chomer of barley and a lesech of barley* (*Hosea* 3:2). Of what significance are these figures of speech?

Rashi interprets: The *gematria* [numerical value] of כֶּסֶף, *silver,* is 160, the same as the *gematria* of נִסָן, *Nissan*. *Fifteen pieces of silver* is an allusion to the fifteenth day of Nissan, the day of the Exodus from Egypt.

The *chomer* (or *kor* which is equal to it) contains thirty *s'ah*, and the *lesech* has half that volume, fifteen *s'ah*. Together these two measures hold forty-five *s'ah*. *Chomer* and *lesech* then, are an allusion to the forty-five days which began on the fifteenth of Nissan until the nation reached Sinai. There Israel made the final preparations to receive the Torah and become the "possession" of God (*Rashi* to *Hosea* 3:2).

19. עֲרָבוֹת — *Aravos* [lit. *willows*].

We have left the word untranslated

טו אֵל נָא בָּרֵךְ בְּעִטּוּר שָׁנָה.
כא-כב אֲמָרַי רְצֵה בְּפִלּוּלִי בְּיוֹם הוֹשַׁעְנָא.
הוֹשַׁעְנָא וְהוֹשִׁיעָה נָּא:

~§ למען תמים

טז אָנָּא אֵל נָא. הוֹשַׁעְנָא. וְהוֹשִׁיעָה נָּא.
א-ב אָבִינוּ אָתָּה:

לְמַעַן תָּמִים בְּדוֹרוֹתָיו. הַנִּמְלָט בְּרוֹב צִדְקוֹתָיו.
מֻצָּל מְשֻׁטָּף בְּבֹא מַבּוּל מַיִם.
לְאוֹם אֲנִי חוֹמָה. הוֹשַׁעְנָא וְהוֹשִׁיעָה נָּא אָבִינוּ אָתָּה:
לְמַעַן שָׁלֵם בְּכָל־מַעֲשִׂים. הַמְנֻסֶּה בַּעֲשָׂרָה נִסִּים.

because the *paytan* intends it as a play on words with the next stich.

20. מֵעֲרָבוֹת — *From Aravos*.
The Talmud (*Chagigah* 12b) describes the loftiest of the seven celestial heavens as עֲרָבוֹת, *Aravos*, where God stores righteousness, justice, and charity. There rest the treasuries of life, peace, and blessing. The highest of the heavenly spheres also holds the souls of the *tzaddikim*, the souls which have not yet come to life, and the dew with which God will resuscitate the dead.
God called it עֲרָבוֹת because the righteous deeds of the *tzaddikim* were עֲרֵבִים, *sweet and desirable*, to Him. He planted their accomplishments in this heaven, where they 'bear fruit' in the sense that they provide the universe with spiritual enrichment (*Midrash Shocher Tov*, 114; see ArtScroll *Tehillim* 68:5).

21. בָּרֵךְ בְּעִטּוּר שָׁנָה — *With a crown bless this year.*
Adorn, this year with every type of blessing (*Rashi*).

22. *Avodas Yisrael* reads: אֲמָרַי בְּפִלּוּלִי שְׁעֵה נָּא, *Please turn to my words as I pray.*

~§ לְמַעַן תָּמִים — **In the Merit of Him who was Perfect.**

In a style reminiscent of *hoshana* 7, the *paytan* recounts the righteousness and love for God which was the hallmark of the righteous people of old. Since that *hoshana* was a prayer for an end to Israel's suffering in exile, it mentioned an incident involving fire in the life of each patriarch. This *hoshana* is a prayer for rain, so the biographical events are related to water.
A double acrostic is used by the *paytan*. Each stich is divided into four parts. The first word of each stich is לְמַעַן, *In the merit of*, followed by an allusion to the righteousness of one of Israel's progenitors. These allusions are contained in the first two parts of each stich and form an alphabetical acrostic going from *tav* to *aleph*. The third section of each stich is reference to a water-related incident.
With the exception of stichs 6 and 13 [see commentary] the final lines of the stichs are an acrostic — beginning with *aleph* — listing praises of Israel, the nation, or of *Eretz Yisrael*. Each stich con-

15
21-22

²¹ *Please God! With a crown bless this year.*

²² *May You find my words favorable as I pray on this day of Hoshana —*

save now and bring salvation now.

◆§ In the Merit of Him Who Was Perfect

16
1-2

Please God, please! Save now and bring salvation now, for You are our Father.

¹ *In the merit of him who was perfect in his generations,*
he escaped by his abundant righteousness,
And was rescued from inundation
upon the arrival of the Flood of water —
For the sake of the nation that declares, 'I am a wall,'
may You save now and bring salvation now,
for You are our Father.

² *In the merit of him who was perfect in all deeds,*
who was proven through ten trials,

cludes with the refrain *may You save now and bring salvation now for You are our Father* (based on *Beis Yaakov*).

The commentary to this *hoshana* will be limited to pointing out the Scriptural allusions and relating the particular praise of Israel to the appropriate person.

1. תָּמִים בְּדוֹרוֹתָיו — *Him who was perfect in his generations.*

Scripture *(Genesis 6:9)* describes Noah this way. For the story of the Flood see *Genesis 6:9-9:17.*

אוֹם אֲנִי חוֹמָה — *The nation that declares, 'I am a wall.'*

[This reference from *Song of Songs* to Israel's steadfast faith in God is explained in commentary to *hoshana* 3, st. 1.]

Israel declares its faith in God to be as sturdy as a wall. The term 'wall' is also used in Scripture's descripton of the waters of the Sea after they were split. They stood up strong and straight:

וְהַמַּיִם לָהֶם חוֹמָה, *the waters were a wall for them (Exodus 14:22, 29).* Thus, in coupling Israel with the merit of Noah, the *paytan* alludes to the protection given both of them from destructive waters *(Rashi).*

2. שָׁלֵם — *Perfect.*

[God told Abraham, *'Walk before me and be perfect' (Genesis 17:1).* Although the Scriptural verse uses the adjective תָּמִים, the *paytan* here uses the term שָׁלֵם (beginning with a *shin*) for the sake of the acrostic. The words are synonyms meaning *perfect.*]

בַּעֲשָׂרָה נִסִּים — *Through ten trials.*

God tested Abraham with ten trials of faith, all of which he withstood. The commentators differ on the precise identity of the 'ten trials', for more than ten incidents in Abraham's life could be so designated.

According to *Avos d'Rabbi Nosson* 33 he was tested (all verses are in *Genesis*):

טז
ג-ד
כַּאֲשֶׁר מַלְאָכִים נָם יֻקַּח־נָא מְעַט־מָיִם.
לְבָרָה כַּחַמָּה. הוֹשַׁעְנָא וְהוֹשִׁיעָה נָּא אָבִינוּ אָתָּה:
לְמַעַן רַךְ וְיָחִיד נֶחֱנַט פְּרִי לְמֵאָה. זָעַק אַיֵּה הַשֶּׂה
לְעוֹלָה. בְּשׂרוּהוּ עֲבָדָיו מָצָאנוּ מָיִם.
לְגוֹלָה וְסוּרָה. הוֹשַׁעְנָא וְהוֹשִׁיעָה נָּא אָבִינוּ אָתָּה:
לְמַעַן קָדַם שְׂאֵת בְּרָכָה. הַנִּשְׁטָם וּלְשִׁמְךָ חִכָּה.
מִיַּחֵם בְּמַקְלוֹת בְּשִׁקְתוֹת הַמָּיִם.
לְדָמְתָה לְתָמָר. הוֹשַׁעְנָא וְהוֹשִׁיעָה נָּא אָבִינוּ אָתָּה:

□ *Twice* when he had to move [once in 12:1, and again in 12:10 when, after God's glowing promise of a good life in Canaan, Abraham was forced to go to Egypt in the face of a famine.]

□ *Twice* in connection with his two sons [the difficult decision to heed Sarah's insistence that he drive away Ishmael (21:10); and second, in the supreme test of binding his beloved son Isaac to the altar in preparation to sacrifice him (22:1-2)];

□ *Twice* with his two wives [when Sarah was taken from him to Pharaoh's palace (12:15); and when he was required to drive Hagar from his home (21:10). An alternate interpretation includes the banishment of Hagar with that of Ishmael as a single test. In its place among the list of the trials is the abduction of Sarah to the palace of Abimelech (20:2)];

□ *Once* on the occasion of his war with the kings (14:14);

□ *Once* at the Covenant between the Parts [(15:7ff) when he was told that his descendants would be enslaved and exiled for four hundred years];

□ *Once* in Ur Kasdim [where he was thrown into a fiery furnace by Nimrod; and

□ *Once* at the covenant of Circumcision (17:9) [which was an unprecedented act and, at his advanced age, a dangerous operation].

[For a complete discussion on the concept and purpose of trials in the life of the righteous see ArtScroll *Genesis*, Overview, pp. 385-388, and commentary, pp. 782-784).

מַלְאָכִים — *Angels.*
Abraham's encounter with the angels is recorded in *Genesis* 18:1-15.

בָּרָה כַּחַמָּה — *Brilliant as the sun.*
[This reference to Israel in its own land, free from foreign domination, is discussed in the commentary to *hoshana* 3, st. 2.]

Scripture describes Abraham's performance of *mitzvos* as taking place in broad daylight. Circumcision was done בְּעֶצֶם הַיּוֹם, *in the strength of the day* [i.e., at midday when the sun is at its strongest (Ibn Janach)] (*Genesis* 17:23); his search for wayfarers to whom he may offer hospitality was כְּחֹם הַיּוֹם, *in the heat of the day* (*Genesis* 18:1). For this reason his offspring are referred to in this stich as *brilliant as the sun* (Rashi).

3. רַךְ וְיָחִיד — *Tender and only.*
Isaac was *tender* in the sense that he was Abraham's younger son. When God told Abraham to sacrifice his son, He described Isaac as בִּנְךָ...יְחִידְךָ, *your son, your only one* (*Genesis* 22:2; Rashi).

Alternatively, Isaac was יָחִיד, *the only son,* of Sarah who had no other children; but Abraham had other children (*Beis Avraham*).

נֶחֱנַט פְּרִי לְמֵאָה — [The] *fruit which blossomed at one hundred.*
Abraham was one hundred years old

16
3-4

Upon seeing the angels he said,
 'Let them be brought some water—
For the sake of the people brilliant as the sun,
  may You save now and bring salvation now,
   for You are our Father.

³ In the merit of the tender and only fruit
 which blossomed at one hundred,
  who cried, 'Where is the lamb for the offering?'
His servants informed him,
 'We have found water' —
For the sake of the exiled and displaced
  may You save now and bring salvation now,
   for You are our Father.

⁴ In the merit of the one who was first
 with gift for the blessing,
Who was hated but who yearned for Your Name,
 he stimulated with rods at the troughs of water—
For the sake of those likened to a palm tree
  may You save now, and bring salvation now,
   for You are our Father.

---

at Isaac's birth *(Genesis 21:5). Avodas Yisrael* omits the word פְּרִי, *fruit*.

אַיֵה הַשֶּׂה — *Where is the lamb?*
[Upon realizing that he was to be offered as a sacrifice, Isaac asked his question. See *Genesis* 22:1-19.]

מָצָאנוּ מָיִם — *We have found water.*
[*Genesis* 26:12-33 relates Isaac's difficulties at the hands of his Philistine neighbors. Jealous of his wealth, they continually stuffed his wells and disputed his ownership of them. For the deeper significance of this 'economic' battle, see Overview to ArtScroll *Genesis*, pp. 1005-1009.]

גָלָה וְסוּרָה — *Exiled and displaced.*
[This reference to Israel is discussed in commentary to *hoshana* 3, st. 3.] It is an apt description of the nation descended from Isaac, who was banished by Abimelech *(Genesis* 26:16) because of the Philistine's jealousy of his success *(Rashi).*

4. קָדַם — *The one who was first.*
[Jacob preceded Esau in bringing delicacies to Isaac. The blessings which he received in return became the cause of an eternal hatred which Esau harbored against him. See *Genesis* 27:1-41.]

מְיַחֵם — *He stimulated.*
[The devices to which Jacob resorted to obtain his rightful share of the flocks are described in *Genesis* 30:37-43.]

דָמְתָה לְתָמָר — *Likened to a palm tree.*
Just as the palm tree has a single heart, which is directed upward [i.e., its trunk does not branch out in many directions], so Israel has a single heart directed only to God. This total sincerity of the Jewish heart was displayed in the story of Jacob and his sons, recounted in the commentary to the verses following *hoshana* 7. Thus, the simile of the palm-tree is aptly related to Jacob *(Rashi;* see also com-

טז
ה-ז

לְמַעַן צָדַק הֱיוֹת לְךָ לְכֹהֵן. כְּחָתָן פְּאֵר יְכַהֵן.
מְנֻסֶּה בְּמַסָּה בְּמֵי מְרִיבַת מָיִם.
לְהָהָר הַטּוֹב: הוֹשַׁעְנָא וְהוֹשִׁיעָה נָּא אָבִינוּ אָתָּה:
לְמַעַן פְּאֵר הֱיוֹת גְּבִיר לְאֶחָיו. יְהוּדָה אֲשֶׁר גָּבַר בְּאֶחָיו.
מִסְפַּר רֹבַע מִדָּלְיָו יִזַּל־מָיִם.
לוֹא לָנוּ כִּי אִם לְמַעַנְךָ.
הוֹשַׁעְנָא וְהוֹשִׁיעָה נָּא אָבִינוּ אָתָּה:
לְמַעַן עָנָיו מִכֹּל וְנֶאֱמָן. אֲשֶׁר בְּצִדְקוֹ כִּלְכֵּל הַמָּן.

mentary to *hoshana* 3, st. 4 and st. 21 below).

5. צָדַק הֱיוֹת לְךָ לְכֹהֵן — *The one worthy of being Your Kohen.*

Levi, son of Jacob, was the progenitor of the priestly tribe from which sprang Aaron the *Kohen* (Rashi).

כְּחָתָן פְּאֵר — *Adorned like a bridegroom.*

[The eight garments of the *Kohen Gadol*, adorned with precious gems in golden settings, are described in *Exodus*, chs. 28 and 39.]

מְנֻסֶּה בְּמַסָּה... — *He was proven at Massah.*

In his blessing of the Levites, Moses praised them as the tribe whom God proved at Massah...at Merivah's water (*Deuteronomy* 33:8). *Sforno* explains that the Levites never joined Israel in any of the ten times the nation questioned God's ability to sustain them in the Wilderness (see *Numbers* 14:22).

לְהָהָר הַטּוֹב — *The good mountain.*

Moses referred to the Temple Mount by this name (*Deuteronomy* 3:25). [In the stich which speaks of the righteousness of the Levites, it is proper that we pray for the return of the Holy Temple in which they served.]

6. יְהוּדָה — *Judah.*

[The commentaries are silent regarding the *paytan's* mention of Judah by name, contrary to the style of the rest of this *hoshana*.]

From among all the children of Jacob [who were equally righteous (see *Rashi* to *Genesis* 35:22)], the *paytan* mentions only Levi and Judah because Scripture relates incidents in their lives relating to water. Alternatively, they are singled out because priesthood and royalty were granted them respectively (*Beis Yaakov*).

גָּבַר בְּאֶחָיו — *Ruled over his brothers.*

Judah is described this way in *I Chronicles* 5:2.

מִסְפַּר רֹבַע — *Though he was fourth* [lit. number four].

The translation follows *Bais Yaakov* and *Tefillah Yesharah*. It is a play on the words of Balaam who spoke of God as מִסְפָּר אֶת־רֹבַע יִשְׂרָאֵל, *He Who counts the* רֹבַע *of Israel* (*Numbers* 23:10). *Rashi*, there, interprets רֹבַע as *the issue of Israel*. The Talmud (*Niddah* 31a) teaches that the Holy One Blessed be He counts the issue of Israel waiting to find the one which will develop into a great and righteous person. Accordingly, Judah was the fourth product of Jacob's issue.

Ibn Ezra, following *Onkelos*, understands רֹבַע as *one-fourth*, a reference to the four sections into which the encampment of Israel was divided, one of which was led by Judah.

מִדָּלְיָו יִזַּל־מַיִם — *From his buckets shall pour water.*

A paraphrase of Balaam's third blessing to Israel (*Numbers* 24:7), the use of this phrase is an allusion to Judah based

16
5-7

⁵ *In the merit of the one worthy of being Your Kohen*
    adorned like a bridegroom he would serve,
He was proven at Massah,
    at Merivah's water —
For the sake of the good mountain
        may You save now and bring salvation now,
            for You are our Father.

⁶ *In the merit of the splendrous one*
    who would be master over his brothers,
Judah who ruled over his brothers
Though he was fourth,
    from his buckets shall pour water —
Not for our sake but for Yours
        may You save now and bring salvation now,
            for You are our Father.

⁷ *In the merit of the humblest of all, and most trusted,*
    for whose righteousness He supplied manna,

on the end of the verse: *And may his kingdom he extended.* Rashi there interprets: May Jacob's royal line be extended with the reigns of David and his son Solomon [who are descended from Judah].

לוֹא לָנוּ כִּי אִם לְמַעַנְךָ — *Not for our sake but for Yours.*
    Paraphrased from *Psalms* 115:1 which reads: *Not for our sake, HASHEM, not for our sake but for Your Name's sake ...*, this stich deviates from the remainder of the *hoshana.* The fourth part of each other stich is a reference to Israel; only here and in stich 13 is the request changed, *not for our sake but for Your sake.* No explanation is offered by the commentaries.

לוֹא — *Not.*
    [Three different spellings for this word may be found. As noted in the prefatory remarks to this *hoshana,* the fourth sections of the stiches follow an alphabetic arrangement. For this reason we have adopted the version found in *Avodas Yisrael* and *Kol Bo* which inserts a ו into the word (לוֹא instead of לֹא) for the sake of the acrostic. Although this spelling is rare, it is found more than thirty times in Scripture, while the more common spelling, לֹא, appears almost five thousand times.]
    Following *Machzor Roma, Iyun Tefillah* reads וְלֹא, *and not.* This spelling includes the ו but deviates from the other stiches which have the alphabet arranged as the second letter of the opening word of the fourth line.
    Finally, *Beis Yaakov* and *Tehillas Hashem* read לֹא but offer no explanation for the deviation. *Tefillah Yesharah* also has this spelling and adds the comment: 'If this line does not contain an error in transcription then the *paytan* must have had an exalted understanding to which we are not privy.'
    [After speaking of the royal line of Judah, we proclaim *not for our sake,* i.e., the kingdom is not ours, *but for Your sake,* for as the Psalmist declares (*Psalms* 22:29): *For the kingship belongs to HASHEM, and He rules the nations.*]

7. עָנָיו מִכֹּל וְנֶאֱמָן — *The humblest of all, and most trusted.*
    In *Numbers* 12:3,7 Moses is referred to as, עָנָו מְאֹד מִכֹּל הָאָדָם, *the very humblest of all men,* and בְּכָל־בֵּיתִי נֶאֱמָן הוּא, *in My entire house he is trusted.*

בְּכַלְכֵּל הַמָּן — *He supplied manna.*
    Three good shepherds arose among

ט-ח **טז** מָשׁוּךְ לְגוֹאֵל וּמָשׁוּי מִמָּיִם.
לְזֹאת הַנִּשְׁקָפָה. הוֹשַׁעְנָא וְהוֹשִׁיעָה נָּא אָבִינוּ אָתָּה:

לְמַעַן **שִׂ**מְתּוֹ כְּמַלְאֲכֵי מְרוֹמִים. הַלּוֹבֵשׁ אוּרִים וְתֻמִּים.
מְצֻוֶּה לָבֹא בַּמִּקְדָּשׁ בְּקִדּוּשׁ יָדַיִם וְרַגְלַיִם
וּרְחִיצַת מָיִם.
לְ**ח**וֹלַת אַהֲבָה. הוֹשַׁעְנָא וְהוֹשִׁיעָה נָּא אָבִינוּ אָתָּה:

לְמַעַן **נְ**בִיאָה מְחוֹלַת מַחֲנָיִם. לִכְמֵהֵי לֵב הוּשְׂמָה עֵינַיִם.
לְרַגְלָהּ רָצָה עָלוֹת וָרֶדֶת בְּאֵר מָיִם.
לְ**ט**וֹבוּ אֹהָלָיו. הוֹשַׁעְנָא וְהוֹשִׁיעָה נָּא אָבִינוּ אָתָּה:

the Israelites: Moses, Aaron, and Miriam. God presented the nation with three gifts in their respective merit: the well in Miriam's merit [see stich 9]; the protective clouds [which surrounded the nation in the Wilderness] in Aaron's; and the manna in Moses' (*Taanis* 9a).

מָשׁוּךְ — *He was drawn.*
Against his will, God drew Moses into the role of leadership (*Iyun Tefillah;* see *Exodus* 3:11-13; 14:13).

מָשׁוּי מִמַּיִם — *Pulled from the water.*
The name Moses means *pulled from the water* (*Exodus* 2:10).

זֹאת הַנִּשְׁקָפָה — *The one who gazes down.*
[*Who is this that gazes down like the dawn? She is beautiful as the moon, brilliant as the sun* (*Song of Songs* 6:10). This verse alluding to Israel is especially apt to the stiches which speak of Moses and his disciple Joshua (st. 10). The Talmud (*Bava Basra* 75a) compares the leadership of Joshua to that of Moses and finds that, great though he was, the disciple was a mere reflection of the master. In the Talmud's words: The face of Moses was like the sun; the face of Joshua was like the moon. Not wishing to cast aspersions on Joshua's greatness, the *paytan* does not call Moses *brilliant as the sun* and Joshua, *beautiful as the moon.* He neutralizes the implications by using the opening of the Scriptural passage for Moses, and then combining יָפָה וּבָרָה, *beautiful and brilliant*, in reference to Joshua (see stich 10).]

8. כְּמַלְאֲכֵי מְרוֹמִים — *Like exalted angels.*
Aaron's holiness is described by the prophet (*Malachi* 2:7): *For the Kohen's lips shall safeguard knowledge; and Torah shall they seek from his mouth, for he is an angel of HASHEM of hosts.*

אוּרִים וְתֻמִּים — *The Urim and Tumim.*
The *Kohen Gadol's* breastplate consisted of twelve precious stones, each inscribed with the name of one tribe.
Contained in the fold of the breastplate was a parchment upon which the Ineffable Name of God was written. When Israel required prophetic advice, the *Kohen Gadol* clad in his sacred garments, would be presented with the question, which he would repeat. Through the power of the Ineffable Name, various letters of the tribal names would light up, spelling the answer to the question (see *Yoma* 73a).
The parchment on which the Ineffable Name was written was called the *Urim* and *Tumim* (*Rashi* to *Exodus* 28:30). The name אוּרִים, *Urim* [lit., *lights*], is an allusion to the illumination of the letters on the breastplate; תֻּמִּים, *Tumim* [lit. *perfect ones*], refers to the perfect advice which it rendered (based on a marginal gloss to *Berachos* 4a).

16
8-9
    He was drawn to be a redeemer
    and pulled from the water —
For the sake of the one who gazes down
      may You save now and bring salvation now,
        for You are our Father.

⁸ *In the merit of the one You emplaced*
    like exalted angels,
He who, wearing the Urim and Tumim,
    is commanded to come to the Temple with
      sanctified hands and feet, and an immersion in water —
For the sake of the one sick with love
      may You save now and bring salvation now,
        for You are our Father.

⁹ *In the merit of the prophetess of the dance of the camps,*
    to those of thirsting heart she was an inspiration,
At her feet ran, rising and descending,
    the well of water —
For the sake of the one of goodly tents
      may You save now and bring salvation now,
        for You are our Father.

... מְצֻוֶּה — *Is commanded ...*

No one may enter the Temple Courtyard without prior immersion (*Yoma* 30a). A *Kohen* is forbidden to perform the Temple service unless he has sanctified his hands and feet in the waters of the בִּיוֹר, *basin*, which stood in the Courtyard (*Exodus* 30:17-21).

חוֹלַת אַהֲבָה — *Sick with love.*

Metzudos to *Song of Songs* 2:5 renders: My soul faints with yearning for the return of the *Shechinah* which is in exile. But as described in *Ezekiel* the withdrawal of the *Shechinah* took place in ten steps — first from the Holy of Holies and finally from the entire land. Thus after mentioning the merit of Aaron who was responsible for the Temple service, we pray for a return of the *Shechinah* to *Eretz Yisrael* and to a rebuilt Temple (based on *Rashi*).

9. ... נְבִיאָה — *The prophetess ...*

Miriam the prophetess ... took the tambourine in her hand; all the women followed her with tambourines and dances (*Exodus* 15:20).

בְּאֵר מַיִם — *The well of water.*

The well which accompanied the Israelites through the Wilderness was granted them in the merit of Miriam (see comm. to st. 7).

טוֹבוּ אֹהָלָיו — *The one of goodly tents.*

Another paraphrase of Balaam's blessing (*Numbers* 24:5). The relationship of this reference to Israel and Miriam's well may be understood from the Midrash (*BaMidbar Rabbah* 19:26). When the nation camped in the Wilderness, the leader of each tribe would take his staff and draw a line from the well through his tribe's encampment. The water would then flow along these twelve paths so that each person had water without exertion. The waters of Miriam's well thus came right to *the goodly tents* of Israel (*Rashi*).

טז
י־יג

לְמַעַן מְשָׁרֵת לֹא־מָשׁ מֵאֹהֶל. וְרוּחַ הַקֹּדֶשׁ עָלָיו אָהַל.
בְּעָבְרוֹ בַיַּרְדֵּן נִכְרְתוּ הַמָּיִם.
לְיָפָה וּבָרָה.   הוֹשַׁעְנָא וְהוֹשִׁיעָה נָּא אָבִינוּ אָתָּה:

לְמַעַן לִמַּד רְאוֹת לְטוֹבָה אוֹת. זָעַק אַיֵּה נִפְלָאוֹת.
מִצָּה טַל מִגִּזָּה מְלֹא הַסֵּפֶל מָיִם.
לְכַלַּת לְבָנוֹן.   הוֹשַׁעְנָא וְהוֹשִׁיעָה נָּא אָבִינוּ אָתָּה:

לְמַעַן בְּלוּלֵי עֲשׂוֹת מִלְחַמְתֶּךָ. אֲשֶׁר בְּיָדָם תִּתָּה יְשׁוּעָתֶךָ.
צְרוּפֵי מִגּוֹי בְּלַקְקָם בְּיָדָם מָיִם.
לְלֹא בָגְדוּ בָךְ.   הוֹשַׁעְנָא וְהוֹשִׁיעָה נָּא אָבִינוּ אָתָּה:

לְמַעַן יָחִיד צוֹרְרִים דָּשׁ. אֲשֶׁר מֵרֶחֶם לְנָזִיר הֻקְדָּשׁ.

10. מְשָׁרֵת — *The servant.*

Joshua's loyalty to Moses is described in *Exodus* 33:11: *But his [Moses'] servant Joshua ... did not move from the tent.* This dedication enabled Joshua to assume the leadership of Israel after Moses' death. For as the Talmud teaches (*Berachos* 7b): *A disciple's service is more significant than his studies* (*Ralbag* to *Joshua* 1:1).

בְּעָבְרוֹ בַיַּרְדֵּן — *When he crossed the Jordan.*

[Israel's entry into the Land of Canaan under Joshua's leadership is recounted in *Joshua* 3:9-4:24.]

יָפָה וּבָרָה — *Beautiful and brilliant.*

[For the relationship between this description of Israel and Joshua's leadership see commentary to st. 7.

Alternatively, this abridgment of the verse *beautiful as the moon, brilliant as the sun* may be a reference to Joshua's command to the heavenly bodies: *Sun in Gibeon remain still, also the moon in the valley of Ayalon* (*Joshua* 10:12).]

11. אוֹת — *Omen.*

Gideon was visited by an angel when Israel was subjugated by Midian. He asked the angel, 'Where are His wonders which our fathers have recounted about Him ...?' In response, God Himself (see *Rashi*) told Gideon to save the nation from the Midianites. Gideon asked for omens which would prove that his mission would be successful, and a sign was given him (see *Judges* 6:1-38 for the complete narrative). He asked for a second sign, one which he specified: *I shall spread a fleece on the threshing floor, if dew falls only on the fleece, and the earth shall all be dry, then I shall know that through my hands will Israel be saved, as You have spoken. And so it was, he awoke in the morning and squeezed the fleece; he pressed dew from the fleece — a full bowl of water* (*Judges* 6:37-38). He subsequently asked for a third sign, that the fleece remain dry while the earth surrounding it becomes wet with dew. This sign was also granted him.

מִצָּה — *He pressed.*

Many *siddurim* read מָץ.

כַּלַּת לְבָנוֹן — *The bride of Lebanon.*

Lebanon is a reference to the Holy Temple [see commentary to *hoshana* 2, st. 9], so called because the [blood-like] sins of the nation are cleansed there [a play on the words לְבָנוֹן, *Lebanon*, and לָבָן, *white*] (*Yoma* 39b).

This whitening of the sins was demonstrated by a scarlet thread which miraculously turned white during the performance of the Yom Kippur Temple services, in fulfillment of the verse (*Isaiah* 1:18): *If your sins are as scarlet,*

16
10-13

¹⁰ *In the merit of the servant who moved not from the tent,*
    upon him the Holy Spirit rested,
When he crossed the Jordan,
    cut was the water —
For the sake of the beautiful and brilliant
    may You save now and bring salvation now,
        for You are our Father.

¹¹ *In the merit of him who showed*
    how to perceive a good omen,
He cried, 'Where are Your wonders,'
    from a fleece he pressed, a bowl full of water —
For the sake of the bride of Lebanon
    may You save now and bring salvation now,
        for You are our Father.

¹² *In the merit of the dedicated fighters in Your war,*
    into whose hands You placed Your salvation,
Proven purest of the nation
    by having lapped from their hand water —
For the sake of those that did not rebel against You
    may You save now and bring salvation now,
        for You are our Father.

¹³ *In the merit of the only child, who thrashed the oppressors,*
    sanctified from the womb as a Nazir,

as snow He will whiten them; if they be red as crimson, they shall become as [white as] wool.

Gideon asked for a good omen involving a woolen thread *(Rashi)*.

12. When Gideon's thirty-two thousand man army prepared for battle with Midian, God told him that the army was too large — Israel would claim that its victory was due to its superior forces. The army was reduced to ten thousand men, but still God demanded a much smaller band. To select only those who were completely loyal to God, the troops were marched to the water where they were told to drink. Those who fell to their knees and brought their faces down to the water were judged unsuitable to serve in God's army [for they were wont to fall on their knees and prostrate themselves before idols *(Rashi)*]. Those who scooped up water and lapped it from their hands were allowed to remain. They numbered only three hundred men (see *Judges* 7:1-8).

לֹא בָגְדוּ בָךְ — *Those that did not rebel against You.*

[The connection between this allusion to Israel from *Isaiah* 33:1 and the loyal troops of Gideon's army is obvious.]

13. יָחִיד — *The only child* [lit., single one].

Samson's parents had only one child *(Iyun Tefillah)*.

מֵרֶחֶם לְנָזִיר — *From the womb he was ... a Nazir.*

[The circumstances preceding Samson's miraculous birth and the in-

טז
יד-טו

מִמַּכְתֵּשׁ לֶחִי הִבְקַעְתָּ לּוֹ מָיִם.
לְמַעַן שֵׁם קָדְשֶׁךָ. הוֹשַׁעְנָא וְהוֹשִׁיעָה נָּא אָבִינוּ אָתָּה:
לְמַעַן טוֹב הוֹלֵךְ וְגָדֵל. אֲשֶׁר מֵעֹשֶׁק עֵדָה חָדֵל.
בְּשׁוּב עַם מֵחֵטְא צִוָּה שְׁאָב־מַיִם.
לְנָאוָה כִּירוּשָׁלָיִם. הוֹשַׁעְנָא וְהוֹשִׁיעָה נָּא אָבִינוּ אָתָּה:
לְמַעַן חַיָּךְ מְכַרְכֵּר בְּשִׁיר. הַמְלַמֵּד תּוֹרָה בְּכָל־כְּלֵי שִׁיר.

structions given his mother to consecrate him as a Nazir even before he was born, are recounted in *Judges* chap. 13.]

מִמַּכְתֵּשׁ לֶחִי — *From the hollow of a jawbone.*

After slaying a thousand Philistines with the jawbone of a donkey, Samson was stricken with an unslakable thirst. *HASHEM split the hollow of the jawbone and water flowed out from it; and he drank. His spirit was refereshed* (Judges 15:18-19).

לְמַעַן שֵׁם קָדְשֶׁךָ — *For the sake of Your Holy Name.*

Once again the *paytan* deviates (see commentary to st. 6) and asks for salvation, not for Israel but for the *Shechinah* in exile.

Rashi, who explains the relationship between each patriarch and the adjacent reference to Israel, has an alternative reading: לְמִי זֹאת עֹלָה, *For the sake of, 'Who is this who rises!'* [See commentary to *hoshana* 13, st. 16 for this reference to Israel in exile.] The angel who foretold Samson's birth ascended to heaven together with the עֹלָה, *burnt offering,* brought by Samson's parents when they heard the good tidings that they would be granted a son (Judges 13:16-20).

14. טוֹב הֹלֵךְ וְגָדֵל — *The good and increasingly exalted one.*

This description of the young Samuel is paraphrased from *I Samuel* 2:26.

מֵעֹשֶׁק — *From robbing ...*

Our reading and translation follows *Beis Yaakov*.

Avodas Yisroel and *Tehillas Hashem*

read: ... מַעְקְשׁוּת לֵב, which the English edition of *Tehillas Hashem* renders: *who restrained the congregation from perverseness.*

חָדֵל ... — *He restrained himself ...*

Samuel gathered the nation asking them to testify whether, at any time during his tenure as judge and prophet, he accepted a bribe or even took the wages to which he was legitimately entitled. None came forward (see *I Samuel* 12:35; *Beis Yaakov*).

שְׁאָב־מַיִם — *Draw water.*

I Samuel 7:5-6 describes how Samuel gathered the nation in prayer and repentance. *They drew water and poured it before HASHEM. Targum* renders: They poured out their hearts before HASHEM as if it were water.

נָאוָה כִּירוּשָׁלָיִם — *Beautiful as Jerusalem.*

Israel is so designated in *Song of Songs* 6:4. Samuel's gathering for repentance took place after the destruction of the Tabernacle of Shiloh. *Psalms* 78:60-68 teaches that Jerusalem was selected after the destruction of Shiloh, hence this epithet for Israel is used here (Rashi).

15. מְכַרְכֵּר בְּשִׁיר — *Dancing with song.*

David danced with all [his] strength before HASHEM (II Samuel 6:14).

The elders of Israel removed the Ark from the Tabernacle at Shiloh, erroneously thinking it would guarantee them protection against Philistine aggression (*I Samuel* 4:35). Instead, thirty thousand Jewish foot soldiers were killed and the Ark was captured (ibid. vs. 10-11). The victorious Philistines brought the Ark from city to city to dis-

16 From the hollow of a jawbone
14-15 You brought him water —
For the sake of Your Holy Name
may You save now and bring salvation now,
for You are our Father.

14 In the merit of the good and increasingly exalted one
who restrained himself from robbing the flock,
When the nation repented
he bade them draw water —
For the sake of the one as beautiful as Jerusalem
may You save now and bring salvation now,
for You are our Father.

15 In the merit of the one who caused You joy,
dancing with song,
Who teaches Torah
accompanied by every sort of instrument,

play their spoils. But whichever city hosted the Ark fell prey to a debilitating epidemic (*ibid.* chap. 5). Finally after seven months, the Philistine chiefs decided that they had had enough. Placing the Ark on a wagon specially constructed for that purpose, they hitched up two cows and allowed them to pull at will. If the cows would pull the Ark to Jewish territory, the Philistines would be assured that the epidemic had been sent by the God of Israel. Should the cows pull the Ark elsewhere, then the epidemic was merely a coincidence.

The Ark was drawn directly to Israelite territory, to the field of Joshua of Beis Shemesh. There the field workers were so jubilant at the Ark's return that they placed the wood of the wagon upon a boulder, lit a fire, and sacrificed the two cows as a burnt offering to God (*ibid.* chap. 6).

The Levites were called to remove the Ark. They brought it to the house of Avinadav in Givah where it remained for twenty years (*ibid.* 7:1-2).

When David attempted to bring the Ark to Jerusalem, tragedy struck. Uzzah inadvertently stretched out his hand, touched the Ark, and died. The festivities ended in mourning and the Ark was left at the house of Oved-edom the Levite for the next three months. At the end of this period it was removed to Jerusalem with great festivities. *And David danced with all [his] strength before HASHEM* (II Samuel 6:1-14).

הַמְלַמֵּד תּוֹרָה בְּכָל־כְּלֵי שִׁיר — *Who teaches Torah accompanied by every sort of instrument.*

The Talmud (*Berachos* 3b) teaches that David had a harp suspended over his bed which would sing every midnight when the north wind rustled its strings. David would immediately awake and engage in Torah study until daybreak. Thus *David taught Torah with the aid of a musical instrument* (*Rashi*).

David taught the Levites תּוֹרַת הַשִּׁיר, *the laws of the Song,* which they sang and played in the Temple, while the Kohanim brought the daily sacrifices (*Beis Yaakov*).

David studied Torah joyously, as if he were listening to a full orchestra (*Shaar HaShamayim*).

Based on *II Chronicles* 15:16 and 16:7, *Tefillah Yesharah* suggests that the proper reading is תּוֹדָה, *thanksgiving,* for David taught the Levites to sing praises of thanksgiving before God.

טז מְנַסֵּךְ לְפָנָיו כִּתְאֹב שְׁתוֹת מָיִם.
טז-יז
לְשָׂמוּ בְךָ סִבְרָם.   הוֹשַׁעְנָא וְהוֹשִׁיעָה נָא אָבִינוּ אָתָּה:

לְמַעַן זָךְ עָלָה בַסְּעָרָה. הַמְקַנֵּא וּמֵשִׁיב עֶבְרָה.
לִפְלוּלוֹ יָרְדָה אֵשׁ וְלִחֲכָה עָפָר וּמָיִם.
לְעֵינֶיהָ בְּרֵכוֹת.   הוֹשַׁעְנָא וְהוֹשִׁיעָה נָא אָבִינוּ אָתָּה:

לְמַעַן וְשֵׁרֵת בֶּאֱמֶת לְרַבּוֹ. פִּי שְׁנַיִם בְּרוּחוֹ נֶאֱצַל בּוֹ.
בְּקַחְתּוֹ מְנַגֵּן נִתְמַלְאוּ גֵבִים מָיִם.
לְפָצוּ מִי כָמְכָה.   הוֹשַׁעְנָא וְהוֹשִׁיעָה נָא אָבִינוּ אָתָּה:

Tefillah Yesharah further suggests that since the phrase הַמְלַמֵּד תּוֹרָה, *He teaches Torah*, appears in the daily Torah blessing, a copyist fell easily into a transcription error.

מְנַסֵּךְ לְפָנָיו — *He poured libations before Him.*

When David thirsted for water in the thick of battle he cried, 'Who will give me water to drink from cistern at the gate of Bethlehem?'
Three bold warriors broke through the Philistine camp and drew water ... When he was given the water David said that to drink water obtained with such potential danger was like drinking the blood of the bold warriors who risked their lives to get it. Such water can only be consecrated to God. And David poured the water as a libation before God (*II Samuel* 23:15-17).

לְפָנָיו — *Before Him.*

[Our translation *before Him*, referring to God is based on the words of Scripture: וַיַּסֵּךְ אֹתָם לַה׳, *he poured them before* (lit. *to*) *HASHEM*.] *Tefillah Yesharah* seems puzzled by this usage and suggests that perhaps לְפָנֶיךָ, *before You*, is the proper text. [Since the entire *hoshana* addresses God in second person (e.g., You are our Father) this emendation seems justified.] *Avodas Yisrael* reads לְפָנֶיךָ, *before You*, commenting, 'This is the manuscript reading.'

שָׂמוּ בְךָ סִבְרָם — *Those who place their hope in You.*

It was David who said: *Praiseworthy is the one at whose side stands the God of Jacob; his hope is to HASHEM his God* (*Psalms* 146:5).

16. [Elijah's ascent to heaven, his vengeance against idolators, and the fire which descended at his behest, are discussed in *hoshana* 7, sts. 13 and 18.]

עֵינֶיהָ בְּרֵכוֹת — *(Her) eyes are* [like] *pools.*

[This description of Israel is paraphrased from *Song of Songs* 7:5. The members of Sanhedrin are called *the eyes of the congregation* (*Leviticus* 4:17; *Numbers* 15:24). Just as the Sanhedrin issued definitive judgment in matters of dispute, so will Elijah, when he arrives to herald the Messiah and resolve the questions whose solutions escaped the Sages of each generation.]

17. שֵׁרֵת בֶּאֱמֶת לְרַבּוֹ — *(He) served his master earnestly.*

Elisha served Elijah faithfully and was therefore worthy to succeed him. The Talmud explains the verse (*II Kings* 3:11), *here is Elisha ben Shafat who poured water at the feet of Elijah:* Scripture does not say 'he studied' at the feet of Elijah, but 'he poured water.' This teaches that a disciple gains more by serving his master than by studying his words (*Berachos* 7b; see also comm. to st. 10).

פִּי שְׁנַיִם — *A double measure.*

Before Elijah was taken to heaven he

16   *He poured libations before Him*
16-17   *though he thirsted to drink water —*
For the sake of those who place their hope in You
      may You save now and bring salvation now,
        for You are our Father.

¹⁶ *In the merit of the pure one who ascended in a storm wind,*
   who avenged and turned back fury,
At his prayer there descended fire
   which consumed dust and water —
For the sake of the one whose eyes are like pools
     may You save now and bring salvation now,
       for You are our Father.

¹⁷ *In the merit of the one who served his master earnestly,*
   a double measure of his spirit was vested in him,
When he summoned a musician
   the cisterns were filled with water —
For the sake of those who exclaimed, 'Who is like You?'
     may You save now and bring salvation now,
       for You are our Father.

---

allowed Elisha one request:

   And Elisha said, 'May there please rest upon me, a double portion of your spirit.'

   [Elijah] replied, 'You have made a difficult request! If you will see me being taken from you — then it shall be so for you. If not, then it shall not be ...'

   Elisha saw — he cried, 'My father, my father! Chariot of Israel and its charioteer.' Then he saw him no longer (II Kings 2:9-12).

Rashi (ibid. v. 14) notes that when Elijah and Elisha were walking together the Jordan split to let them pass (ibid. v. 8). On the return trip Elisha was alone, yet the water split for him. Thus, Elisha's double portion was granted, for Elisha's own merit accomplished what had earlier required the merit of both.

בְּקַחְתּוֹ מְנַגֵּן — *When he summoned a musician.*

The kings of Judea, Israel and Edom formed an alliance against Moab. After their armies had marched seven day's journey into the wilderness they ran out of water. Jehosaphat, king of Judea, summoned Elisha who said:

   'Now bring me a musician.' As the musician played, the Hand of HASHEM came upon him [Elisha] and he said, 'So says HASHEM: "This valley shall be filled with cisterns, cisterns." For thus says HASHEM: "You shall not see wind, you shall not see rain, but this valley shall be full with water. You shall drink — you, your cattle and your pack-animals" (II Kings 3:9-17).

פָּצוּ מִי כָמֹכָה — *Those who exclaimed, 'Who is like You?'*

[Israel sang these words twice in the Song of the Sea (*Exodus* 15:11). The Sea of Reeds split for Israel, the Jordan twice split for Elisha.]

Hoshanos / **In the Merit of Him Who Was Perfect**

טז לְמַעַן הִרְהֵר עֲשׂוֹת רְצוֹנֶךָ. הַמַּכְרִיז תְּשׁוּבָה לְצֹאנֶךָ.
יח-כב אָז בְּבֹא מְחָרֵף סָתַם עֵינוֹת מָיִם.
לְצִיּוֹן מִכְלַל יֹפִי.   הוֹשַׁעְנָא וְהוֹשִׁיעָה נָּא אָבִינוּ אָתָּה:

לְמַעַן דָּרְשׁוּךָ בְּתוֹךְ הַגּוֹלָה. וְסוֹדְךָ לָמוֹ נִגְלָה.
בְּלִי לְהִתְגָּאֵל דָּרְשׁוּ זֵרְעוֹנִים וּמָיִם.
לְקוֹרְאֶיךָ בַצָּר.   הוֹשַׁעְנָא וְהוֹשִׁיעָה נָּא אָבִינוּ אָתָּה:

לְמַעַן גָּמַר חָכְמָה וּבִינָה. סוֹפֵר מָהִיר מְפַלֵּשׁ אֲמָנָה.
מְחַכְּמֵנוּ אֲמָרִים הַמְשׁוּלִים בְּרַחֲבֵי מָיִם.
לְרַבָּתִי עָם.   הוֹשַׁעְנָא וְהוֹשִׁיעָה נָּא אָבִינוּ אָתָּה:

18. הִרְהֵר עֲשׂוֹת רְצוֹנֶךָ — *Who meant to do Your will.*

Hezekiah, king of Judea committed six halachically questionable acts. Of three of them, the Sages approved; of the other three they disapproved (*Pesachim* 56a; *Berachos* 10b). Although they did not consent to all of Hezekiah's actions, they repudiated only the particular acts, not the man, for they knew that (*II Kings* 18:5) *he had faith in HASHEM, God of Israel* (*Iyun Tefillah*).

הַמַּכְרִיז תְּשׁוּבָה — *He cried out, 'Repentance.'*

The runners went, with letters [signed] by the king's hand and [that of] his officials, throughout Israel and Judea, and in accordance with the king's order they said: Children of Israel! Return to HASHEM, God of Abraham, Isaac and Israel!' (*II Chronicles* 30:6).

מְחָרֵף — *The blasphemer.*

Ravshakeh, the Assyrian general, cried out blasphemously to the Jewish king and army to abandon their faith in God (*II Kings* 18:19-35).

סָתַם עֵינוֹת מָיִם — *He sealed the springs of water.*

When Sennacherib's army, led by Ravshakeh threatened, Hezekiah ordered that the springs which supplied Jerusalem with water be sealed. *Why should the Assyrian kings come and find abundant water* (*II Chronicles* 32:4)? Hezekiah contended.

Since this is one of the three acts of which the Sages disapproved (see citation above from *Pesachim* 56a), why does the *paytan* plead for salvation in its merit? The answer may be found in *Avos d'R'Nosson* 2:4. Hezekiah performed four acts in which his wisdom coincided with Divine wisdom. One of these was the sealing of the springs, as Scripture states (*II Chronicles* 32:30): *And he, Hezekiah, sealed the mouth of the upper waters of Gichon* [a spring outside Jerusalem (*Rashi*)] *causing them to flow downward to the west of the city of David; and Hezekiah was successful in all his deeds.*

[For a reconciliation of the divergent teachings of *Pesachim* and *Avos d'R'Nosson* see *Maharsha* to *Berachos* 10b.]

צִיּוֹן מִכְלַל יֹפִי — *Zion, perfect in beauty.*

[The description of Jerusalem as *perfect in beauty* is from *Psalms* 50:2. It is discussed in commentary to *hoshana* 2, sts. 10-11. A prayer for Jerusalem is apt at this point, since the stich speaks of Hezekiah's defense of the city.]

19. בְּתוֹךְ הַגּוֹלָה — *In midst of the exile.*

Daniel, Chananiah, Mishael, and Azaryah were taken from among the exiles of Judah (*Daniel* 2:25) to live in Nebuchadnezzar's palace. Their refusal to partake of the conqueror's food, their

**16
18-20**

¹⁸ *In the merit of the one who meant to do Your will,*
    he cried out, 'Repentance,' to Your sheep,
Then when the blasphemer came
    he sealed the springs of water —
For the sake of Zion, perfect in beauty
        may You save now and bring salvation now,
            for You are our Father.

¹⁹ *In the merit of those who sought You in midst of the exile,*
    Your secret was uncovered to them,
Not to defile themselves,
    they requested pulse and water —
For the sake of those who call in distress
        may You save now and bring salvation now,
            for You are our Father.

²⁰ *In the merit of the one who studied*
    wisdom and understanding,
    a skillful scribe, expounder of faith,
He made us wise with sayings that are likened
    to expanses of water —
For the sake of the city great with people
        may You save now and bring salvation now,
            for You are our Father.

---

insistence on eating a vegetarian diet of pulse and water (*ibid.* 1:8-16), and their prayers to God (*ibid.* 2:18 and 6:11-12) are sure signs that they sought closeness to God even in the midst of the exile.

וְסוֹדְךָ לָמוֹ נִגְלָה — *Your secret was uncovered to them.*

[This refers to Daniel's interpretation of Nebuchadnezzar's dream recounted in *Daniel* chap. 2.]

לְקוֹרְאֶיךָ בַצָּר — *Those who call in distress.*

Israel cries to God when in distress just as did Daniel and his companions (*Rashi*).

20. סוֹפֵר — *Scribe.*

Ezra prepared his heart to expound HASHEM's Torah and to fulfill [its commandments]; to teach Israel statute and law (*Ezra* 7:10).

He is Ezra who came up from Babylon; he is a scribe accomplished in Moses' Torah ... (*ibid.* v. 6).

מְחַכְּמֵנוּ — *He made us wise.*

Ezra was worthy enough that the Torah could have been given through him, had not Moses preceded him (*Sanhedrin* 21b). When the Torah was almost forgotten by Israel, Ezra came up from Babylon and re-established it (*Succah* 20a).

הַמְּשׁוּלִים בְּרַחֲבֵי מַיִם — *That are likened to expanses of water.*

Proverbs 5:16 compares the Torah to water: *May your wellsprings burst forth outwardly, in broad channels of water* (*Proverbs* 5:16; *Rashi*). [See commentary to *hoshana* 17, st. 10, for an explanation of the comparison.]

רַבָּתִי עָם — *[The city] great with people.*

The translation of this description of Jerusalem is based on its use in *Lamen-*

טז לְמַעַן בָּאֵי לְךָ הַיּוֹם בְּכָל־לֵב. שׁוֹפְכִים לְךָ שִׂיחַ בְּלֹא לֵב
כא-כב וָלֵב. שׁוֹאֲלִים מִמְּךָ עֹז מַטְרוֹת מָיִם.
לְשׁוֹרְרוּךָ בַיָּם.   הוֹשַׁעְנָא וְהוֹשִׁיעָה נָּא אָבִינוּ אָתָּה:

לְמַעַן אוֹמְרֵי יְגַדַּל שְׁמֶךָ. וְהֵם נַחֲלָתְךָ וְעַמֶּךָ.
צְמֵאִים לְיִשְׁעֲךָ. כְּאֶרֶץ עֲיֵפָה לַמָּיִם.
לְתָרְתָּ לָמוֹ מְנוּחָה.   הוֹשַׁעְנָא וְהוֹשִׁיעָה נָּא אָבִינוּ אָתָּה:

◆§ תענה אמונים

Some put aside the lulav and esrog and take up the hoshana-bundle of five willow twigs. This is held until it is beaten at the end of the service. Others retain the lulav and esrog and do not take up the hoshana-bundle until it is to be beaten (see commentary).

הוֹשַׁעְנָא. אֵל נָא אָנָּא הוֹשִׁיעָה נָּא: הוֹשַׁעְנָא סְלַח נָא וְהַצְלִיחָה נָּא וְהוֹשִׁיעֵנוּ אֵל מָעֻזֵּנוּ:

tations 1:1 where the phrase is preceded by the word הָעִיר, *the city*.

Just as Ezra led Israel back to Jerusalem from the exile, so may we merit to see Jerusalem once again *great with people (Shaar HaShamayim)*.

Alternatively, רַבָּתִי עָם alludes to Israel and means *the greatest of peoples (Avodas Yisrael)*.

21. הַיּוֹם — *Today*.

This stich refers to the congregants who are reciting the *Hoshana* prayers.

בְּלֹא לֵב וָלֵב — *With undivided heart* [lit., *without heart and heart*].

Radak (to I Chronicles 12:33) renders this phrase as synonymous with לֵב אֶחָד, *one heart (ibid. v. 38)*. [Perhaps the phrase לֵבָב שָׁלֵם, *perfect heart (ibid.)* is also synonymous. See also commentary to st. 4.]

Midrash Tehillim to Psalms 12:3 explains בְּלֵב וָלֵב יְדַבֵּרוּ, *with heart and heart they speak*, as אֶחָד בְּפֶה וְאֶחָד בְּלֵב, *one with the mouth, one with the heart*, i.e., the heart does not mean what the mouth says. We, however, are not that way, we are בְּלֹא לֵב וָלֵב, *with undivided heart*, i.e., our heart agrees with our mouth.

עֹז מַטְרוֹת מָיִם — *Powerful rains of water*.

This expression is paraphrased from Job 37:6: וְגֶשֶׁם, *and rain*, מְטְרַת עֻזּוֹ, *rain of His strength*.

שׁוֹרְרוּךָ בַיָּם — *Those who sang to You at the Sea*.

Israel at the Sea of Reeds sang: עָזִּי, *Strength and song is to God and He shall be my salvation (Exodus 15:2)*. We pray for the rains to be brought by that same strength *(Rashi)*.

22. נַחֲלָתְךָ וְעַמֶּךָ — *Your heritage and Your nation*.

Israel is God's *heritage* by virtue of its Patriarchs, and His *nation* for He freed it from Egyptian slavery *(Ibn Ezra to Deuteronomy 9:29)*.

Alternatively, *Your heritage* refers to the select among the nation, while *Your nation* includes all the common folk *(Etz Yoseph)*.

כְּאֶרֶץ — *As a land*.

16 21-22

²¹ For the sake of those who came to You today
with all their heart,
Pouring prayer before You with undivided heart,
asking You for powerful rains of water —
For the sake of those who sang to You at the Sea
may You save now and bring salvation now,
for You are our Father.

²² For the sake of those who say,
'May Your Name be exalted!'
they are Your heritage and Your nation,
They thirst for Your salvation
as does a land that thirsts for water —
For the sake of those for whom You scouted a resting place
may You save now and bring salvation now,
for You are our Father.

✥ Answer the Faithful

Some put aside the *lulav* and *esrog* and take up the *hoshana*-bundle of five willow twigs. This is held until it is beaten at the end of the service. Others retain the *lulav* and *esrog* and do not take up the *hoshana*-bundle until it is to be beaten (see commentary).

**Save now, please God, please bring salvation now.
Save now, forgive now, bring success now, and save us, God, our Fortress.**

Shaar HaShamayim reads בְּאֶרֶץ, *in a land*. This, then, is a prayer for the Jews living in *Eretz Yisrael* which is described as *a land ... which drinks water from the rains of heaven* (Deuteronomy 11:11).

תַּרְתָּ לָמוֹ מְנוּחָה — *Those for whom You scouted a resting place.* The Ark of HASHEM's Covenant traveled a three day journey before them, to scout a resting place for them (Numbers 10:33).

✥ תַּעֲנֶה אֱמוּנִים — Answer the Faithful

At this point, *Maharam* would lay aside the Four Species and pick up the *hoshana*-bundle, consisting of five willow twigs, and hold it until the end of the service. *ARIzal* would hold the Four Species until the end of the service; only then would he lay them aside and pick up the *hoshana*-bundle to beat it on the ground. He strongly opposes taking up the *hoshana*-bundle until the end of the service. Both *Maharam* and *ARIzal* agree that Four Species and the *hoshana*-bundle should not be held simultaneously.

Beis Yaakov follows *Maharam*, while *Tefillas Hashem* follows *ARIzal*.

Tefillah Yesharah and *Shaar HaShamayim* reconcile the opinions: Those who say the *Hoshana* prayers after *Mussaf*, as did *Maharam*, should follow his view and take up the *hoshana*-bundle here; those who say the *Hoshana* prayers immediately after *Hallel*, as did *ARIzal*, should not take up the *hoshana*-bundle until the end of the service. Both customs are valid and have profound Kabbalistic implications.

יז
א-יא תַּעֲנֶה אֱמוּנִים. שׁוֹפְכִים לְךָ לֵב כַּמַּיִם. וְהוֹשִׁיעָה נָּא:
לְמַעַן בָּא בָאֵשׁ וּבַמַּיִם.
גָּזַר וְנָם יֻקַּח־נָא מְעַט־מַיִם. וְהַצְלִיחָה נָּא. וְהוֹשִׁיעֵנוּ אֵל מָעֻזֵּנוּ:

תַּעֲנֶה דְגָלִים גָּזוּ גּוֹזְרֵי מַיִם. וְהוֹשִׁיעָה נָּא:
לְמַעַן הַנֶּעֱקַד בְּשַׁעַר הַשָּׁמַיִם.
וְשָׁב וְחָפַר בְּאֵרוֹת מַיִם. וְהַצְלִיחָה נָּא. וְהוֹשִׁיעֵנוּ אֵל מָעֻזֵּנוּ:

תַּעֲנֶה זַכִּים חוֹנִים עֲלֵי מַיִם. וְהוֹשִׁיעָה נָּא:
לְמַעַן חָלָק מְפַצֵּל מַקְלוֹת בְּשִׁקֲתוֹת הַמָּיִם.
טָעַן וְגָל אֶבֶן מִבְּאֵר מַיִם. וְהַצְלִיחָה נָּא. וְהוֹשִׁיעֵנוּ אֵל מָעֻזֵּנוּ:

תַּעֲנֶה יְדִידִים נוֹחֲלֵי דָת מְשׁוּלַת מַיִם. וְהוֹשִׁיעָה נָּא:
לְמַעַן כָּרוּ בְּמִשְׁעֲנוֹתָם מַיִם.

Following the theme of the preceding *hoshana*, we again ask for rain in the merit of our righteous forebears. The Talmud teaches that during Succos the Heavenly Tribunal judges the world with regard to its water supply for the following year. The Holy One Blessed be He ordained the water libations of Succos as a source of merit; as if He said, 'Pour water before Me on this festival, that you be blessed with the year's rains' (*Rosh Hashanah* 16a). These prayers for rain are not recited until the last day of the festival because 'rain is but a symptom of curse during Succos,' for it makes it impossible to sit in the *Succah* (*Taanis* 2a).

1. שׁוֹפְכִים לְךָ לֵב כַּמַּיִם — *Who pour out their heart to You like water.*

Pour out your heart like water in the Presence of the Lord (*Lamentations* 2:19). Since the gates of tears we never closed (*Berachos* 32b), sincere weeping assuredly will reach the Presence of the Lord (*Yismach Moshe*).

2. בָּא בָאֵשׁ וּבַמַּיִם — *The one who entered fire and water.*

[Abraham allowed himself to be thrown by Nimrod into a blazing furnace. See commentary to *hoshana* 7, st. 1.] When Abraham was on the way to the *Akeidah* with Isaac, Satan appeared in the form of a wide, deep river, attempting to block their path. They braved the obstacle and plunged into the water until it was up to their necks — then the river was removed and they proceeded on their mission undeterred (*Tanchuma, Vayeira* 22).

3. יֻקַּח־נָא ... — *Let there now be taken...*

[See commentary to *hoshana* 16, st. 2, for this allusion to Abraham's hospitality to the angels.]

4. דְגָלִים — *The banners.*

[The Israelite tribes in the Wilderness were distinguished by the colors and emblems of their banners. See commentary to *hoshana* 7, st. 4.]

גּוֹזְרֵי מַיִם — *Divisions of water.*

17
1-11

¹ **A**nswer the faithful who pour out their heart to You like water — and bring salvation now
² In the merit of the one who entered fire and and water —
³ who decreed, saying, 'Let there now be taken some water;'
and bring success now and save us, God, our Fortress.

⁴ Answer the banners who passed through divisions of water — and bring salvation now,
⁵ In the merit of the one bound at the gateway of Heaven,
⁶ who returned and dug wells of water;
and bring success now and save us, God, our Fortress.

⁷ Answer the pure ones who encamped near the water — and bring salvation now,
⁸ In the merit of the smooth-skinned one who peeled rods at the troughs of water,
⁹ Who lifted and rolled away a boulder from a well of water;
and bring success now and save us, God, our Fortress.

¹⁰ Answer the beloved heirs of the mandate likened to water — and bring salvation now,
¹¹ In the merit of those who dug with their staffs for water,

A reference to the Splitting of the Sea.

5-6. הַנֶּעֱקַד...וְחָפַר — *The one bound ...who... dug.*

[These references to Isaac are discussed in the commentary to *hoshana* 7, st. 2, and *hoshana* 16, st. 3.]

7. חוֹנִים עֲלֵי מָיִם — *Who encamped near the water.*

After leaving Marah where it was taught a number of *mitzvos*, the nation arrived at Eilim. There the people found twelve wells and seventy date trees. The seventy elders each sat under one of the trees and expounded the Torah to the twelves tribes, each of which encamped around one of the wells. *And the nation rested there near the water* (Exodus 15:27; see Rashi).

8. חָלָק — *The smooth-skinned one.*

Jacob called himself smooth-skinned in comparison to his hairy brother Esau (Genesis 27:11).

מְפַצֵּל מַקְלוֹת — *Who peeled rods.*

[This was one of the devices to which Jacob resorted to gain a just share of the flocks from Laban (Genesis 30:37-43).]

9. טָעַן וְגָל — *Who lifted and rolled.*

[Upon meeting Rachel, Jacob displayed his strength by rolling a huge stone from the mouth of a well. See Genesis 29:7-10.]

10. דָּת מְשׁוּלַת מַיִם — *The mandate likened to water.*

The Torah is compared to water: just as water runs from a high to a low place, so does Torah run from the haughty and find its place with the humble of spirit (*Taanis* 7a).

11. כָּרוּ בְמִשְׁעֲנוֹתָם — *Those who dug with their staffs.*

[This refers to the tribal princes who

יז
יב-כד

לְהָכִין לָמוֹ וּלְצֶאֱצָאֵימוֹ מָיִם. וְהַצְלִיחָה נָא.
וְהוֹשִׁיעֵנוּ אֵל מָעֻזֵּנוּ:

תַּעֲנֶה **מִ**תְחַנְּנִים כְּבִישִׁימוֹן עֲלֵי־מָיִם. וְהוֹשִׁיעָה נָּא:
לְמַעַן **נֶ**אֱמַן בַּיִת מַסְפִּיק לָעָם מָיִם.
סֶלַע הָךְ וְיָזוּבוּ מָיִם. וְהַצְלִיחָה נָא.
וְהוֹשִׁיעֵנוּ אֵל מָעֻזֵּנוּ:

תַּעֲנֶה **עוֹ**נִים עֲלֵי בְאֵר מָיִם. וְהוֹשִׁיעָה נָּא:
לְמַעַן **פָּ**קַד בְּמֵי מְרִיבַת מָיִם.
צְמֵאִים לְהַשְׁקוֹתָם מָיִם. וְהַצְלִיחָה נָא.
וְהוֹשִׁיעֵנוּ אֵל מָעֻזֵּנוּ:

תַּעֲנֶה **קְ**דוֹשִׁים מְנַסְּכִים לְךָ מָיִם. וְהוֹשִׁיעָה נָּא:
לְמַעַן **רֹ**אשׁ מְשׁוֹרְרִים כְּתָאַב שְׁתוֹת מָיִם.
שָׁב וְנָסַךְ לְךָ מָיִם. וְהַצְלִיחָה נָא.
וְהוֹשִׁיעֵנוּ אֵל מָעֻזֵּנוּ:

תַּעֲנֶה **שׁוֹ**אֲלִים בְּרִבּוּעַ אֶשְׁלֵי מָיִם. וְהוֹשִׁיעָה נָּא:
לְמַעַן **תֵּ**ל תַּלְפִּיּוֹת מוֹצָא מָיִם.
תִּפְתַּח אֶרֶץ וְתַרְעִיף שָׁמַיִם. וְהַצְלִיחָה נָא.
וְהוֹשִׁיעֵנוּ אֵל מָעֻזֵּנוּ:

drew the water to their respective tribes. See commentary to *hoshana* 16, st. 9.]

14. נֶאֱמַן בַּיִת — *The most trusted of the household.*

[This reference to Moses is discussed in the commentary to *hoshana* 16, st. 7.]

15. סֶלַע הָךְ — *Who struck the rock.*

[Soon after the Exodus, the people were without water. God commanded Moses to strike a rock, whereupon water would gush forth (*Exodus* 17:6). Although Moses struck a rock to bring water on a second occasion (*Numbers* 20:11), it is unlikely that the *paytan* refers to that incident, because there Moses was commanded to *speak*, not

strike, and he was punished for not doing so.]

16. עֲלִי בְאֵר — *Ascend, O well.*

[The song of the well is found in *Numbers* 21:17-20. It thanks God for miracles through which He saved Israel from death, among which is the well which followed them throughout their wanderings.]

17-18. [Moses was given the assignment of supplying water to the thirsty nation at a place called מַסָּה וּמְרִיבָה, *Masah and Merivah*, literally, *trial and dispute*, it was so named because of the dispute of the Children

17
12-24

¹² *to prepare, for themselves
and for their offspring, water;
and bring success now and save us, God, our Fortress.*

¹³ *Answer those who beseech as in the Wilderness
for water —   and bring salvation now,*
¹⁴ *In the merit of the most trusted of the household,
who supplied the people with water,*
¹⁵ *Who struck the rock and there flowed water,
and bring success now and save us, God, our Fortress.*

¹⁶ *Answer those who responded, 'Ascend, O well
of water' —   and bring salvation now,*
¹⁷ *In the merit of the one assigned at Merivah's waters,*
¹⁸ *to give drink to those thirsting for water;
and bring success now and save us, God, our Fortress.*

¹⁹ *Answer the holy ones who pour before You
libations of water —   and bring salvation now,*
²⁰ *in the merit of the foremost singer, who,
though thirsting to drink water,*
²¹ *poured before You a libation of water;
and bring success now and save us, God, our Fortress.*

²² *Answer those who ask with a quartet of species
planted near water —   and bring salvation now*
²³ *In the merit of the Hill of Talpios, source of water,*
²⁴ *may the earth open wide and the heavens give rain;
and bring success now and save us, God, our Fortress.*

---

of Israel and their testing of HASHEM in that place *(Exodus 17:7).*]

19. מְנַסְּכִים לְךָ מָיִם — *Who pour before You libations of water.*

[I.e., the special water libations of Succos. See commentary to *hoshana* 12, st. 31 and *hoshana* 15, st. 11.]

20⁻21. *II Samuel* 23:15-17 tells of David thirsting for water. When three of his bravest warriors risked their lives to bring him water from the cistern in Bethlehem, David refused to drink water purchased at such danger. Instead he used the water for a libation to God (see commentary to *hoshana* 16, st. 15).

22. בְּרִבּוּעַ אֶשְׁלֵי מָיִם — *With a quartet of species planted near water.*

[A reference to the *lulav, esrog,* myrtle, and willow which are held while the *hoshana* prayers are uttered.]

23. תֵּל תַּלְפִּיּוֹת — *Hill of Talpios.*

[For a selection of commentaries on this obscure reference to the Temple in Jerusalem see commentary to *hoshana* 2, st. 22.]

אָז כְּעֵינֵי עֲבָדִים

יח רַחֶם־נָא קְהַל עֲדַת יְשֻׁרוּן סְלַח וּמְחַל עֲוֹנָם.
א-י   וְהוֹשִׁיעֵנוּ אֱלֹהֵי יִשְׁעֵנוּ:

אָז כְּעֵינֵי עֲבָדִים אֶל־יַד אֲדוֹנִים.
בָּאנוּ לְפָנֶיךָ נְדוֹנִים.   וְהוֹשִׁיעֵנוּ אֱלֹהֵי יִשְׁעֵנוּ:

גֵּאֶה אֲדוֹנֵי הָאֲדוֹנִים. נִתְגָּרוּ בָנוּ מְדָנִים.
דָּשׁוּנוּ וּבְעָלוּנוּ זוּלָתְךָ אֲדוֹנִים.   וְהוֹשִׁיעֵנוּ אֱלֹהֵי יִשְׁעֵנוּ:

הֵן גַּשְׁנוּ הַיּוֹם בְּתַחֲנוּן. עָדֶיךָ רַחוּם וְחַנּוּן.
וְסִפַּרְנוּ נִפְלְאוֹתֶיךָ בְּשִׁנּוּן.   וְהוֹשִׁיעֵנוּ אֱלֹהֵי יִשְׁעֵנוּ:

זָבַת חָלָב וּדְבַשׁ. נָא אַל־תִּיבָשׁ.
חָשְׁרַת מַיִם בְּאֻבֶּיהָ תֶחְבָּשׁ.   וְהוֹשִׁיעֵנוּ אֱלֹהֵי יִשְׁעֵנוּ:

טַעֲנוּ בְשֶׁמְנָה. בְּיַד שִׁבְעָה וּשְׁמוֹנָה.
יָשָׁר צַדִּיק אֵל אֱמוּנָה.   וְהוֹשִׁיעֵנוּ אֱלֹהֵי יִשְׁעֵנוּ:

◆§ אָז כְּעֵינֵי עֲבָדִים — **Then, like the Eyes of Slaves.**

1. אָז — *Then.*

Then, in bygone days, when the Temple stood in all its glory, the nation turned only to You (*Beis Yaakov*).

כְּעֵינֵי עֲבָדִים — *Like the eyes of slaves.*

Slaves have no avenues of support other than the largesse of their master. Likewise, Israel has no source of sustenance other than its faith in God to whom it turns its eyes (*Radak to Psalms 123:2*).

Alternatively, just as the slaves cannot escape יַד אֲדוֹנֵיהֶם, *the hand of their master,* for they can turn to no one else, so we recognize that our suffering and troubles are punishments issued by Your hand, and our eyes turn to none but You for relief (*Radak* citing his father).

4. וּבְעָלוּנוּ זוּלָתְךָ אֲדוֹנִים — *Lords have ... become our masters, excluding You.*

HASHEM, our God, בְּעָלוּנוּ, they have *become our masters,* אֲדוֹנִים, *lords,* זוּלָתְךָ, *excluding You, yet [we strive] only to You, we mention Your Name (Isaiah 26:13).* The translation of זוּלָתְךָ, *excluding You,* follows *Targum. Rashi* interprets *contrary to Your will.* [This is not to say that something can be done against God's will. It is God's will that a sinful Israel be punished by exile and subjugation to human masters. However, the ultimate purpose of creation is that Israel bring holiness into a sin-free world. In attaining this perfect state Israel, and each of its members, is free to choose between right and wrong.]

6. בְּשִׁנּוּן — *And repeated* [lit. *with repetition*].

The translation is based on *Iyun Tefillah,* who interprets it as a reference to the two *Shemoneh Esrei* prayers, *Shacharis* and *Mussaf.* This is based on the Ashkenazic custom of placing the *Hoshana* service after *Mussaf.*

৽৪ Like the Eyes of Slaves

**18
1-10**   Be Merciful, please, with the congregation of Jeshurun's flock; forgive and pardon their inquities; and save us, God of our salvation.

¹ Then, like the eyes of slaves looking to
their master's hand,
² so did we come before You for judgment —
so save us, God of our salvation.

³ Proud One, Lord of lords,
they have stirred up strife within us;
⁴ Lords have trodden upon us
and become our masters, excluding You —
so save us, God of our salvation.

⁵ Indeed we have approached with supplication today,
before You, O merciful and gracious One.
⁶ And we have recounted, and repeated Your wonders
so save us, God of our salvation.

⁷ Where milk and honey flow please make not arid.
⁸ With watering clouds clothe her produce —
and save us, God of our salvation.

⁹ Plant us in the fertile land,
by the hand of seven and eight;
¹⁰ O just and righteous One, O trustworthy God
and save us, God of our salvation.

Tefillah Yesharah uses the same translation, but understands it as a reference to the two-fold praises of the *Hallel*. The first part of *Hallel* sings of the redemption from Egypt, while the second part relates to Messianic times.

Alternatively, שנון means *clearly, lucidly* (*Beis Yaakov*).

7. זָבַת חָלָב וּדְבָשׁ — *Where milk and honey flow.*

This description of *Eretz Yisrael* appears no less than twenty times in Scripture. It is first mentioned to Moses in his initial contact with God at the Burning Bush (*Exodus* 3:8). *Sforno* there explains it as a promise of a fertile land where herds of cattle will thrive [milk] and bumper crops will grow [honey refers to the sweetness of dates].

9. שִׁבְעָה וּשְׁמֹנָה — *Seven and eight.*

In prophesying about Messianic times, *Michah* 5:4 speaks of *seven shepherds and eight chiefs of humanity*. The Talmud (*Succah* 52b) identifies the seven shepherds as: David in the center, Adam, Seth and Methuselah to his right, Abraham, Jacob and Moses to his left. The eight chiefs of humanity are: Jesse, Saul, Samuel, Amos, Zephaniah,

יח כָּרַתָּ בְרִית לָאָרֶץ. עַד כָּל־יְמֵי הָאָרֶץ.
יא-כ לְבִלְתִּי פְּרָץ־בָּה פָּרֶץ. וְהוֹשִׁיעֵנוּ אֱלֹהֵי יִשְׁעֵנוּ:

מִתְחַנְּנִים עֲלֵי־מָיִם. כַּעֲרָבִים עַל־יִבְלֵי מָיִם.
נָא זְכָר־לָמוֹ נְסוּךְ הַמָּיִם. וְהוֹשִׁיעֵנוּ אֱלֹהֵי יִשְׁעֵנוּ:

שִֹיחִים בְּדֶרֶךְ מַטָּעָתָם. עוֹמְסִים בְּשַׁוְעָתָם.
עֲנֵם בְּקוֹל פְּגִיעָתָם. וְהוֹשִׁיעֵנוּ אֱלֹהֵי יִשְׁעֵנוּ:

פּוֹעֵל יְשׁוּעוֹת. פְּנֵה לְפִלּוּלָם שְׁעוֹת.
צַדְּקֵם אֵל לְמוֹשָׁעוֹת. וְהוֹשִׁיעֵנוּ אֱלֹהֵי יִשְׁעֵנוּ:

קוֹל רְגָשָׁם תִּשָּׁע. תִּפְתַּח אֶרֶץ וְיִפְרוּ יֶשַׁע.
רַב לְהוֹשִׁיעַ וְלֹא חָפֵץ רֶשַׁע. וְהוֹשִׁיעֵנוּ אֱלֹהֵי יִשְׁעֵנוּ:

שַׁעֲרֵי שָׁמַיִם פְּתַח.
וְאוֹצָרְךָ הַטּוֹב לָנוּ תִפְתַּח.
תּוֹשִׁיעֵנוּ וְרִיב אַל תִּמְתַּח.
וְהוֹשִׁיעֵנוּ אֱלֹהֵי יִשְׁעֵנוּ:

Zidkiyahu (an alternate reading has Hezekiah), Elijah and the Messiah. *Rashi* comments that he does not know from where the Talmud derives these particular lists *(Iyun Tefillah).*

Alternatively, *seven and eight* alludes to the Talmud's interpretation of the verse in *Ecclesiastes* 11:2: *Give a portion to seven and also to eight.* Seven are the days of Pesach, eight are the days of Succos [including Shemini Atzeres] *(Eruvin* 40b). Thus we ask for salvation in the merit of our observance of these two festivals *(Iyun Tefillah).*

11. עַד כָּל־יְמֵי הָאָרֶץ — *Continuously, all the days of the earth.*

After inhaling, so to speak, the sweet smell of Noah's sacrifice, God used these words in declaring that He would never again cause a cessation of the normal rotation of the seasons (see *Genesis* 8:21-22).

15. בְּדֶרֶךְ מַטָּעָתָם — *In the direction of their growth.*

Every *mitzvah* prescribed with a specific type of plant must be performed in the direction of that plant's natural growth *(Succah* 45b). For example, the Four Species must be held with their lower parts down and their upper parts up, just as they grew on their respective trees *(Rashi).*

20. וְלֹא חָפֵץ רֶשַׁע — *And desires not wickedness.*

Rashi interprets *Psalms* 5:5, from which this stich is paraphrased, as a call to rid the world of evildoers.

Alternatively, the stich may be understood according to the interpretation of *Midrash Tehillim* which relates the above verse from *Psalms* to *Ezekiel* 33:11: *I do not desire the death of the wicked one, but the wicked one's return from his way, that he may live. Repent,*

> ¹¹ *You have made a covenant with the earth,*
> *continuously, all the days of the earth,*
> ¹² *Not to cause a breach in it —*
> *so save us, God of our salvation.*
>
> ¹³ *Those who supplicate for water*
> *like willows alongside streams of water,*
> ¹⁴ *Please, remember for their sake the libations of water —*
> *and save us, God of our salvation.*
>
> ¹⁵ *Trees, in the direction of their growth,*
> *they carry as they supplicate —*
> ¹⁶ *Respond to the sound of their entreaties —*
> *and save us, God of our salvation.*
>
> ¹⁷ *Worker of salvations,*
> *heed their prayers and turn to them,*
> ¹⁸ *Adjudge them righteous, O God of salvations —*
> *and save us, God of our salvation.*
>
> ¹⁹ *To the voices of their multitudes turn,*
> *open the earth and let salvation sprout,*
> ²⁰ *O He Who is bounteous in salvation,*
> *and desires not wickedness —*
> *and save us, God of our salvation.*

Open the gates of heaven,
  and Your goodly treasure trove may You open for us,
Save us, do not let accusations be drawn out,
  and save us, God of our salvation.

---

repent from your evil ways; why should you die, O Family of Israel?

שַׁעֲרֵי שָׁמַיִם פְּתַח — *Open the gates of heaven.*

As can readily be seen from the acrostic, these next two lines are actually the final two stiches of the *hoshana*. However, they are set off from the others to be read responsively with the *chazzan*. Since these lines have been borrowed from this *hoshana* for use in the Yom Kippur *Neilah* service, where they stand alone, they are accorded the same honor here *(Beis Yaakov)*.

ARIzal explains the divergent liturgies which have arisen among the Jews: There are twelve gateways in heaven, corresponding to the twelve tribes. These are the gateways referred to in Ezekiel [48:31-34]. ARIzal teaches that each of these gateways differs from the others, therefore the prayers of each tribe [entering through these gateways] are different *(Pri Etz Chaim)*. It is these gateways that we ask God to open, that our prayers may enter *(Iyun Tefillah)*.

וְאוֹצָרְךָ הַטּוֹב — *And Your goodly treasure trove.*

[This stich is based on *Deuteronomy* 28:12 which appears at the very end of the *Hoshana* service and is explained in the commentary there.]

קול מבשר

יט
א-ה

קוֹל מְבַשֵּׂר מְבַשֵּׂר וְאוֹמֵר:

אֹמֶץ יֶשְׁעֲךָ בָּא.
קוֹל דּוֹדִי הִנֵּה־זֶה בָּא. מְבַשֵּׂר וְאוֹמֵר:
קוֹל בָּא בְּרִבְבוֹת כִּתִּים.
לַעֲמוֹד עַל הַר הַזֵּיתִים. מְבַשֵּׂר וְאוֹמֵר:
קוֹל גִּשְׁתּוֹ בַּשּׁוֹפָר לִתְקֹעַ.
תַּחְתָּיו הַר יִבָּקַע. מְבַשֵּׂר וְאוֹמֵר:
קוֹל דָּפַק וְהֵצִיץ וְזָרַח.
וּמָשׁ חֲצִי הָהָר מִמִּזְרָח. מְבַשֵּׂר וְאוֹמֵר:
קוֹל הֵקִים מִלּוּל נְאֻמוֹ.
וּבָא הוּא וְכָל־קְדוֹשָׁיו עִמּוֹ. מְבַשֵּׂר וְאוֹמֵר:

קוֹל מְבַשֵּׂר — The Voice of the Herald

Upon concluding the prayers for rain we proclaim our faith in תְּחִיַּת הַמֵּתִים, *the resurrection of the dead*, which will follow the coming of the Messiah. *Iyun Tefillah* explains the connection between these events and the rain:

R' Abuhu teaches *(Taanis 7a)*: Greater is the day of the rains than the resurrection of the dead. The resurrection will benefit only the righteous; while the rains benefit both the righteous and the wicked.

R' Chiyah bar Abba *(Bereishis Rabbah 13:6)* adds: The resurrection will benefit only man; while the rains benefit both man and beast.

Another connection between the rains and the resurrection is found in *Sanhedrin 97a*:

[These are the events which will occur] in the seven-year period preceding the arrival of the scion of David [i.e., the Messiah]: In the first year will be fulfilled the verse *(Amos 4:7): I shall pour rain upon one city, but upon another city I shall not pour rain...* [i.e., there will be bountiful areas and hunger-stricken areas*(Rashi)*]; in the second year, arrows of hunger will be dispatched; in the third, a great hunger will cause the death of men, women, and children, people of loving-kindness and good deed, and Torah will be forgotten by its students; the fourth year will bring an incomplete bounty; the fifth year [will have heavy rainfall *(Iyun Tefillah)* and] great satiety in which people will eat, drink, and make merry, and Torah will return to its students; the sixth year will be replete with rumors [of the coming of the Messiah *(Rashi)*]; the seventh will be a year of battles; in the eighth year the scion of David shall come.

The Talmud *(Pesachim 5a)* teaches that the Messiah is alluded to in the verse *(Isaiah 41:27): The first to come to Zion will say, 'Behold! Here they are!' And to Ierusalem, 'I shall dispatch*

The Voice of the Herald

19
1-5

The voice of the herald heralds and proclaims:

¹ *The strength of Your salvations comes,*
a voice — my Beloved, behold He comes —
heralds and proclaims.

² *A voice — He comes among myriad bands,*
to stand upon the Mount of Olives —
heralds and proclaims.

³ *A voice — To the blast of the shofar, He draws near,*
beneath Him the mountain shall be split —
heralds and proclaims.

⁴ *A voice — He knocks, He peers and He shines,*
and half the mountain moves from the east —
heralds and proclaims.

⁵ *A voice — He has verified the words of His utterance,*
He has come, and all His holy ones with Him —
heralds and proclaims.

מְבַשֵּׂר, *herald.*' Based on the verse (*Malachi* 3:23): *Behold! I send you Elijah the prophet, before the arrival of the great and awesome day of HASHEM,* the מְבַשֵּׂר, *herald,* is identified as אֵלִיָּהוּ, *Elijah* (*Kol Bo*).

The voice of this 'herald' will proclaim many things about the coming of the Messiah and the subsequent resurrection. The *paytan* constructs each line (except the first) of this *hoshana* similarly — first comes the word קוֹל, *a voice;* then a parenthetical stich, and finally מְבַשֵּׂר וְאוֹמֵר, *heralds and proclaims* [lit. *says*]. These three words קוֹל מְבַשֵּׂר וְאוֹמֵר, *a voice heralds and proclaims,* should be treated as one phrase despite the intervening words of the stich (*Avodas Yisrael*).

1. אֹמֶץ — *The strength.*
Most *siddurim* contain this reading. However *Kol Bo* and *Avodas Yisrael* follow the reading of *Machzor Roma:* אָמֵן, *the faithfulness,* i.e., Your salvation for which we have striven faithfully.

2-5. The next four stiches are based on Zechariah 14:4-5, which reads:

His feet shall stand that day upon the Mount of Olives, which is to the east of Jerusalem, and the Mount of Olives shall be split in half, along the east-west line, a very great rift. Half the mountain shall move northward, and its other half, southward... HASHEM, my God, has come, all His holy ones with Him.

2. רִבְבוֹת כִּתִּים — *Myriad bands.*
This refers to bands of ministering angels (see comm. to st. 5).

3. שׁוֹפָר — *Shofar.*
And it will come to pass on that day, a great shofar will be blown; those lost in the land of Assyria will come, and those ousted to the land of Egypt; and they will bow to HASHEM upon the holy mountain in Jerusalem (Isaiah 27:13).

5. *Avodas Yisrael* reads קְדוֹשִׁים, *holy ones,* omitting the pronoun *His.*

יט	קוֹל **וּ**לְכָל־בָּאֵי הָעוֹלָם.	
ו-טז	בַּת־קוֹל יִשָּׁמַע בָּעוֹלָם.	מְבַשֵּׂר וְאוֹמֵר:
	קוֹל **ז**ֶרַע עֲמוּסֵי רַחֲמוֹ.	
	נוֹלְדוּ כְיֶלֶד מִמְּעֵי אִמּוֹ.	מְבַשֵּׂר וְאוֹמֵר:
	קוֹל **ח**ָלָה וְיָלְדָה מִי זֹאת.	
	מִי שָׁמַע כָּזֹאת.	מְבַשֵּׂר וְאוֹמֵר:
	קוֹל **ט**ָהוֹר פָּעַל כָּל־אֵלֶּה.	
	וּמִי רָאָה כָּאֵלֶּה.	מְבַשֵּׂר וְאוֹמֵר:
	קוֹל **י**ֶשַׁע וּזְמַן הַוּחַד.	
	הֲיוּחַל אֶרֶץ בְּיוֹם אֶחָד.	מְבַשֵּׂר וְאוֹמֵר:
	קוֹל **כ**ַּבִּיר רוֹם וָתַחַת.	
	אִם־יִוָּלֵד גּוֹי פַּעַם אֶחָת.	מְבַשֵּׂר וְאוֹמֵר:
	קוֹל **ל**ְעֵת יִגְאַל עַמּוֹ נָאוֹר.	
	וְהָיָה לְעֵת־עֶרֶב יִהְיֶה־אוֹר.	מְבַשֵּׂר וְאוֹמֵר:
	קוֹל **מ**וֹשִׁיעִים יַעֲלוּ לְהַר צִיּוֹן.	
	כִּי־חָלָה גַּם־יָלְדָה צִיּוֹן.	מְבַשֵּׂר וְאוֹמֵר:
	קוֹל **נ**ִשְׁמַע בְּכָל־גְּבוּלֵךְ.	
	הַרְחִיבִי מְקוֹם אָהֳלֵךְ.	מְבַשֵּׂר וְאוֹמֵר:
	קוֹל **שׂ**ִימִי עַד דַּמֶּשֶׂק מִשְׁכְּנוֹתַיִךְ.	
	קַבְּלִי בָנַיִךְ וּבְנוֹתַיִךְ.	מְבַשֵּׂר וְאוֹמֵר:

7. עֲמוּסֵי רַחֲמוֹ — *Borne [by Him] from the womb.*

Listen to Me, O House of Jacob, and the remnant of the House of Israel, who have been borne from the belly, who have carried from the womb (Isaiah 46:3). God has carried the Jewish nation since its inception, unlike the false gods which are borne by their adherents' animals (*Mahari Kara*).

8-13. Who has heard the like of this? Who has seen the like of these? Can the earth deliver issue in but one day? Can a nation be born in a trice? For Zion has delivered and borne her children (Isaiah 66:8). Can it be imagined that the complete nation would arise from the exile in one day to populate the desolate land of Israel? (*Metzudos*).

8. מִי זֹאת — *Who is this?*
[For an interpretation of this reference to Israel, see comm. to *hoshana* 13, st. 16.]

12. וְהָיָה לְעֵת־עֶרֶב יִהְיֶה־אוֹר — *At*

19
6-15

⁶ *A voice — To all who walk the earth,*
a heavenly voice is heard on the earth —
heralds and proclaims.

⁷ *A voice — The seed borne by Him from the womb,*
born like a child from its mother's innards —
heralds and proclaims.

⁸ *A voice — She delivered and gave birth: 'Who is this?*
Who has heard the likes of this?' —
heralds and proclaims.

⁹ *A voice — The pure One has done all these;*
and who has seen the like of these? —
heralds and proclaims.

¹⁰ *A voice — Salvation and its moment were ordained.*
Can the earth deliver issue in a single day? —
heralds and proclaims.

¹¹ *A voice — He Who is mighty above and below,*
can a nation be born in a trice? —
heralds and proclaims.

¹² *A voice — when the resplendent One redeems His nation,*
at evening time there will be light —
heralds and proclaims.

¹³ *A voice — Saviors shall ascend upon Mount Zion,*
for Zion has delivered and given birth —
heralds and proclaims.

¹⁴ *A voice — It is heard within all your boundaries,*
'Expand the area of your tents!' —
heralds and proclaims.

¹⁵ *A voice — Set up your dwellings until Damesek,*
receive your sons and your daughters —
heralds and proclaims.

---

evening time there will be light.
R' Elazar cites *Zechariah* 14:7 from which this stich is taken verbatim, to prove that the entire duration of Israel's exile under the Four Kingdoms [see ArtScroll *Daniel*, p. 102ff; and ArtScroll *Zemiroth*, p. 170ff)] is but one day in the eyes of God. And before that day draws to a close the radiance of the redemption will shine for Israel, and *at evening time there will be light* (*Yalkut Shimoni* II, 585).

13. מוֹשִׁיעִים — *Saviors.*
[For an explanation of the plural usage see comm. to *hoshana* 15, st. 13.]
Avodas Yisrael reads בְּהַר, lit., in Mount...

14-15. הַרְחִיבִי מְקוֹם אָהֳלֵךְ...עַד דַּמֶּשֶׂק — *Expand the area of your tents...until Damesek.*
Isaiah 54:2 calls upon the desolate Jerusalem to expand its boundaries to enable it to accommodate all those

יט	קוֹל עָלְזִי חֲבַצֶּלֶת הַשָּׁרוֹן.
טז-כב	
מְבַשֵּׂר וְאוֹמֵר:	כִּי קָמוּ יְשֵׁנֵי חֶבְרוֹן.
	קוֹל פְּנוּ אֵלַי וְהִוָּשֵׁעוּ.
מְבַשֵּׂר וְאוֹמֵר:	הַיּוֹם אִם בְּקוֹלִי תִשְׁמָעוּ.
	קוֹל צֶמַח אִישׁ צֶמַח שְׁמוֹ.
מְבַשֵּׂר וְאוֹמֵר:	הוּא דָוִד בְּעַצְמוֹ.
	קוֹל קוּמוּ כְּפוּשֵׁי עָפָר.
מְבַשֵּׂר וְאוֹמֵר:	הָקִיצוּ וְרַנְּנוּ שׁוֹכְנֵי עָפָר.
	קוֹל רַבָּתִי עָם בְּהַמְלִיכוֹ.
מְבַשֵּׂר וְאוֹמֵר:	מִגְדּוֹל יְשׁוּעוֹת מַלְכּוֹ.
	קוֹל שָׁם רְשָׁעִים לְהַאֲבִיד.
מְבַשֵּׂר וְאוֹמֵר:	עֹשֶׂה־חֶסֶד לִמְשִׁיחוֹ לְדָוִד.
	קוֹל תִּנָּה יְשׁוּעוֹת לְעַם עוֹלָם.
מְבַשֵּׂר וְאוֹמֵר:	לְדָוִד וּלְזַרְעוֹ עַד עוֹלָם.

קוֹל מְבַשֵּׂר מְבַשֵּׂר וְאוֹמֵר:
קוֹל מְבַשֵּׂר מְבַשֵּׂר וְאוֹמֵר:
קוֹל מְבַשֵּׂר מְבַשֵּׂר וְאוֹמֵר:

returning from the exile. Zechariah 9:1 prophesies that these new boundaries will reach all the way to Damesek (see Rashi there). [For a discussion on the location of Damesek and whether it is identical with the present day city of Damascus, see ArtScroll Ezekiel 47:16.]

16. חֲבַצֶּלֶת הַשָּׁרוֹן — *Rose of Sharon.*

חֲבַצֶּלֶת and שׁוֹשַׁנָּה both means *rose.* When the flower is still a freshly-emerged bud covered by its own shadow [חֲבוּיָה בְּצִלּוֹ] it is called חֲבַצֶּלֶת, *chavatzeles,* literally, *covered by shadow,* when it is in full bloom it is called שׁוֹשַׁנָּה.

שָׁרוֹן, *Sharon,* is midrashically identified with שִׁירָה, *song.* Israel, as an emergent nation, covered by the shadow of Egyptian exile, was redeemed and sang שִׁירָה, *a song of thanksgiving,* at the Sea of Reds (*Midrash Shir HaShirim* 2:1).

יְשֵׁנֵי חֶבְרוֹן — *Those sleeping in Hebron.*

This refers to the Patriarchs and Matriarchs of the nation [Adam and Eve, Abraham and Sarah, Isaac and Rebecca, Jacob and Leah], who are buried in the Cave of Machpelah in Hebron (*Avodas Yisrael; Iyun Tefillah*).

17. פְּנוּ אֵלַי וְהִוָּשֵׁעוּ — *Turn to Me and you shall be saved.*

This verse from *Isaiah* 45:22 reads in full: *Turn to Me and you shall be saved, all who dwell at the ends of the earth, for I am God, there is no other.*

18. צֶמַח שְׁמוֹ — *Tzemach is his name.*

In *Zechariah* 6:12 (see commentaries there) this phrase refers to both

19 ¹⁶ *A voice — Be joyous, O rose of Sharon,*
16-22   *for those sleeping in Hebron have arisen —*
                              heralds and proclaims.
 ¹⁷ *A voice — Turn to Me and you shall be saved*
   this very day — if you will but heed My voice —
                              heralds and proclaims.
 ¹⁸ *A voice — A man has sprouted, Tzemach is his name,*
      He is David himself —heralds and proclaims.
 ¹⁹ *A voice — Arise, you who are covered with dust;*
      awake and sing, you who lie in the dust —
                              heralds and proclaims.
 ²⁰ *A voice — When he rules the city great with people,*
   his king shall be a tower of salvations —
                              heralds and proclaims.
 ²¹ *A voice — The name of the wicked He will cause to be lost,*
   but he will show loving-kindness to His anointed,
   to David —   *heralds and proclaims.*
 ²² *A voice — Grant salvations to the eternal nation,*
   to David and to his descendants, forever —
                              heralds and proclaims.

The voice of the herald heralds and proclaims.
The voice of the herald heralds and proclaims.
The voice of the herald heralds and proclaims.

Zerubavel, builder of the Second Temple, and his descendant, the Messiah, who will build the Third Temple.

הוּא דָוִד בְּעַצְמוֹ — *He is David, himself.*

If Tzemach is the Messiah, scion of David, how can the *paytan* call him 'David himself'? *Sanhedrin* 98b discusses the Messiah's name. After various opinions are stated, R' Yehudah cites Rav: The Holy One Blessed be He will in the future enthrone a second David [i.e., the Messiah's name will be David] who will be the ruler, while the first David will be his viceroy (*Iyun Tefillah*).

Alternatively, David's pure soul will be reincarnated in the body of the Messiah so that he is truly David himself (*Beis Yaakov; Shaar HaShamayim;* see also *Overview* to ArtScroll *Psalms,* p. 51).

20-22. He Who is a tower of salvations to His king and shows loving-kindness to His anointed, to David and his descendants forever (II Samuel 22:51). This same verse is found in *Psalms* 18:51 where the word מַגְדִּל, *He Who makes great,* is substituted for מִגְדּוֹל, *He Who is a tower.* *Midrash Tehillim* explains that salvation of the Jews will come in gradual stages, similar to the rising sun whose first rays appear across the horizon as a weak light, which keeps growing in intensity. Initially, the sign of salvation will be barely discernible, but God will *make great the salvation* so that when the Messiah does come, *He will be a tower of salvations.*

Avodas Yisrael reads מַגְדִּיל, *make great.*

רַבָּתִי עָם — *The city great with people.*
[This description of Jerusalem is from *Lamentations* 1:1.] See *hosh.* 16 st. 20.

הוֹשִׁיעָה אֶת־עַמֶּךָ וּבָרֵךְ אֶת־נַחֲלָתֶךָ, וּרְעֵם וְנַשְּׂאֵם עַד־הָעוֹלָם: וְיִהְיוּ דְבָרַי אֵלֶּה אֲשֶׁר הִתְחַנַּנְתִּי לִפְנֵי יהוה קְרֹבִים אֶל־יהוה אֱלֹהֵינוּ יוֹמָם וָלָיְלָה, לַעֲשׂוֹת מִשְׁפַּט עַבְדּוֹ וּמִשְׁפַּט עַמּוֹ יִשְׂרָאֵל דְּבַר־יוֹם בְּיוֹמוֹ: לְמַעַן דַּעַת כָּל־עַמֵּי הָאָרֶץ כִּי יהוה הוּא הָאֱלֹהִים, אֵין עוֹד:

[The Ark is closed and the chazzan says Kaddish.]

קדיש

יִתְגַּדַּל וְיִתְקַדַּשׁ שְׁמֵהּ רַבָּא. (אמן)

בְּעָלְמָא דִּי בְרָא כִרְעוּתֵהּ. וְיַמְלִיךְ מַלְכוּתֵהּ. (וְיַצְמַח פֻּרְקָנֵהּ וִיקָרֵב מְשִׁיחֵהּ. אמן)

בְּחַיֵּיכוֹן וּבְיוֹמֵיכוֹן וּבְחַיֵּי דְכָל בֵּית יִשְׂרָאֵל. בַּעֲגָלָא וּבִזְמַן קָרִיב. וְאִמְרוּ אָמֵן: אמן

יְהֵא שְׁמֵהּ רַבָּא מְבָרַךְ לְעָלַם וּלְעָלְמֵי עָלְמַיָּא:

יִתְבָּרַךְ וְיִשְׁתַּבַּח וְיִתְפָּאַר וְיִתְרוֹמַם וְיִתְנַשֵּׂא וְיִתְהַדָּר וְיִתְעַלֶּה וְיִתְהַלָּל שְׁמֵהּ דְּקֻדְשָׁא בְּרִיךְ הוּא. בְּרִיךְ הוּא [אמן]

לְעֵלָּא מִן כָּל בִּרְכָתָא וְשִׁירָתָא תֻּשְׁבְּחָתָא וְנֶחֱמָתָא. דַּאֲמִירָן בְּעָלְמָא. וְאִמְרוּ אָמֵן: אמן

קהל: קַבֵּל בְּרַחֲמִים וּבְרָצוֹן אֶת תְּפִלָּתֵנוּ:

תִּתְקַבֵּל צְלוֹתְהוֹן וּבָעוּתְהוֹן דְּכָל בֵּית יִשְׂרָאֵל קֳדָם אֲבוּהוֹן דִּי בִשְׁמַיָּא. וְאִמְרוּ אָמֵן: אמן

קהל: יְהִי שֵׁם יהוה מְבֹרָךְ מֵעַתָּה וְעַד עוֹלָם:

יְהֵא שְׁלָמָא רַבָּא מִן שְׁמַיָּא. וְחַיִּים (טוֹבִים). עָלֵינוּ וְעַל כָּל יִשְׂרָאֵל. וְאִמְרוּ אָמֵן: אמן

קהל: עֶזְרִי מֵעִם יהוה עֹשֵׂה שָׁמַיִם וָאָרֶץ:

עֹשֶׂה שָׁלוֹם בִּמְרוֹמָיו. הוּא יַעֲשֶׂה שָׁלוֹם עָלֵינוּ וְעַל כָּל יִשְׂרָאֵל. וְאִמְרוּ אָמֵן: אמן

22. עַם עוֹלָם — *The eternal nation.*
In his commentary to Isaiah 44:7, Rashi, followed by most commentators, translates עַם עוֹלָם as *the nation of the world,* i.e., all of God's creatures. The *paytan* obviously does not use the term in this manner. *Iyun Tefillah* sees this as a reference to עַם ה׳, HASHEM's nation, [perhaps interpreting עוֹלָם as *Eternal One.*]

Save Your nation and bless Your heritage, tend them and elevate them forever. May these words of mine, which I have supplicated before HASHEM, be near to HASHEM, our God, by day and by night; that He bring about justice for His servant and justice for His people, Israel, each day's need in its day; that all the peoples of the earth shall know that HASHEM is God, there is no other.

[The Ark is closed and the chazzan says Kaddish]

⋄§ Kaddish

May His great Name be exalted and sanctified
            Congregation responds: *Amen.*
in the world He created according to His will;
And may He establish His Kingship
  (and cause His salvation to sprout and bring near His Messiah —
           Congregation responds: *Amen.*)
During your lifetime and during your days
  and during the lifetime of the entire Family of Israel,
  swiftly and soon.   **Now respond: Amen.**
            Congregation responds: *Amen.*

 Congregation responds following stich aloud, and *chazzan* repeats:
 May His great Name be blessed forever and ever.
Blessed, lauded, glorified, extolled,
  upraised, honored, elevated, and praised
Be the Name of the Holy One, Blessed be He —
    Congregation responds: *Blessed be He.* (Some respond: *Amen*).
Beyond all blessings, songs, praises, and consolations
  that are uttered on earth. **Now respond: Amen.**
            Congregation responds: *Amen.*

 Congregation: *Accept our prayers with mercy and favor.*
May the prayers and supplications
  of the entire Family of Israel
Be accepted before their Father
  Who is in Heaven.   **Now respond: Amen.**
            Congregation responds: *Amen.*

 Congregation: *May the Name of HASHEM be blessed from now to eternity.*
May there be abundant peace from Heaven,
  and (good) life, upon us and upon all Israel.
           Now respond: Amen.
            Congregation responds: *Amen.*

 Congregation: *My help is from HASHEM — Maker of heaven and earth.*
He Who makes peace in His heights,
  may He make peace upon us,
  and upon all Israel.   **Now respond: Amen.**
            Congregation responds: *Amen.*

יְהִי רָצוֹן

[Some recite Psalm 29 which speaks of seven voices alluding to the prayers said during the hakafos.] The Hoshana-bundle is beaten on the ground [ARIzal used exactly five twigs and beat them exactly five times], after which the following is said:

יְהִי רָצוֹן מִלְּפָנֶיךָ יהוה אֱלֹהֵינוּ וֵאלֹהֵי אֲבוֹתֵינוּ, הַבּוֹחֵר בִּנְבִיאִים טוֹבִים וּבְמִנְהֲגֵיהֶם הַטּוֹבִים, שֶׁתְּקַבֵּל בְּרַחֲמִים וּבְרָצוֹן אֶת־תְּפִלָּתֵנוּ וְהַקָּפוֹתֵינוּ, וְזָכָר־לָנוּ זְכוּת שִׁבְעַת תְּמִימֶיךָ, וְתָסִיר מְחִיצַת הַבַּרְזֶל הַמַּפְסֶקֶת בֵּינֵינוּ וּבֵינֶיךָ, וְתַאֲזִין שַׁוְעָתֵנוּ, וְתֵיטִיב לָנוּ הַחֲתִימָה, תֹּלֶה אֶרֶץ עַל־בְּלִימָה. וְחָתְמֵנוּ בְּסֵפֶר חַיִּים טוֹבִים. וְהַיּוֹם הַזֶּה תִּתֵּן בִּשְׁכִינַת עֻזֶּךָ חֲמִשָּׁה גְּבוּרוֹת מְמֻתָּקוֹת עַל־יְדֵי חֲבִיטַת עֲרָבָה מִנְהַג נְבִיאֶיךָ הַקְּדוֹשִׁים. וְתִתְעוֹרֵר הָאַהֲבָה בֵּינֵיהֶם, וּתְנַשְּׁקֵנוּ מִנְּשִׁיקוֹת פִּיךָ, מַמְתֶּקֶת כָּל־הַגְּבוּרוֹת וְכָל־הַדִּינִין, וְתָאִיר

יְהִי רָצוֹן — May It be Favorable

וּבְמִנְהֲגֵיהֶם הַטּוֹבִים — **And their good customs.**
The beating of the willow is a custom ordained by the prophets [see Overview]. Tehillas Hashem reads וּבְמִנְהָגִים טוֹבִים, and good customs.

שִׁבְעַת תְּמִימֶיךָ — **Your seven perfect ones.**
This is an allusion to the seven patriarchs: Abraham, Isaac, Jacob, Moses, Aaron, Joseph, and David (see commentary to end of hoshana 1).

מְחִיצַת הַבַּרְזֶל — **The iron partition.**
Sinful acts build and maintain partitions between the sinner and the spark of holiness which is his source of spiritual life. As one gets deeper and deeper into the ways of evil the partition built by his actions is strengthened until it has the strength of iron, while the prison in which his spark of holiness is confined becomes more and more impermeable. Only repentance can breach the partition and extricate that spark of holiness (see Tanya 1:17).

הַחֲתִימָה — **The seal.**
On Hoshanah Rabbah the final seal is placed on the verdict issued on Rosh HaShanah and tentatively sealed on Yom Kippur (see preface to hoshana 1).

תֹּלֶה אֶרֶץ עַל־בְּלִימָה — **He Who suspends the earth upon silence.**
The word בְּלִימָה, here translated silence, is a combination of two words, בְּלִי, without, מָה, anything (Ibn Ezra to Job 26:7; see commentary to hoshana 5, st. 22).

בְּסֵפֶר חַיִּים טוֹבִים — **In the Book of Good Life.**
Three books are opened by the Heavenly Tribunal on Rosh HaShanah; one for the totally wicked, one for the perfectly righteous and one for those between these extremes. The perfectly righteous are inscribed and immediately sealed with a verdict of life. The totally wicked are inscribed and immediately sealed with a verdict of death. The judgment of those in between stands suspended from Rosh HaShanah until Yom Kippur. If [during that period] they prove worthy they are inscribed

◆§ May it be Favorable

[Some recite *Psalm* 29 which speaks of seven voices alluding to the prayers said during the *hakafos*.] The *Hoshana*-bundle is beaten on the ground [ARIzal used exactly five twigs and beat them exactly five times], after which the following is said:

May it be favorable before You, HASHEM, our God and God of our fathers, He Who opts for good prophets and their good customs, that You accept with mercy and favor our prayers and our hakafah-circuits. Remember for our sake the merit of Your seven perfect ones. Remove the iron partition separating us from You. Hearken to our pleas and grant us the good seal, He Who suspends the earth upon silence. Seal us in the Book of Good Life. Today may You place, with the manifestation of Your strength, five strict powers which have been sweetened through the beating of willows, the custom ordained by Your holy prophets. May You awaken love among them and kiss us with the kisses of Your mouth, which sweeten all the strict powers and all the harsh judgments. May

for life. If they are not found worthy they are inscribed for death (*Rosh HaShanah* 16b).

וְהַיּוֹם הַזֶּה... — *Today*...
The entire section beginning *Today may You place*... and ending בִּתְשׁוּבָה שְׁלֵמָה לְפָנֶיךָ, *with wholehearted repentance before You*, is omitted by *Avodas Yisrael*.[1]

חֲמִשָּׁה גְבוּרוֹת — *Five strict powers*.
Five of the twenty-two letters of the *aleph-beis* have two forms: כְּפוּפָה, *bent*, and פְּשׁוּטָה, *straight*. They are the letters [מנצפ״ך סוֹףְ״ץ]. Their straight forms are usually called סוֹפִית, *concluding* [letters], because they are used at the end of a word. Since these letters are in a sense restraining forces which force a halt in speaking they are called גְבוּרוֹת, *strict powers*. These letters are the כֵּלִים, *vessels*, within which are contained that minute portion of God's infinite being which can be conceived by finite people (*Tanya* 2:4).

[The five-time beating of the aravah branches symbolizes the breaking of the five vessels which restrain the revelation of the full force of holiness. The beating of the branches thus causes a 'sweetening' of the strict powers.]

בֵּינֵיהֶם — *Among them*.
Tehillas Hashem omits this word.

נְשִׁיקוֹת פִּיךָ — *The kisses of Your mouth*.
God's love for Israel is expressed in terms of embrace (*Song of Songs* 2:6) and kisses (*ibid* 1:2). Embrace is an action and refers to the coupling of acts of man with acts of God through the performance of *mitzvos* and deeds of kindness. Such action brings God to embrace Israel. Kissing brings mouth to mouth — the word of man unites with the word of God through the study of the holy Torah (*Tanya* 1:45).

[Torah study is the superior method by which the vessels containing the contracted Divine manifestation may be broken, that the full glory of the *Shechinah* may be revealed.]

---

1. In place of the omitted portion which is heavy in Kabbalistic overtones, *Avodas Yisrael* has: וּתְהִי חֲשׁוּבָה לְפָנֶיךָ מַחֲשַׁבְתֵּנוּ בַּחֲבִיטַת הָעֲרָבָה כְּאִלּוּ כִּוַּנּוּ בָהּ בְּכָל הַכַּוָּנוֹת כְּתִקּוּנָן וְתַשְׁפִּיעַ לָנוּ אוֹר הַחַיִּים, *May our thoughts upon beating the willow be reckoned before You as if we had all the proper intentions in mind while doing it, and may You endow us with the light of life.*

לִשְׁכִינַת עֻזֶּךְ בְּשֵׁם יוּ״ד הֵ״א וָא״ו שֶׁהוּא טַל אוֹרֹת טַלָּךְ, וּמִשָּׁם תַּשְׁפִּיעַ שֶׁפַע לְעַבְדְּךָ הַמִּתְנַפֵּל לְפָנֶיךָ, מְחִילָה, שֶׁתַּאֲרִיךְ יָמַי וְתִמְחָל־לִי חֲטָאַי וַעֲוֹנוֹתַי וּפְשָׁעַי, וְתִפְשׁוֹט יְמִינְךָ וְיָדְךָ לְקַבְּלֵנִי בִּתְשׁוּבָה שְׁלֵמָה לְפָנֶיךָ, וְאוֹצָרְךָ הַטּוֹב תִּפְתַּח לְהַשְׂבִּיעַ מַיִם נֶפֶשׁ שׁוֹקֵקָה, כְּמוֹ שֶׁכָּתוּב, יִפְתַּח יהוה לְךָ אֶת־אוֹצָרוֹ הַטּוֹב אֶת־הַשָּׁמַיִם לָתֵת מְטַר־אַרְצְךָ בְּעִתּוֹ וּלְבָרֵךְ אֵת כָּל־מַעֲשֵׂה יָדֶךָ: אָמֵן:

יוּ״ד הֵ״א וָא״ו — *Yud Hei Vav.*
These three letters are the beginning of the Ineffable Name of God and represent the descent of the Divine to the corporeal. The fourth letter ה׳ represents the *Shechinah.*

More specifically, the י, *yud*, is a mere dot, symbolizing Divine Wisdom. As this seminal wisdom expands, it develops into a revelation which the human intellect can grasp and understand. This expansion is represented by the letter ה, *hei.* The top of the *hei* resembles a widened *yud*, indicating a broadening of understanding, while the legs extending downward indicate a downward flow of this wisdom. The continued downward flow is represented by the shape of the ו, *vav.* The numerical value of *vav* is six, alluding to the first six of the *sefirah*-emanations. The seventh *sefirah* מלכות, *Kingship* [see commentary following *hoshana* 1], is represented by the final ה, *hei*, of the Holy Name *(Tanya* 3:4). God's Kingship on earth is manifested through the *Shechinah* which represents His Presence in a perceptible manner. Thus we pray that the *Shechinah*, represented by the final *hei*, be illuminated by the Divine Wisdom represented by the *yud, hei, vav,* of the Ineffable Name, thus bringing about a perfect unification of the Holy Name (see commentary to *hoshana* 1, st. 6).

טַל — *Dew.*
The numerical value of יוּ״ד הֵ״א וָא״ו, *yud hei vav*, is thirty-nine. the same as the value of טַל, *dew.*

טַל אוֹרֹת טַלָּךְ — *Your dew is the dew of lights.*
This phrase is borrowed from *Isaiah* 26:19. *Rashi* there explains: It is fitting that the dew given as a reward for Torah study and performance of *mitzvos* be an illuminating dew. *Ibn Ezra* renders *dew with light.*
Radak, however, translates אוֹרֹת as a species of vegetable. Thus טַל אוֹרֹת is *dew capable of sustaining vegetables.* Just as the dew brings the plants to life so does God awaken the dead to eternal life.

עַבְדְּךָ — *Your servant.*
Kol Bo has the worshiper insert his name and the name of his mother — e.g., Your servant Isaac the son of Sarah — at this point. [This usage is based on the verse: *Please, HASHEM, for I am Your servant the son of Your maid (Psalms* 116:16), *Rashi* explains: The performance of a servant bought at the auction block cannot compare to that of one born into the household.]

הַמִּתְנַפֵּל — *Who prostrates himself.*
Some *siddurim* read הַמִּתְפַּלֵּל, *who prays (Tefillah Yesharah; Kol Bo; Tehillas Hashem).*

מְחִילָה — *Forgiveness.*
Tehillas Hashem omits this word.

לְהַשְׂבִּיעַ מַיִם נֶפֶשׁ שׁוֹקֵקָה — *To satisfy with water a thirsty soul.*
שׁוֹקֵקָה is an intensified form of שׁוֹק which means *desire.* Our translation of *thirsty* is based on the reference to water here, and on the use of this word in

you illuminate the manifestation of Your strength with the Name Yud Hei Vav which corresponds to the dew — Your dew is the dew of lights. From there endow Your servant, who prostrates himself before You, with forgiveness, that my days may be lengthened. Forgive me my sins, my iniquities, and my transgressions. Spread wide Your right arm and Your hand to accept me, with my wholehearted repentance before You. Open Your goodly treasure trove to satisfy with water a thirsty soul — as it is written: May HASHEM open for you His goodly treasure trove, the heavens, to give your land rain in its season and to bless all of your handiwork. Amen.

Psalms 107:9 where נֶפֶשׁ שׁוֹקֵקָה, a thirsty soul, appears in apposition to נֶפֶשׁ רְעֵבָה, a hungry soul.

Although on a simple level this part of the prayer must be taken in its obvious meaning as a prayer for rain, if the tenor of this prayer, which until this point has dealt exclusively with spiritual matters, is to continue on that lofty plane, then the reference to thirst and water must be seen as more than of just material nature.

My soul thirsts for God, the living God (Psalms 42:3). The prophet compares the perception of God achieved through Torah study to the satisfaction derived by a thirsty man drinking water: הוֹי כָּל־צָמֵא לְכוּ לַמַּיִם, Ho, everyone who thirsts, go to water (Isaiah 55:1).

Radak explains that just as the world cannot exist without water, so it cannot exist without Torah.

Amos 8:11 is even more specific.

'Behold, days are coming,' says HASHEM / ELOHIM, 'when I shall send a hunger upon the land; neither a hunger for bread nor a thirst for water, but only to hear the words of HASHEM.'

כְּמוֹ שֶׁכָּתוּב — As it is written.

Avodas Yisrael reads וִיקַיֵּם בָּנוּ מִקְרָא שֶׁכָּתוּב, and fulfill for us the verse in which is written...

יִפְתַּח ה׳ לְךָ... — May HASHEM open for you...

This verse (Deuteronomy 28:12) is elucidated in the Talmud:

Only God Himself can open the floodgates of rain. Three keys were not given over to the angels but are held in God's hand, so to speak. One of these is the key to the storehouse of rain, as it is written: May HASHEM [personally, not His emissary (Rashi)] open for you His goodly treasure trove...to give your land rain in its season (Taanis 2a).

תם ונשלם
שבח לאל בורא עולם

APPENDIX
The Custom of Hakafos on Succos and Hoshana Rabbah

by Rabbi Hersh Goldwurm

◆§ Sources of the Custom

On each day of Succos, a Torah Scroll is brought to the *bimah* [the table from which the Torah is read] and the congregation, each person with his Four Species in hand circles the *bimah* while reciting the *Hoshana* liturgy of the day. On the first six days of Succos, one *hakafah* [circuit] is made, and on Hoshana Rabbah seven *hakafos* are made.

Though this custom is not mentioned in the Talmud it is found in the *siddurim* of *R' Amram* and *R' Saadyah* and, indeed, it may very well have been practiced even in Talmudic times.[1] The liturgy said during the *hakafos* by Ashkenazic communities was composed by *R' Elazar HaKalir*, one of the earliest composers of liturgy (according to *Tosafos, Chagigah* 13a s.v. ורגלי, he was a tanna). *Rambam (Hilchos Lulav* 7:23) writes: All Israel has adapted the custom to place the *bimah* in the middle of the synagogue and circle it every day as they did in the Temple, in commemoration of the Temple service.

Vilna Gaon (Orach Chaim 660:1) adduces a source from the Midrash (*Yalkut Shimoni, Psalms* 26) where R' Chiya, a first generation amora, says of the practice of *hakafah*-circuits around the altar that it was in memory of the circuits made around Jericho. He continues, 'This is well in the days of the Temple, but in our days the *chazzan* of the synagogue stands like an angel of God, Sefer Torah on his arm, the people circling him as if he were the altar. *Ohr Zarua, Rokeach* and *Shibbolei HaLeket* cite R' Chiya's statement as appearing in *Yerushalmi*, although it is not found in presently available editions.

However R' Sherira Gaon (in a responsum quoted by R' Yitzchak ibn Giath, *Meah Shearim* p. 114) maintains that even in the Temple they did not walk around the altar, but merely stood around it in a circle. He concludes that the accepted custom of making a procession around the *bimah* is an innovation [חידוש הוא]. Nevertheless, this responsum demonstrates that the custom of *hakafos* was universally known and accepted in R' Sherira's time.

In Temple times, the *hakafos* were done around the altar; nowadays they are made around the *bimah*, where one of the congregants stands, *Sefer Torah* in hand (as described in the above cited *Yalkut*). *Vilna Gaon* (660:2) explains that the Torah Scroll serves as our substitute for the altar and its sacrifices. As the Sages teach (*Megillah* 31b): God promised Abraham at the 'Covenant between the Parts' that in post-Temple times, study of the סֵדֶר הַקָּרְבָּנוֹת, *procedure of sacrifices*, would take the place of actual sacrifices.

◆§ Does one make hakafos even without a lulav?

This question is involved in the controversy between R' Elazar and R' Chanina (*Succah* 43b) as to whether the

---

1. *Ba'al Halttur (Asseres HaDibros* p. 186) asserts that the מִנְהַג נְבִיאִים, *custom of the prophets,* alluded to in the Gemara (*Succah* 44a) includes the *hakafos* around the *bimah*. However he limits this to the seven *hakafos* made with willow twigs on Hoshana Rabbah. Thus even according to him, the *hakafos* on the first six days of Succos have no Talmudic basis. Indeed *Shibbolei HaLeket* (369), who cites *Ba'al Halttur* testifies that the custom of Italian communities in his time was to make *hakafos* on Hoshana Rabbah only. On the other days, *Hoshanos* were recited without making the circuit around the *bimah*.

hakafah in the Temple was done with the lulav in hand [i.e., all Four Species] or only with the willow branches (see commentary to ArtScroll Mishnah Succah 4:5). This appears to be tied by the Gemara to the question (discussed loc. cit.) of whether the willows were בְּנְטִילָה, taken, i.e., held in hand during the circuits, or whether they were merely בִּזְקִיפָה, set up, around the altar. If the willows were merely 'set up' in place around the altar, then surely the lulav was held in hand during the Temple hakafos. Assuming that the current custom is related to the aravah custom, the Gemara's conclusion that the willow-branches were 'taken' points to a decision in favor of the opinion that the lulav, was not 'taken' during the hakafah around the altar.

Rashi (in a responsum quoted by Ohr Zarua 315; Machzor Vitri 382) had originally been of this opinion, but then concluded that holding the lulav was not part of the hakafos custom. Thus if one did not have a lulav he could still participate in the hakafos.

Ba'al Halttur (Asseres HaDibros p. 186) agrees. He goes further and rules that on Hoshana Rabbah the hakafos must be done holding the willow. R' Yosef Karo (Orach Chaim 664:3; see Ran to Succah 44) accepts this opinion as Halachah. However, Rashi later rejected this opinion (cf. Rashi, Succah 42b s.v. לולב and Sfas Emes), taking the view that the Gemara's conclusion that the willow was 'taken' need not yield the corollary that the hakafah as well was done with the willow. Even if the willow was 'taken', this need not mean that it was held during the hakafah; it may mean only that the aravah was held in hand, shaken [נענוע], or beaten on the ground as part of the service, but not that it was held while the hakafos were made (see comm. to ArtScroll Mishnah Succah 4:3 and 5). Thus we can still accept the view that this hakafah was done with the lulav. This seems to be Rambam's view (Hilchos Lulav 7:22-3). R' Yosef Karo (Orach Chaim 660:2, consistent with his opinion in 664:3 cited above) rules that the hakafah is made even without a lulav, while Rama (loc. cit.) rules that one must have a lulav in hand. However, R' Yosef Karo rules that the lulav and aravah may be taken together during the hakafos. Rama (loc. cit.) testifies that such was the prevailing custom and he seems to approve of it. Presumably (see Mishnah Berurah 664:15; Beur HaGra 660:7), this custom is based on the premise that we should perform the mitzvah in a way agreeable to both views. However, Rama rules (664:7) that it is preferable that the hakafos be done holding only the lulav. The willows should be taken only after the hakafos have been completed and the lulav put away.

Sfas Emes (42b) advances the novel view that everyone agrees that the lulav was held during the hakafah around the altar. The question is only whether the willow, too, was held.

☙ Who participated in the hakafos in the Temple?

Rashi (43b s.v. והביאום), Tosafos (43b s.v. שלוחי), and others assume that only Kohanim eligible for the sacrificial service took part in the procession around the altar. All others were prohibited to enter the area between the western wall of the altar and the Temple (Kelim 1:9)[1]. This is the apparent intent also of Succah 44a which ostensibly permits only Kohanim — even physically blemished ones [בעלי מומין] — to participate in the procession (see Tosafos loc. cit. s.v. כהנים). This creates a difficulty, for the prevalent custom is that everybody, Israelite and Kohen alike, takes part in the procession around the bimah. Vilna Gaon (Beur HaGra 360:1) finds it difficult to reconcile this difficulty. However, Ohr Zarua (2:315) has already touched upon this and says

---

1. R' Sherira Gaon in the above cited responsum disagrees with this. Since he holds that they did not walk around the altar, but merely stood around it in a circle, it was perfectly permissible for Israelites to participate in the mitzvah. They would stand on the eastern, northern, and southern sides of the altar, leaving the western side exclusively for the Kohanim.

simply that the *mitzvah* of circling the altar overrides the prohibition against Israelites entering the space west of the altar. Otherwise, he argues, how could blemished *Kohanim* enter this space which, under normal circumstances, they too are prohibited to enter. The Talmud (*Succah* 44a) clearly permits them to do this for the sake of *hakafos*, the same principle which makes an exception for blemished *Kohanim* could be used for Israelites.

[It may also be that Israelites are not exempted categorically from the *mitzvah* of *hakafos*. In the Temple they could not perform it because the halachah prevents them from entering the inner Temple Courtyard. But in synagogues, they are not barred from participating in the *mitzvah*.]

BIBLIOGRAPHY

This bibliography is not a complete catalogue of all the works cited in this book. Rather it is a listing, mostly *siddurim*, of sources specifically commenting on the *Hoshana* prayers.

Avodas Yisrael

A *siddur* grammatically corrected by the eminent grammarian **R' Yitzchak Zeligman Baer**. R' Yitzchak appended a commentary named **Yechin Lashon** to this *siddur* concentrating on the establishment of correct textual readings, and elucidation of the plain meaning. Rodelheim 5628 (1868), Photo-reproduction, Tel Aviv 5717 (1957).

Beis Avraham

Siddur with a basically kabbalistic commentary by **R' Avraham ben R' Aharon Yosef**. Jerusalem 5692 (1932).

Beis HaOtzar

A *siddur* containing the commentaries כַּוָּנוֹת פְּשׁוּטִיּוֹת, *Kavanos Pashtiyos* [lit. plain meanings] by an anonymous author, plus *Margalis Tovah, Knesses Yisrael,* and *P'ninim Ykarim* by **R' Tzvi Yechezkel Michelsohn** (one of the rabbis of pre-World War II Warsaw; author of *Sh'eilos U'Teshuvos Tirosh VeYitzhar* and many other writings).

Photo reproduction by Reinman Seforim Center (New York). No date given.

Beis Yaakov

This *siddur*, first published in Lemberg 5664 (1904), contains, with numerous additions, the famous *siddur Amudei Shamayim* by **R' Yaakov Emden** (1697-1776). Hence this *siddur*, which has enjoyed great popularity and has been reprinted numerous times, has been known as *The R' Yaakov Emden Siddur*. The publisher has in great measure contributed to this misconception. The commentary to *Hoshanos* contained in this *siddur* is not by R' Yaakov Emden, but was added from an unspecified source.

Bnei Yisaschar

A compilation of Torah thoughts arranged according to the calendar, by **R' Zvi Elimelech of Dynow** (1785-1841), combining brilliant Talmudic insights and Biblical exegesis with profound Kabbalistic and chassidic thought regarding the Sabbath, the New Moon, the festivals and the fast days. R' Hirsch Meilech, as he was commonly called, was a towering figure in the chassidic life of Galicia and progenitor of many chassidic dynasties including Blushev and Munkacz.

Iyun Tefillah

Analytical commentary to the *siddur* by **R' Aryeh Leib ben Shlomo Gordon** of Jerusalem; incorporated into *Siddur Otzar HaTefillos* (first published 1915). The commentary to *Hoshanos* contains an annotated version of a manuscript, credited variously to *Rashi*, one of his disciples, or one of his colleagues.

Kol Bo

The commentary to this *siddur* and *machzor* is taken from the commentary *Hadras Kodesh* in the *Sulzbach Machzor*, by **R' Yitzchak ben Yaakov Yosebel Segal** of Herlisheim. This commentary is itself taken from commentaries printed in the old editions of the *machzor* whose roots can be traced back to commentators as early as **Ravan** (R' Eliezer ben Nathan — late 10th to early 11th century).

Otzar HaTefillos

See *Iyun Tefillah*.

Shaar HaShamayim

Commentary to the *siddur* by **R' Yeshayah HaLevi Horowitz** (born 1565 in Prague), celebrated author of *Shaloh* (an acronym for *Sh'nei Luchos HaBris*), first published in 1717 by the author's great-grandson.

Shaar Yisaschar

A compilation of Torah thoughts arranged according to the calendar, by **R' Chaim Elazar Shapira** (1872-1937) of Munkacs, written in the style of his forebear R' Zvi Elimelech of Dynow's *Bnei Yisaschar*.

Rashi

See *Iyun Tefillah*.

Tefillah Yesharah VeKesser Nehorah HaShalem

A *siddur* which contains the commentary *Kesser Nehorah* to the prayers, by **R' Aharon HaKohen** preacher and *dayan* in Zelichov (Poland). R' Aharon was a disciple of R' Uziel Meizels, one of the outstanding disciples of the famed chassidic mentor, R' Dov Ber of Mezeritch. The commentary to *Hoshanos* printed in this *siddur* is probably not by this author.

Tehillas Hashem

A *siddur* containing the prayers according to Nusach Ari as established by **R' Shneur Zalman of Liadi** — the founder of the Chabad branch of Chassidus.

An English translation of this *siddur* by **R' Nissen Mangel** appeared in Brooklyn, 5738 (1978).

This volume is part of
THE ARTSCROLL SERIES®
an ongoing project of
translations, commentaries and expositions
on Scripture, Mishnah, Talmud, Halachah,
liturgy, history and the classic Rabbinic writings;
and biographies, and thought.

For a brochure of current publications
visit your local Hebrew bookseller
or contact the publisher:

Mesorah Publications, ltd

4401 Second Avenue
Brooklyn, New York 11232
(718) 921-9000